Other Half of the Society

Backward Caste and Politics of Bihar

Other Half of the Society

Backward Caste and Politics of Bihar

Sushil Kumar Sinha
Research Officer, NCBC
Ministry of Social Justice and Empowerment
Government of India, New Delhi

Raj Publications
New Delhi - 110002 (INDIA)

Other Half of Society: *Backward Caste and Politics of Bihar*

First Published in 2018

` 995

ISBN 978-81-86208-48-9

Published by : **Raj Publications**

108, 4855/24, Ansari Road,

Daryaganj, New Delhi - 110002

Tel. : 011- 23250939, 09811010939

Laser Typesetting : Aarati Computers, Delhi-110 009

Printed at : Balaji Offset, Delhi

Preface

Sometimes unusual happens in one's life and same is the case with me. I had never dreamt of working for the causes of backward classes. But by sheer luck or chance, got selected as Research Officer in the National Commission for Backward Classes.After working for few months in the organization, I develop interest in different aspects of OBCs and the person who arose interest in me in the initial stage was the then chairperson of the Commission, Hon'ble Justice (Retd.) R.S. Singh. The outcome of this interest came in form of a book, i.e.; Backward Classes in India: Various Dimensions. I came very close to the OBCs of Bihar due to my frequent official visits and interaction with different backward castes associations, individuals as well as some prominent persons, which created curiosity in me to know more about them and it prepared ground for writing this book. People come to know Bihar from various sources, such as, from newspapers and television which shows it as a land of caste wars and natural disasters, some knew it from experience that it is the most difficult place to live in, some hate it and want to wish it away and finally those who love to talk of its past, its rich cultural history, its educational brilliance, its role in the freedom struggle and its relative well being for some years after independence. Myself belong to this place and wish for its betterment in various fields of activities. This can not be done without taking help of approximately 39.0 percent of OBCs population, because they plays an important role in its development. So the answer lies in social justice and their empowerment. But this also depends on the approach which State adopt to achieve its goal. One example in this regard is sufficient to show the adhoc approach of the State government, i. e; the Bihar Government had setup Justice Amir Das Commission in 1997 to probe the massacre of 61 dalits by Ranveer Sena in Laxmanpur – Bathe Village in Jehanabad district, but nothing came out of it in the last nine years(as the State Government think so) and ultimately government wind it up. If the reports had came out it would have been valuable one to chalk out programmes and policies for the MBCs and dalits.

As we Know that the caste in India has acquired a very important place in social life and in present scenario it is in process of transformation. Now the caste status is not solely based on the notion of purity and pollution but other considerations such as economic and occupational status, educational achievement, and political power also plays an important role. Besides this, Social scientists are also confronted with lots of problems which are going on due to the process of transformation including social mobility, and social reforms in the social, economic, political and ideological fields. During the last fiftynine years of independence transformation in social sector has been phenomenal.

In case of Bihar, not much has changed for MBCs and in this context I want to quote from V. Ramakrishnan article appeared in the "Frontline" about Ramji Malha, a resident of Bansperi village of Sitamarhi district and a member of extremely backward community (Kewat). In his word, "Twenty years ago, I began fishing in this stream with a small hand-held fishing net. I used to earn about Rs. 10. I continue to do the same job and earn more or less the same amount. Now my children, aged 18 and 15, also do the same job. Our lot has not changed. If anything, it has worsened. There are more mouths to feed and less and less to eat". This statement indicate that much has to be done for their socio-economic upliftment.

The slogans of social justice and empowerment of the weaker sections have dominated Bihar politics for the last 17 years, but there has not been much change in the life of Ramji Malha's family, or those from the EBC groups. The only beneficial groups are the upper backwards, both on socio-economic and political front, due to the political leadership except a few from the upper backward castes who in turn empowered their own communities, providing very little to the EBC groups thus leaving on their own .

Without making balance between these two backward communities, the State can not achieve its required development neither on social or economic front nor can achieve its political goal.

The present study makes an attempt to understand the ongoing process of social transformation in context of backward classes of Bihar. The introductory chapter gives a bird's eyes view about the Indian caste system including the meaning of backward castes in legal as well as sociological context, their place in social hierarchy of Bihar and their occupation as well as their population district-wise and in the end SWOT analysis of backward castes has been done which helps in chalking out programmes and plans for OBCs welfare as well as for its better understanding. Till date we have not defined OBC in text book form, what we have done, i.e; given a workable definition of backward classes. In view of Marc Galanter, A backward community is a community which is backward in the opinion of the Government. And what is the opinion of the Government is determinative only of the groups under representation and not of its backwardness seems to beg the question: who then would determine backwardness. It is an important issues confronting social scientists and others and this should also be looked into.

The second chapter 'Mobilization of Backward castes', provides a broad view about different backward castes of Bihar, especially the three upper backward castes, i.e; Kurmi, Koeri, and Yadava, their occupation and position in agrarian society of Bihar and also the role played by their respective caste associations in achieving higher socio-economic, educational and political status, both during pre-independence and post-independence period. In the case of Bihar, where agrarian society exist, the above mentioned castes have been categorized under 'Intermediate Caste' alongwith some other backward castes, i.e; castes under Annexure-II in the State list. Only Castes under Annexure-I who are most backward alongwith SCs and STs, have suffered in the past at the hand of upper castes and in many cases their occupation had stigma attached to it and to heel their past injuries, Government has provided compensation in the form of protective discrimination, but this applies on the whole categories of OBCs irrespective of whether they are in Annexure-I or Annexure-II. In many cases, these intermediate castes did not resort to sanskritization as a means to climb higher in the social ladder, may be in the initial stage they have resorted to but later on left it. This may be due to liberal attitude among north as well as some East Indian societies in comprasion to the South Indian society. It also provides sufficient background to think about reformulation of reservation policy. Protective discrimination has also led to polarization of society in the State leading to formation of private armies based on castes, which has reference in this chapter and in many cases it has restricted the socio-economic development of the State.

The third chapter deals with the history of Mungerilal Commission setup by the Bihar Government to identify backward castes of the State and to suggest measures for their social and educational upliftment. It also analysed the reservations policy for the backward castes in the State Government services. Later on acting on the Mandal judgment, the State Government setup a permanent Commission, which promulgated guidelines and procedures for inclusion and exclusion (through creamy layer) of backward castes of Bihar in the State List and from time to time suggest on different issues of the backward castes. It also speaks of constraints faced by the State Backward Classes Commission and remedial measures for it. It hints at lacuna that has crept in the Commission and whose removal is necessary for its healthy growth, besides co-ordination between the State and National Commission to serve the backward communities in the best possible way, for example; there is a gap in the State and Central list of OBCs for Bihar (16 Castes/sub-castes/Communities/ Synonyms etc; donot find place in the Central list , whereas it exists in the State list)

In the fourth chapter Protective Discrimination has been dealt in the light of theoretical as well as practical aspects in context of Bihar. It is a tool in the hand of Government, which has been used discriminately, sometimes in the name of atrocities meted out by the backward communities in the past or to raise the social, educational and economic status of the said communities. No sincere efforts have been made to use it judiciously in this era of globalization and liberalization, where maket economy dominates the State or Central economy and where efficiency counts. As there is a provision of creamy layer, but it has its own difficulties in implementation and in the State of Bihar case of Ashok Kumar Thakur Vs.

State of Bihar proves it. In the initial stage a separate approach had been adopted by the State Government on creamy layer, which was later on modified at the instance of Court order and at present creamy layer promulgated by the National Commission for Backward Classes, is in vogue in the State with certain addition by the State Government. Another case pertaining to reservation in higher educational institutions of Bihar, known as Ajay Kumar Vs. State Government has been dealt in this chapter for having more insight into it.

The fifth chapter of this book deals with various welfare measures initiated by the State Government as well as the Central Government in its different five years plan. It also looks it in analytical framework and provides suggestions to remove anomalies.

Finally, I want to quote the famous saying of Swami-Vivekananda, one of the greatest social reformer of India- "The solution is not by bringing down the higher, but by raising the lower up to the level of the higher. And that should be found in all our works, in spite of what you may hear from some people whose knowledge of their own scriptures and whose capacity to understand the mighty plans of the ancients are only zero". And this should reflect in one's deeds.

I owe my sincere gratitude to the Member-Secretary of the Commission, from whom I learnt a lot. Also, I am thankful to my colleagues in the Research Wing with whom I shared my views on different aspects of backward castes and they provided me valuable informations and suggestions from time to time. I am thankful to the librarian (acting) Sh. Pushkar of NCBC for giving me free hand to use the Commission library during my work. My wife Pratibha who went through the manuscript and my son Aayush who at his leisure period typed it, my thanks goes to them also.

I am grateful to the authors, editors as well as State and Central Government personnels whose works, reports and notifications, I have used in this book.

Finally, I thank Ms. Poonam Goel of Raj Publications, New Delhi for taking keen interest in the publication of the book.

—Sushil Kumar Sinha

Contents

1

Introduction: Caste & OBCs

One of the most widely known and commented upon features of Indian society is the caste system. The origin of this particular usage of the term "Caste" is traced by Basham(1967) to the 16th century when the Portuguese came to India and found the Hindu community divided into many separate groups which they called Castas, meaning tribes, clans or families. The well known four fold classifications –Brahmin, Kshatriya, Vaishya and Sudra – in descending order of social status, is believed to have been first enunciated by the ancient law-giver Manu some time in the vedic period (1500-1000 BC).These four varnas, aggregated macro groupings, which were further divided into a myriad castes and sub castes.Each Varna, caste and sub caste has an internal hierarchical social order.

Historians who have attempted to draw a straight line between the Manusmriti and post-independence India are clearly unfamiliar with those patterns of Indian history that contradicts such a linear view. While some of the social evils of modern India may have ancient roots, many others have a fairly recent history. And even those that may have ancient precedence were modulated and modified as a result of numerous struggles for social equality that have taken place throughout Indian history, such as construction of temples was one of the means to move higher in social mobility and in 18th and 19th century, mostly temples were built by the low castes but during the British period restriction in temple entry for lower castes began as the means to construct and control through **Trust** went in hand of upper castes.

Economic factors were also crucial in determining caste rank and its relationship. In period of intense economic exploitation, caste discrimination intensified and the reverse took place in period of economic expansion. Most historians are in agreement that the Gupta period was a period of rising prosperity and also a period of increasing social mobility. Improvements in agricultural productivity led to improvements in the social ranks of the cultivators and later on these agriculturist castes led social movement for their upliftment in social hierarchy and their assertion for political identity (reference chapter: 2).

i. On the whole our understanding of caste system as a system of inequality is primarily derived from:

   (a) Indological Sources, i.e; from the Hindu sacred literature; and

   (b) From census reports, Gazetteers and Ethnographic glossaries as well as accounts based on intensive field works. As we know that Indian society has been organized on the principle of heredity and ascription.

Caste has been defined in numerous way by social scientists but universally it has been defined as a "system of groups within the class which are normally endogamous, commensal, and craft-exclusive" (Basham, 1967).

In the 20th century, the problem of social stratifications or inequality has led to the development of two schools of thought:

a) Functional, and

b) Structural

The exponent of functional theory saw inequality as a functional necessity for all human societies. In case of India, for example, in older times, the artisans guild system helped in the development and preservation of specialized knowledge and perfection of important manufacturing skills. These guilds were closely corelated to jati or caste. It was not Brahmins and upper castes who favoured hereditary continuity, but skilled carpenters, weavers, metalworkers, painters and numerous categories of other artisans also saw certain benefits in maintaining their jati identities. While the artisan's castes often fought for greater social equality - the complete breakdown of caste identities was never a serious option except for those at the very bottom of the caste totem pole.

The caste system survived not just because it was enforced by the legal writ of an elite class, but as much because it served a social purpose in an era in which it was difficult if not impossible to organize the educational and productive activities of society in a more flexible and democratic way.

If we take the views of western sociologists on Indian caste system, most of them perceived it in religious form. As Emile Senart, on Indian caste system wrote that "Hindu society is regulated by religious customs and the law books are essentially collections of religious precepts. Henry Maine found it difficult to detach Hindu law from Hindu religion, and the belief became widely established that Hindu society was unchangeable because it was rooted in immutable religious observance. Max Weber defined social identity of the Hindu in term of caste and of caste in terms of ritual. He was of the opinion that it was the product of Brahamanical theodicy. Bougle's also supported this view, i.e; caste is basically a religious institution and Hinduism is defined more by the observance of caste rules than by fidelity to some precise dogma. Louis Dumont has carried Bougle's perspective further forward and greatly enriched it by his mastery of Indian ethnography and language. He defined it in the form of 'Purity' and 'Impurity'. Whereas, Indian writers supported Varnadharma. According to this, castes are divided into four varnas, i.e; Brahmin, Kshatriya, Vaishya and Shudra and accordingly they inherit qualities (Satya, Rajas, Tamas etc;). Conventionally caste has had at least two distinct meanings: Varna and jati.But people perceive more of jati than Varna. This also lead to some sort of confusion.Though most frequently paired with varna in the ethnographic literature, the term jati has other associations as well.It is commonly used to cover a series of identities of increasing degrees of inclusiveness from sub subcastes through caste to religion and language. Based on varna (in sense of jati) Hindus have their marriage system of Anuloma and Pratiloma Vivaha and other restrictions. Restriction of caste rules became more rigid during post-vedic period (600 BC- 300 AD) and continued during the British rule in India.As G.S Ghurye in his book **"Caste and Class in India"** has written about the plights of the lower castes, but intermediate castes had some freedom in this respect, because most of them were from serving classes and under Jajmani system they always have interactions with the higher castes. These intermediate castes alongwith lower castes consists most of the backward castes / classes in India.

As backward castes are also referred to as backward classes and vice versa in the context of OBCs. Their synonymity can be seen in the official documents throughout the 19th and 20th centuries. The following statement made by Dr. Ambedkar in the parliament in defining the term "backward classes", shows that castes and classes have been used interchangeably. In his words, "What we call backward classes are nothing else but a collection of certain castes".

In historical perspective the term Backward Classes had started acquiring meaning at the end of 19th century with the commencement of special treatment to some and communal representation to others in early 20th century. From the St. George Gazetteer No. 40 of November 5, 1895 to Poona Pact, Simon Commission and other Acts provided platform for the backward castes in pre-independence period which continued after gaining independence.

In pre-Constitution period the expression "class" and "caste" were used interchangeably and that caste was understood as an enclosed class. As a matter of fact Dr. Ambedkar made it clear in his speech in the parliament at the time of the first amendment to the constitution that "Backward classes are nothing else but a collection of certain castes." A caste is an enclosed class. Issuing clarification of the use of the word class in Article 16(4) Kania, CJ. and Venkatachaliah, Ahmadi and Jeevan, Reddy, JJ. pointed out in Mandal case that the obvious reason of using the expression "class" in Article 16(4) was that otherwise non-Hindus would have been excluded from its purview as they do not use caste. Therefore, from the use of the word class in Article 16(4), it cannot be concluded either that class is antithetical to caste or that a caste cannot be a class or that a caste as such can never be taken as a backward class of citizens. As Article 15(4) do not speak of castes, but only speaks of classes, and that caste and class are not synonymous. Therefore exclusion of caste to ascertain backwardness does not vitiate classification if it satisfies other tests. However Marc Galanter and A Beteille has interpreted it in Balaji case i.e., equating class with caste and referred low caste as backward classes. Similarly Late Pandit Jawahar Lal Nehru had divided society in high castes and lower castes. Lower caste has been further divided into SCs, STs and OBCs. A representative from Bihar also explained that backward classes were a section of society between the higher caste and the scheduled caste. At the time of functioning of the Constituent assembly the term backward classes by and large denoted intermediate class. Sociologists including M.N.Srinivas, supported and propagated the perception that caste sans class represented modern India. In spite of this, caste and class divide has never been rigid. Basic differences between caste and class are given below:

Class	Caste
1. Progresive, flexible and changeable	1. Obscurant, rigid and unchangeable
2. Comprised individual as distinct basis social unit.	2. No existence of an individual as a social unit.
3. Membership on the basis of merit.	3. Membership acquired by birth.
4. Alterable hierarchy.	4. Fixed hierarchy.
5. Occupational variety and mobility permitted.	5. Occupational variety and mobility not permitted.

It is thus obvious that notwithstanding the use of the term class, at the time of the functioning of the Constituent assembly, Backward Classes (other than SC/ST) by and large denoted intermediate castes and analogous social groups.

The proliferation of OBCs group was necessarily created because of the Constitutional opportunities and not the other way round. As the OBCs are a legal – constitutional category in the post–independence period that has been striving to obtain acceptance of the identity of an independent social category. The term "OBC" itself was not used in the Indian Constitution until amendment of Article 338 where it came to be used for the first time. Until then, even legal-Constitutional designation wise, the OBC had only a derived status either as a part of weaker sections (Article 46) or SEBCs (Article15 (4) i, e; socially and educationally backward classes or Article 16(4). Also, their accorded inferior status is visible in the nature of provisions made for the other two clearly defined BC categories of SCs and STs for whom all the provisions are mandatory. In case of the OBCs all the provisions have been left to the discretion and convenience of the governments of the day at Central and State level. This derived status has continued even through the 73rd and 74th Constitutional amendment Acts (Article 243D(6) and 243T(6) in reservation of seats in the PRIs and urban municipal bodies.

Mungerilal Commission also kept in mind various parameters and in accordance with Article 15(4) of the Indian Constitution determined backwardness of any caste/ community who were socially and educationally backward. For this their literacy level, condition of work, i.e; low and unprofitable work or stigma attached to it, their percentage in the government services including government undertakings, involvement in social and political activities etc; were kept in mind.

Marc Galanter (1991) indicates that the term "backward Classes" had a less fixed and definite reference. It had been there with a variety of referents, it had shifted rapidly in meaning and came to mean different things in different places. He goes on to specify ten such denotations of the term 'backward classes'. These include depressed classes, untouchables, SCs, aboriginals and hill tribes, criminal tribes, all communities deserving special treatment except untouchables, all communities above the untouchables but below the most advanced ones, communities other than the highest or most advanced, communities meeting non-communal tests of backwardness etc; (Ibid:155). Galanter proceeds to provide historical examples of different States at different points of time in the pre-independence period to conclude that the term had never acquired a definite meaning at all-India level. There had been no attempts until then to define or employ it on the national level. The term had definite meanings in local contexts although these differed somewhat. After separating SCs and STs, he stated that two major species emerged (i) as the more inclusive group of all those who need special treatment; and (ii) as a stratum higher than the untouchables but nonetheless depressed. This double usage continues even today: the former in the usage of Backward Castes in the wider sense (including SCs and STs) and the latter in the usage as equivalent to OBCs (Ibid:159). Related to the (ii) aspect mentioned above insertion of the word 'backward' at a later stage, i.e., in drafting of Article 10(3) by the drafting committee of the Constitution brought two important features, as had been mentioned by Dr. B.R. Ambedkar, firstly that there shall be equality of opportunity and secondly, there shall be reservation in favour of certain communities which have not so far been provided.

However, backwardness as understood in the Indian context has a number of distinctive features:

(i) It is viewed as an attribute not of individuals but of certain clearly defined social segments, in which membership is generally acquired by birth,

(ii) Membership of the backward classes entitles one to certain advantages and concessions specifically conferred by the government.

The working group for the development and welfare of the backward classes, set up by the planning commission to recommend measures for the empowerment of the OBCs during the ninth five-year plan, in its report in May 1996, grouped the OBCs into following five occupational sub-categories:

(a) Castes/communities of poor peasantry including poor peasantry of former zamindar and other intermediary tenures.

(b) Castes/communities providing traditional services (i.e., hair-cutting and grooming, washing of clothes, scavenging, etc.).

(c) Castes/communities of artisans producers (i.e; fisher folk, toddy tapers, stone cutters, earth workers, etc.).

(d) Artisans/Castes/communities with traditional skills engaged in various traditional crafts providing a variety of goods at family/cottage scale (i.e., potters, weavers, blacksmiths, carpenters, etc.). These are the original and true manufacturing classes of Indian society who were engaged in secondary production even at a time when many of the major industrial houses of today were money lenders and hundi operators.

(e) Communities without resources or skills: a good number of castes or communities are indigent and their traditional occupations has been (and still is) begging, sometimes with religious overtones. Many of them are nomadic or semi-nomadic.

These communities comprise of people who follow different religions, speak different languages, live in different socio-cultural-geographical locales but they share same traditional occupations.

On the basis of SWOT (strength, weakness, opportunities and threat perception) analysis of OBCs one can come to know about their different facets that will be helpful in development, empowerment and welfare of the OBCs in India, which is as follows:

Strength of the OBCs

Among all social categories, the OBCs posses largest pool of social capital. This is based on commonly observed rules and mutual self-help. These social links discourage deviant behaviour through ostracism and other social penalties, create a climate of trust in which agreements are honoured, grievances are redressed, and facilitate collective action against threat from outsiders and risks from natural disasters. These communities cover a huge range-one that cannot be covered either by the governmental organizations or the NGOs. Enormous economic benefits(i.e., high level of trust, greatly reduced risks, encouragement to innovation and enterprise, reduction of costs, etc.) flow from social capital if this can be properly harnessed.

Quite a few of the OBCs communities do have an economic asset base, i.e.land and occupational skills. Although a steady increase in their population, changes in the technology, commercialization and globalization have dented its importance somewhat and provides them the cushion of something to fallback upon and use it in their favour. Moreover it is a great asset base on which successful future strategies can be worked out taking advantages of available local resources.

Among the backward classes, the OBCs are the only category that has thrown up a larger number of regional political parties in many states. Although their tenure in the offices have not been for very long duration. Inspite of that they have reached a threshold destination in the nation's political history where ruling parties dominated by the upper castes /classes have forced to take note of the strength of the OBCs, at least at the State levels. This bound to play an important role at Centre in the next stage of political development.

Weakness of the OBCs

The OBCs display persistence of the culture of backwardness. There is an absence of concern beyond hearth and home. Most of the OBC communities continue to be steped in obscurantism and, therefore, have generally opted to travel on the sanskritization route in search of dignity, voice and space. Sanskritization doesn't offer independent identity. On the contrary, it provides only false sense of prestige and does not free them from the oppressive grip of Brahmanism. It also prevent them from developing their own cultural text, something that confers on them the freedom to act as they feel like. The psyche of the mass of the OBC communities continues to be fatalist, resigned to its miserable fate, docile, submissive, and not ready to fight its own battles against oppression and exploitation. It lacks collective initiatives and has kept its mental horizons closed, and cut them off any hope of freedom and decent existence. These characteristics make them an easy prey to the nefarious designs of the Hindutva forces that use them as "executioners" in their periodic partisan campaigns in different theatres to achieve their goals. This culture of backwardness has emboldened the ruling class fractions and they continue to indulge in oppression and exploitation of the OBCs.

The OBCs have been engaged in hard, relentless and demanding manual work. Their work and knowledge associated with it are downgraded. The elites in the Indian society have maintained their position precisely through creating a sphere of knowledge separated from understanding based on practicals of everyday life. Therefore, the OBCs became an "underclass" which was practically bereft of "cognitive ability" and remained excluded from the exercise of power. Nehru, who set out to create an egalitarian society, ended up creating one of the most unequal educational societies in the world. The out come is there for all to see. Whereas India's highly educated upper crust is a world class, the underclass, consisting of the SCs, STs and OBCs, is educationally one of the most ill equipped in the world. Thus, in the run up to India becoming the 'developed' society, the chances of the underclass securing any better bargain in near future are not very bright. Use of Hindi only and other regional languages, absence of good educational institutions in the rural areas, and the fright of English and Mathematics among the OBCs have greatly reduced their access to professional and quality education that could help them in their occupational mobility.

The fact that the peasants among the OBCs possess landed assets has made them complacent and prevented them from pursuing other occupations.

As a single category, they possess the largest pool of occupational skills but they have not kept themselves in tune with the changing requirements of a changed social, economic, technological and political enviornment. Their younger generation has not been as dedicated and is fast losing its occupational skills. Since some of the new generation OBCs have gained entry into other gainful professions, others have become vagabonds. The consequences have been disastrous. In the changed socio-economic environment, quite a few of the OBC communities find that their traditional occupations are no longer viable to be pursued: either their demand has almost vanished or others with better capital and technological innovations have appropriated their terrain.In the era of globalization and liberalization of market economy OBCs have become even more pauperized.

Vulnerability-to the natural elements, the input vendors, output marketing, and other vultures who live off their hard labour has been their greatest bane. Conscientization about the causes of their 'unfreedoms'has generally not been witnessed from within. Systematically addressing various types of vulnerabilities through collective initiatives, as, for example, was done by the Raigars of Jawaja in Rajasthan with the help of a team of management experts from IIM, Ahmedabad in the mid –seventies (Mathai, 1977), is something that has still not occurred to the OBCs. Vulnerability multiplied by significant increase in population has averaged out even the meager gains, which some sections among them had succeeded in achieving.

Except a few large OBC communities like the Ahirs and Kurmis, the OBC don't possess a pan-Indian character. Even those having pan-Indian presence are characteristically different in different locals. There is no active all India organization of the OBCs that can take up their causes and fight their battles. There is also no effective linkage of the OBC communities' with the non-OBC communities that have been forming part of the regional ruling class in many of the States. As results, the later have formed alliances with the upper castes much to the disadvantage of the OBC interests.

During the last 59 years of post-independence period, leadership drawn from the OBC communities have lacked the vision and dedication, which was shown by the OBC ideologues like Sri Narayan Guru, Jyoti Rao Phule, Shahuji Maharaj, and Perriyar E.V.Ramaswami Naicker. Therefore the OBCs have not progressed much on indicators such as education, health, political power and economic well- being. As a consequence, the upper castes/classes switch over to the knowledge economy and reaped immense benefits at a very fast rate and speed, the OBCs continue to remain in the rut of subsistence economy.

Threat Perceptions

A consequential change has taken place in the composition of the ruling class coalition itself. In quite a few States of the Indian union, now the upper backwards, who have not been listed in the OBC lists, have assumed controlling positions in the levers of governance at the State level. Their quid pro quo with the Brahmins, Kshatriyas and Vaishyas from the traditional varna order on the one hand and privileges of the industry, bureaucracy, media and knowledge based institutions on the other has also changed. The terms vary in different locales but one undeniable element in the emerging scenario is perceptible decline of the clout of the traditional power axis. The impact at the national level, where the traditional axis continues is not so significant. However, the earlier arrogance and constant 'lecturing' postures of those ruling at the Centre has gone- perhaps forever- and replaced by one of 'consultation' and 'persuasion'. A logical consequence of this development should have been a stronger bonding between the non-OBC backwards and such numerically preponderant upper backwards, listed among the OBC communities, and enjoying power in some of the states. Two factors appear to have played a crucial role in preventing its emergence: one, having acquired some of the cultural habits of the upper castes and classes much earlier than the 'dominant'OBCs, the non-OBC backwards, therefore, find it easier to deal with the upper castes and classes and have arrived at an understanding with them that allows them better share of the cake; and secondly, there is considerable internal jostling among the upward mobile 'dominant' OBC communities and this is exploited both by the upper non-OBC backwards on the one side and the upper castes and classes on the other.

The ruling elites have been playing games with the OBC identity formation, identity assertion and sharing of power in the classical Machiavellian mode. This has reduced the gains of the OBCs. On the other hand a clutch of policies directly affecting key segments of the OBCs(i.e., agricultural credit, subsidies, agricultural produce pricing, public distribution system, fuel policy, exports and imports, custom and excise duties, etc.) has been introduced during the structural adjustment phase of the economic reforms. Because of these the OBCs find themselves squeezed out from different sides. Whereas the government is very prompt in listening to the demands of the organized industry and trade, the cries of help from the farmers, weavers, artisans, etc., consistently fell on deaf ears of the government. As it is supposedly carrying the country to the comity of 'developed' world, a tiny 5.0 percent of the upper crust of the population is receiving the top priority and the needs of the 95.0 percent are being consistently ignored. The OBCs- and other under classes-would need to take such steps that force this insensitive government to see reason.

There has been enormous proliferation of the NGOs in India. Both the international lending and funding institutions as well as the Central government-and at their behest the State governments- have funneled huge sums of funds to them to carry out 'development' programmes on the plea that the NGOs are more successful in securing people's participations. Where as some among these are indeed carrying out good work but for the overwhelming majority this has become a business in which no taxes have to be paid. There is a partnership going on between various elements of the ruling coalition to share the funds in the name of empowering the poor: the poor themselves are, it for all, very rarely represented in these outfits. No one seems to have asked any questions about the social composition of these NGOs.

The OBCs must internalize the fact that the ruling class attaches maximum importance to this fact that there is an inverse relationship between the conditions of the OBCs and the dominance of the ruling classes. Therefore, the ruling coalition might be giving assurances of 'accommodating' the OBCs and forced by compulsions of power may even give them some space and voice but would not be very much inclined to share substantive power with them. The OBCs, and other marginalized segments, i.e., SCs, STs, and the minorities, would not be allowed to remain together since their prolonged friendship and social axis would mean end of the upper caste rule.

Opportunities for OBC Communities

In this context some examples from different parts of the country can be cited, such as the Nadars of Tamil Nadu demonstrated one route to the transformation of the identity and status of a community from the lowest rungs of the ritual hierarchy to the position of power. They have increasingly abandoned their traditional occupation of toddy tapping and as they have risen in education and wealth, the community has differentiated occupationally and economically. After being ridiculed following the sanskritization route, they adopted the secular economic and political goals in the creation of Nadar Mahajan Sangham that became the agent of the community integration and mobilization. This transformation came in three stages: one, where the community was dependent and there was no community self-consciousness; second, when the community moved to urban areas and for trading and organizational skills and in this process help in arising community consciousness for integration and mobilization puropse and thirdly, when the community became differentiated and formation of new class interests and associations took place. Politically also, the community become far more assertive.

The Ezhavas of Kerala demonstrated another story of transformation of a community which too was traditionally engaged in the occupation of toddy tapping, and was ritually placed at par with the SCs. In their case, the colonial rule, the communist movement, the cultural impact of Sri Narayan Guru's work, the organizational accomplishments of the Sri Narayan Dharma Paripalan Yogam (SNDP), the educational attainments, migration to differents parts of the country and international migration first to East Asian and next to the Gulf countries helped the Ezhavas to develop their own alternate cultural text, acquire land and other assets, diversify occupationally in the State itself and become politically an influential entity in Kerala.

There are success story of upper backward communities from different states also, these include the Reddys, Kammas and Velamas from Andhra Pradesh, the Patels and Patidar from Gujarat and some of the leading Maratha communities from Maharashtra, who have all established themselves well in the society, economy and polity of their respective States by diversifying their occupational pursuits through impulses generated by higher education, external orientation and heightened political participation. To begin with, all of them had the advantages of number as well as asset base. These communities are now treated as the 'dominant' castes but still do not form part of the upper castes. However, the best available success story of a backward community having graduated to the status of upper castes is that of the Kayasthas. They are now considered to be part of upper castes, not on the axis of purity and pollution but on the substantive grounds of actual exercise of social, economic and political power in the live quarters of the Indian society. Although they constitute less than one percent of population, yet they are very visibly prominent in bureaucracy, education, Bar and judiciary, and political structures. The community possesses large and varied social capital. Its journey of emancipation began with their gravitation to the seat of power during the rule of the Mughal period first and the British later. Their mastery of Urdu and English languages and their ability to adapt themselves quickly to the changing requirements and scenarios facilitated them to set with the rulers at different points of time. Education of both the sexes, occupational positioning in the knowledge based professions, early migration to the urban areas and distant places offering new opportunities are some of other characteristics of the community that helped it move miles ahead of the other backward communities. Over a period of time, they evolved their own cultural sub-text that established them in the upper echelons of the society, economy and polity. Their leadership is diffused; the mass base itself is mentally quite capable, open and empowered and above all possesses enormous coping abilities. The community itself is deemed to be very clever and they have demonstrated the capacity to scale dizzy heights and continue to stay there comfortably meeting all the challenges of doing so. It is true that they have taken a very long time to change the cultural profile of the community but the fact remains that they are the only backwards community that has achieved such a status.

The peasantry forms the largest chunk of the OBC population. They are deemed to be the most notorious economic group in adapting to change, especially technological change. Whereas this may indeed be true for the mass of peasantry in most part of the country, some of these OBCs as for Kurmi, Koeri and Yadavas of Bihar spotted the opportunity early, actualized it and reaped the benefits in an environment where most other farmers, not moving out from their tradition, are bleeding, quite a few even committing suicide in large numbers. Farmers near the metropolitan towns like Pune, Mumbai, New Delhi and Kolkata have realized the importance of agricultural crop diversification and gone in for horticulture, floriculture, vegetable farming and food processing. In fact, some prosperous among them have gone on packaged tours to Australia, New Zealand and Israel to learn more about such innovative practices first hand. After coming back to their native place, they have opted for floriculture and horticulture and benefited immensely. They now favoured for a third crop, hold back menthol oil for better prices at a later date, and get rid of the worries of crop not being purchased. These are isolated forays and yet, what they demonstrate is that the close minds are getting open, opportunities are getting spotted and localized mass type adoptions and adaptations are beginning to take shape.

The weavers are the second largest sub- group among the OBCs. Powerlooms, mechanized cotton and synthetic textile industry and free imports have ruined them beyond recognition. However, as Kanak Lata Mukund and B.Shyamsundari (2002) demonstrated, even in such a bleak scenario, we see many expressions of this traditional skill such as sambhalpuri of Orrisa, jamdhani of West Bengal, leheria of Gujarat, ikkat of Andhra Pradesh and triple ply silks of Kanchi-Puram (Tamil Nadu) are vibrantly alive today. In a globalized era, where market is flooded with textiles from China and other countries, these provide a well-defined product identity and saleable brand names. There is additional advantage of availability of local markets. They can rapidly grow by leveraging the major assets. The disadvantages they suffer from are the absence of market intelligence, grip on the retailers and wholesalers deciding what they would like to sell-Depending chiefly on their profit margins-Government policy that focus only on exports ignoring massive domestic market, and the competition from the powerlooms and the mechanized cotton textile industry. In case of Khadi, the Khadi and village Industries Commission has now demonstrated that by changing its product range and proper promotion, this turn around can be done very successfully. This trend is also seen sporadically among the chikan(Lucknow), dargozi (Hydrabad), and the metal/brass metal artisan groups (Aligarh, Moradabad, Ferozabad)wherever they have been able to organize themselves as collectives and taken due care of the backward and forward linkages.

As the country moves ahead and the economic structure reaches a scale where it can reconfigurate the social structure, the opportunities for other smaller sub-groups among the OBCs would be available where their native skills would come handy (i.e., the stonecutters in the booming building industry). What they need to do is to group themselves as organized 'vendors' who can benefit from the up gradation of technology, organizational strength and economies of scales.

The problem in most of the foregoing opportunity structures has been the absence of entrepreneurial initiatives focusing on the entire collectivities and intertwining of the social, economic and political interests of the concerned communities. Therefore, quite a few of these successes have not been replicated on wide enough geographical and economic scales.

Subject of study: Bihar

Bihar is located in the eastern part of the country (between 83°.30' to 88°.00' longitude). It is entirely land-locked State, although the outlet to the sea is through the port of Kolkatta, not far away. It lies mid-way between the humid West Bengal in the east and the sub humid Uttar Pradesh in the west which provides it with a transitional position in respect of climate, economy and culture. It is bounded by Nepal in the north and Jharkhand in the south. The State plain is divided into two unequal halves by the river Ganga which flows through the middle from west to east.

It finds mention in the Vedas, Puranas, and Epics. It is the land where the seeds of the first republic were sown and which cultivated the first crop of democracy. It has given birth to innumerous intellectuals, which spread the light of knowledge and wisdom not only in the country but in the whole world. The state as it is today has been shaped from its partition from the province of Bengal and most recently after the separation of the tribal southern region now called Jharkhand. Earliest myths and legends of hinduism the Sanatana (Eternal) Dharma - are associated with Bihar. The original author of the Hindu epic - **The Ramayana** - Maharishi Valmiki - lived in ancient Bihar. It was here that Prince Gautam attained enlightenment, became the Buddha- at the present Bodh Gaya- a town in central Bihar; and the great religion of Buddhism was born. It is here that Lord Mahavira, the founder of another great religion - Jainism - was born and attained nirvana (death). It is here that the tenth and the last Guru of the Sikhs, Guru Gobind Singh was born and attained the sainthood of sikhism. The ancient kingdoms of Magadh and of Licchavis, around about 7-8th century B.C., produced rulers who devised a system of administration that truly is progenitor of the modern art of statecraft, and of the linkage of statecraft with economics. Kautilya, the author of Arthashastra, the first treatise on the modern science of Economics lived here.

Another Mauryan king, Ashok, (also known as Priyadarshi or Priyadassi: around 270 B.C.) was the first

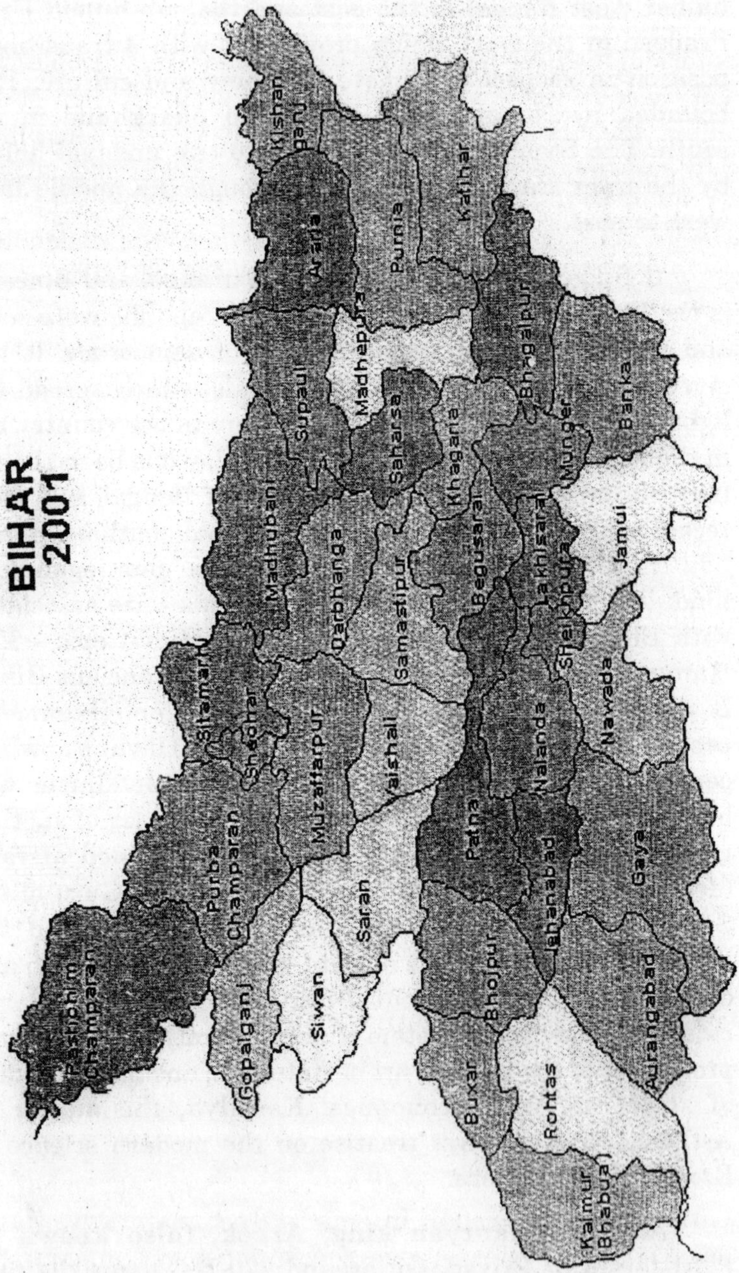

BIHAR
2001
Pashchim Champaran
Purba Champaran
Gopalganj
Siwan
Saran
Sitamarhi
Sheohar
Muzaffarpur
Vaishali
Madhubani
Darbhanga
Samastipur
Supaul
Saharsa
Madhepura
Araria
Kishanganj
Purnia
Katihar
Khagaria
Begusarai
Bhagalpur
Munger
Banka
Jamui
Lakhisarai
Sheikhpura
Nalanda
Patna
Jehanabad
Nawada
Gaya
Bhojpur
Buxar
Rohtas
Aurangabad
Kaimur (Bhabua)

to formulate firm tenets for the governance of people. He had these tenets, the Edicts of Ashok, inscribed on stone pillars which were planted across his kingdom. The pillar were crowned with the statue of one or more lions sitting on top of a pedestal which was inscribed with symbols of wheels. As the lion denoted strength, the wheel denoted the eternal (endless) nature of truth (dharma), hence the name Dharma (or Dhamma) Chakra. This figure of lions, atop a pedestal, with inscription of a wheel, was adopted as the Official Seal of the independent Republic of India (1947). Also, Ashok's dharma chakra was incorporated into the national flag of India, the Indian tricolor.

Ancient Bihar also saw the glorification of women in matters of state affairs. It was here that Amrapali, a courtesan of Vaishali in the kingdom of the Lichhavis, attained and wielded enormous power.

At Nalanda, the world's first seat of higher learning, an university, was established during the Gupta period. It continued as a seat of learning till the middle ages, when the muslim invaders burned it down.

In medieval times Bihar lost its prestige as the political and cultural centre of India. The Mughal period was a period of unremarkable provincial administration from Delhi. The only remarkable person of this time in Bihar was Sher Shah, or Sher Khan Sur, an Afghan.. several acts of land reform are attributed to him.

During British period, Bihar was a part of the Presidency of Bengal, and was governed from Calcutta. As such, this was a territory very much dominated by the people of Bengal. All leading educational and medical centres were in Bengal. In spite of the unfair advantage that Bengalis possessed, some sons of Bihar rose to positions of prominence by dint of their intelligence and hard labour, such as Dr. Rajendra Prasad, native of Ziradei, in the district of Saran. He became the first President of the Republic of India.

When separated from the Bengal Presidency in 1912, Bihar and Orissa comprised a single province. Later, under the Government of India Act of 1935, the Division of Orissa became a separate province; and the Province of Bihar came into being as an administrative unit of British India. In 1956 the district of Purulia, was separated and incorporated into West Bengal as a part of the Linguistic Reorganization of Indian States.

Resurgence in the history of Bihar came during the struggle for India's independence. It was from Bihar that Mahatma Gandhi launched his civil-disobedience movement, which ultimately led to India's independence.

We cannot forget the JP's substantial contribution to modern Indian history which continued up until his death in 1979. The movement started by JP, however, brought the Emergency to an end, led to the massive defeat of Indira Gandhi and her Congress Party at the polls, and, installation of a non-Congress government -The Janata Party - at Delhi, for the first time. Subsequent bickerings in the Janata Party led to the formation of a breakaway political party - the Janata Dal. It was also from this party that Laloo Prasad Yadav, the Chief Minister of Bihar was elected. The bickering continued. A new party led by Mr. Yadav was formed i.e., the Rashtriya Janata Dal - which went on to rule for almost 15 years in Bihar.

Bihar apart from being one of the biggest States (183.0 million population in 2001) is also the poorest in term of both per capita income and human development indicators (BIMARU State). The human development report of 1990 clubbed Bihar with the world's six most underdeveloped countries-all in Africa. A recent ranking of India's 569 districts by the National Population Commission on a composite index of socio-demographic progress placed all of Bihar's 37 districts below 300. It presents a paradoxical picture with regard to the available resources and development. The bar chart given below indicate the per capita development expenditure (2000-03) in case of Bihar, which is the lowest, i.e; below Rs.4000.

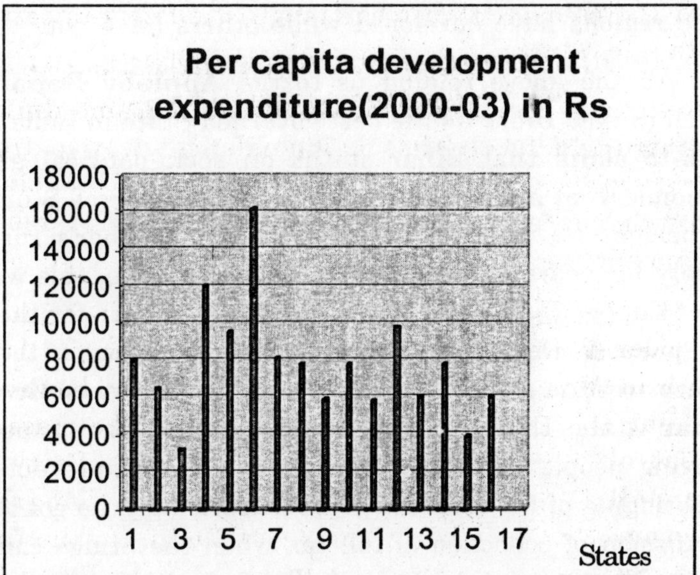

1.AP, 2.Assam, 3.Bihar, 4.Gujarat, 5.Haryana, 6.HP, 7.Karnataka, 8.Kerala, 9.MP, 10.Maharashtra, 11.Orissa, 12.Punjab, 13.Rajasthan, 14.TN, 15.UP, 16. W.Bengal.

On the one hand, it has rich and fertile land, numerous rivers, abundant rain, skilled handicraft, rich cultural heritage, eminent institutions for learning while on the other hand male and female literacy in 2001 were as low as 60.0% and 34.0% respectively (National: 76.0% & 54.0% respectively), Bihar alongwith UP, MP, Orissa etc; have been categorized under BIMARU States.With a per capita income growth close to zero in the last decade, the situation has only deteriorated since. It has also not made social adjustment within the castes. As a result of social instability, a conducive atmosphere to build proper infrastructure is absent, and thereby leading to low investment. The fruits of democracy are far away from the majority of the population. This is a pivotal point why some regions have developed while others have not.

All the above remind us to the **Appleby Report-** which ranked Bihar **as** the best governed State in India in 1949-to claim that Bihar status on socio-political and economic front has declined over the years.But Prof. Stuart Corbridge of LSE, who has been studying Bihar's rural society for years do not think so. In his opinion, this was due to upper caste control over land and politics for their own purpose. Development would have ended some of their enterprises. As Arvind Das in his book, **"The Republic of Bihar"** states that, A landlord who ran a prolific business ferrying people across the Ganga from Patna prevented the bridging of the river for years.(surprisingly, he got the permission of collection of toll tax when the bridge came up).

In the absence of other alternative policies to reach social stability, reservation remains the only policy that can pave the way for development of the backward castes leaving aside upper castes of the State.

It is the second largest State in the country in term of population. There has been a good deal of mixture among various castes. Though Brahmins and Kshatriyas belong to the same racial stock, the later are more mixed because of their marriage with various stocks of people. Besides the above castes others are Bhumihar and, Kayastha who alongwith formers forms upper castes (13.2*) in the State.The percent of these castes in total population of the State is given below:

a) Brahmin: 4.7%

b) Kshatriya: 4.2 %

c) Bhumihar: 2.9%

d) Kayastha: 1.4%

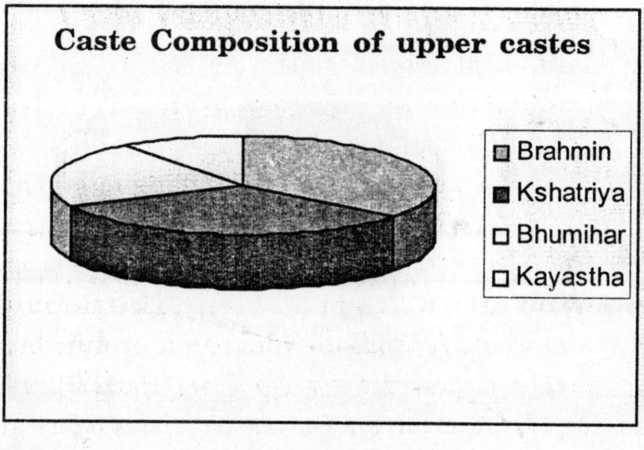

(* Report of the Backward Classes Commission (B.P.Mandal): 1980, Part-1, Government of India, N.Delhi)

The backward castes like Koeri, Kurmi, Kahar and Ahir represent various racial strains. Caste rivalries and prejudices are numerous in Bihar. It also has a large percentage of population belonging to SCs (14.51%) after creation of Jharkhand in 2000. Risley has grouped these people under Arya - Dravidian race and among the lower castes, Dravidian character is found mostly. However anthropologists have rejected Risley's classification. Anthropologist such as, Dr. B.S.Guha is of the opinion that the lower castes of Bihar represent the basic dolico type, having dark complexion, pointed chin and deep pigmentation. He classifies them under the palaeo-mediterranean group but Eickstedt prefers to call them the melanid type because in some physical characters they represent the Melanesian Negroids. But this view has not gained acceptance in India. These castes are spread all over the State, which is shown below in the table.

Table: 1.1

Caste	Percentage of total population
Upper caste	
Brahmin	4.7
Bhumihar	2.9
Rajput	4.2
Kayasta	1.2
Sub total	13.0
upper backwards	
Bania	0.6
Yadav	11.0
Kurmi	3.6
Koeris	4.1
Sub total	19.3
Lower backwards	
Barai	1.0
Dhanuk	1.8
Hajjam	1.4
Kahar	1.7
Kandu	1.6
Kumhar	1.3

Lohar	1.3
Mallah	1.5
Tatwa	1.6
Teli	2.8
Others	16.0
Sub total	32.0
Scheduled castes	14.4
Scheduled tribes	9.0
Muslims	12.5
Total	100.0

Source; (Blair, 1980)

Similarly derived District wise distribution of castes for 1961 can be seen in the table given below:.

Table: 1.2

Percentage distribution of castes by District, Bihar 1961

Districts	Upper castes	Lower castes	SCs	STs	Muslims
Saran	22.65	55.02	10.33	—	12.00
Champaran	11.79	57.75	14.56	0.10	15.80
Muzaffarpur	16.84	59.57	14.89	—	8.70
Darbhanga	15.80	56.35	14.67	—	13.20
Saharsa	10.00	66.08	17.18	0.44	6.30
Purnia	5.27	42.38	12.24	03.91	36.20
Sahabad	26.59	49.81	16.01	0.69	06.90
Patna	15.19	59.47	16.09	0.05	09.20
Gaya	16.64	49.10	24.54	0.02	09.70
Monghyr	21.28	53.23	15.81	1.38	08.30
Bhagalpur	10.66	62.59	11.58	3.77	11.40
*Santhalpraganas	04.18	40.62	07.56	38.24	09.40

*Hazaribagh	07.03	58.12	12.55	11.30	11.00
*Palamu	09.24	36.09	25.93	19.24	09.50
*Ranchi	02.62	25.92	04.55	61.61	05.30
*Dhanbad	20.27	41.09	17.86	11.08	09.70
*Singhbhum	02.93	43.59	02.97	47.31	03.20
All Bihar	13.22	52.16	14.07	09.05	11.50

* Now in Jharkhand State

Source: 1- Figure for upper castes projected from1931 caste census, figures for SCs & STs taken from census of India 1961, vol-VI, Bihar part-II A, figures for Muslims census of India 1951, vol-IV, Bihar.

A 2- Lower caste includes the entire castes intermediary between upper and the SCs.

Over all the backward castes account 52.0 percent of the population (according to 1st Backward Classes Commission report, total Backward Castes population of the State is 38.1 %). The largest single other names, i.e; Ahirs and Gwalas they comprise 11.0% of the population and are spread in all districts of the State. Earlier, their main occupation was cattle grazing and sale of milk and milk products but in course of time, bulk of them have acquired land and in most cases they constitute small, medium and in some cases rich farmers. In some districts like Saharsa, they form the dominant caste. The next largest caste is that of the Kurmi, who forms 3.6 percent of the population. They have been traditionally landholders and in some districts they constitute medium and rich peasantry agricultural development in Patna and Nalanda districts has been largely successful due to their efforts. Koeri/ Kushwaha is the caste traditionally devoted to vegetable growing. Yadav, Kurmi, Koeri and 40 other castes comprise the advanced sections of the backward castes in Bihar and figure in Annexure-II of the backward classes list of the State. L.R.Naik, member of the Mandal Commission has

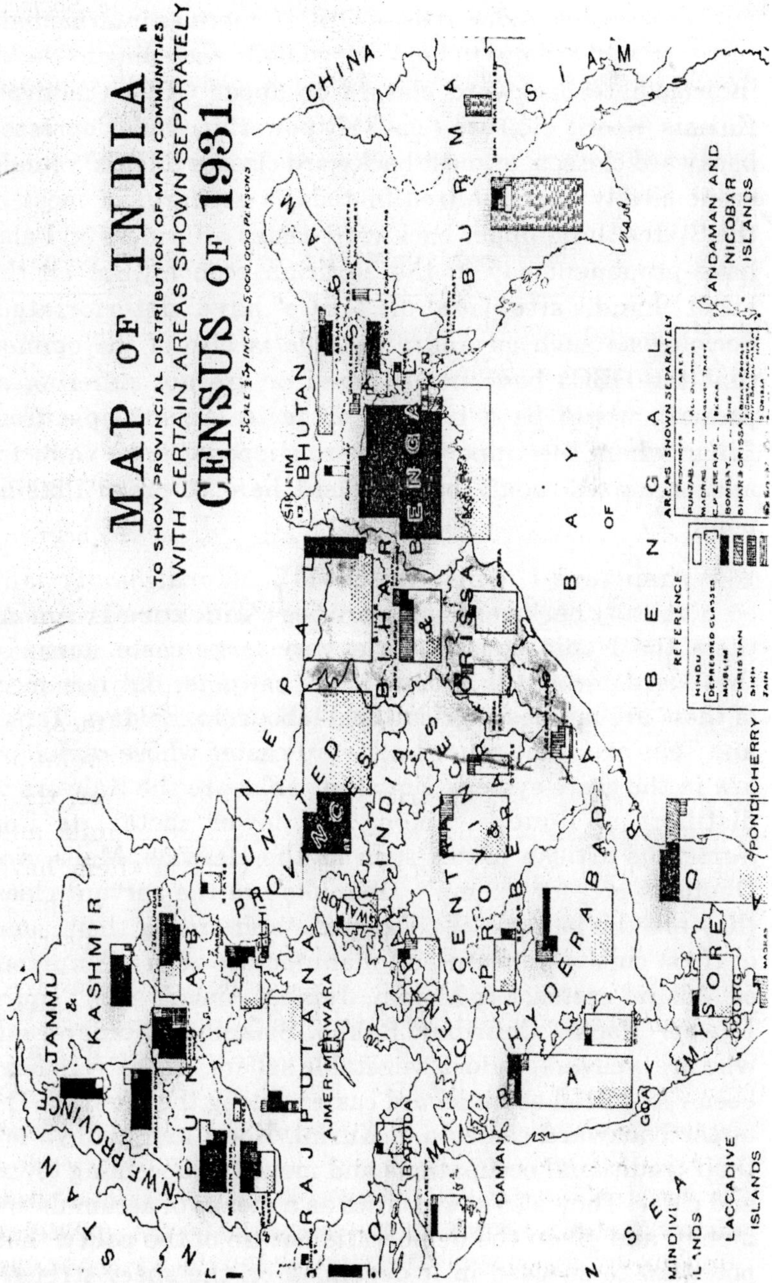
MAP OF INDIA
TO SHOW PROVINCIAL DISTRIBUTION OF MAIN COMMUNITIES
WITH CERTAIN AREAS SHOWN SEPARATELY
CENSUS OF 1931.
REFERENCE
HINDU
DEPRESSED CLASSES
MUSLIM
CHRISTIAN
SIKH
JAIN
AREAS SHOWN SEPARATELY
JAMMU & KASHMIR
N.W.F. PROVINCE
PUNJAB
RAJPUTANA
AJMER-MERWARA
UNITED PROVINCES
NEPAL
SIKKIM
BHUTAN
BIHAR & ORISSA
BENGAL
ASSAM
CHINA
BURMA
SIAM
CENTRAL PROVINCES & BERAR
CENTRAL INDIA
GWALIOR
BARODA
HYDERABAD
MYSORE
COORG
GOA
DAMAN
PONDICHERRY
BAY OF BENGAL
ARABIAN SEA
LACCADIVE ISLANDS
ANDAMAN AND NICOBAR ISLANDS

put these castes under artisan OBCs, where as intermediate castes mostly belongs to landowing OBCs.According to Naik's intermediate backward classes or upper OBCs (Yadavas, Kurmis, Koeris etc;) are relatively powerful, while depressed backward classes, or most backward classes (MBCs) remain economically marginalized.In today's scenario in most of the States these upper backward castes are rulers and also have prominent say in the agrarian economy.But on the other hand, situation of MBCs have deterioriated. Sociologists such as Andre Beteille is also of the opinion that the OBCs have not suffered or are not suffering at present, would be a travesty of facts. An example from Bihar, where the Upper OBCs are supposed to be powerful and organized would be pertinent here to prove Beteille point.

Annexure-I consists of 112 educationally and economically backward communities (**Annexure-I**). Among them the Nonia constitutes a very large caste. Initially, they were devoted to production of saltpeter but now most of them are landless agricultural labourers. Beldars, Tantis and Telis are some other backward castes whose ranks are low in the caste system, Equal in ranks are the Kalwars or distillers of liquors. Among the lower castes we find numerous artisan castes such as the Halwais, Malis, and Dhanuks etc; for example Dhanuks are the servant class, they are the bearers of palanquins and among them some of them cultivate hemp and manufacture ropes. A number of Muslim castes, i.e; Momin, Julaha, Ansari, Sai/ Faquir/ Dewan/ Madar/ Churihar, Bakho, Saikailgar, Rangrej etc; who are weavers, tailors, vegetable sellers, cloth dyers have been recognized as backward castes among the Muslims.The upper backward castes, i.e; Kurmi, Koeri and Yadava left their traditional occupations and moved to upcoming towns and cities. They also saw politics as a means of accumulating money, and given the democratic nature of the polity, their potential to succeed in it depended on the sheer strength of their numbers. This was the beginning of a process that gave Bihar its large crop of casteist leaders, starting with Karpoori Thakur and now including the likes of Lalu Prasad Yadav, Nitish Kumar and Sushil Kumar Modi. Most of these backward caste leaders emerged on the scene through the JP movement of the 1970s, but their rise was part of a larger social churning. Their numbers have indeed proved sufficient for electoral success, albeit, given their own inner schisms, not without a subtle juggling of caste combinations.

But the rise of the backward caste leaders has failed to end Bihar's own backwardness. They joined politics as a means of money accumulation, and have stuck to their task – strengthening the nexus of caste, politics, under-development and crime like their predecessors. A good example of this continuity is the Fodder scam. At present caste rules both mainstream and extremist politics in Bihar.It will rule as long as Bihar remains inegalitarian and under-developed. And until Bihar remain such; crime will prosper as the only means of moneymaking and improving social status (ex; Kidnapping as an industry).

Now the Nitish government has appointed persons of eminence in different fields, such as Dr. S.C.Jha to tackle the State problems and provide guidelines for its development. Besides this one can tap the rich cultural heritage of these OBCs, so that they can go hand in hand with the upper strata of society, for example in the realm of dance there are several of them. One can be kept spellbound by their performance, like dhobinach, jhumarnach, manjhi, gondnach, jitiyanach, more-morni, dom-domin, bhuiababa, rah baba, kathghorwa nach etc. Subaltern tradition with ethnic identity is not only alive in their action packed dances but can be found in the melodious songs as well with folk aesthetic grammer, No cultural or religious function is complete in certain social groups without the melody of the shivnarayani, harpauri, birha, lorikayan. Even in the realm of theatre and musical instruments subaltern culture has rich tradition in Bihar.

District wise population of these castes including MBCs are given below :

Table: 1.3

District-Wise population of backward castes of Bihar

Districts	Backward Castes	Percent, out of total population
Araria	Ahir	8.0
	Tantis	4.0
Aurangabad	Ahirs 16.0	Koeris 6.0
Banka	—	—
Begusarai	Ahirs	11.0
	Dhanuks, Koeris, Tantis	4.0 each
	Kurmis	sizable number
Bhabhua	—	—
Bhagalpur	Ahirs	13.0
	Kurmi, Dhanuk,	
	Koeri, Tanti	5.0 each
	Teli	sizable number
Bhojpur	Ahirs	18.0
	Kurmi, Koeri	5.0 each
Buxar	Ahir	13.0
	Koeri	6.0
	Kurmi, Kahar, Kandu	sizable number
Darbhanga	Ahir	13.0

	Kewat, Koeri, Dhanuk	5.0 each
	Teli	sizable number
Gaya	Ahir	14.0
	Kahar, Koeri	6.0 each
Gopalganj	Ahir	11.0
	Koeri	7.0
	Kandu, Teli	sizable number
Jehanabad	Ahir	18.0
	Koeri	8.0
	Kahar	5.0
	Teli	sizable number
Katihar	Ahir	6.0
	Tanti	4.0
Khagaria	Ahir	16.0
	Dhanuk, Koeri, Tanti	5.0 each
	Teli	sizable number
Kishanganj	Ahir	8.0
	Tanti	sizable number
Madhepura	Ahir	20.0
	Dhanuk, Koeri, Tanti, Teli	5.0 each
Madhubani	Ahir	13.0
	Kewat	8.0
	Koeri, Dhanuk	5.0 each
	Teli	sizable number
Munger	Ahir	15.0
	Dhanuk, Koeri, Tanti	5.0 each
Muzaffarpur	Ahir	12.0
	Kewat	6.0
	Koeri, Kurmi, Kandu, Teli	5.0 each

Nalanda	Ahir	13.0
	Kurmi	11.0
	Kahar	6.0
	Koeri	5.0
	Teli	sizable number
Nawada	Ahir	15.0
	Koeri	7.0
	Kahar,	Teli 5.0
Purbi & Paschmi Champaran	Ahir, Kandu, Kewat, Teli, Kurmi,	—
Patna	Ahir	18.0
	Kurmi	7.0
	Koeri, Kahar	5.0
Purnea	Ahir	8.0
	Tanti	4.0
	Dhanuk	sizable number
Rohtas	Ahir, Koeri, Kurmi, Kahar, Kandu	sizable number
Saharsha	Ahir	15.0
	Dhanuk, Koeri, Tanti, Teli	5.0 each
Samastipur	Ahir	12.0
	Kewat	7.0
	Koeri, Dhanuk	5.0 each
Chapra	Ahir	18.0
	Koeri	7.0
	Kurmi	5.0
	Nuniya, Kandu, Teli	sizable number
Sheohar	Ahir	11.0
	Koeri	6.0
	Kurmi, Kewat	5.0 each
	Teli, Kandu	sizable number
Sitamarhi	Ahir	13.0

	Kewat, Koeri, Kurmi	5.0 each
	Teli, Kandu	sizable number
Siwan	Ahir	14.0
	Koeri	7.0
	Kurmi	5.0
	Nuniya, Kandu, Teli	sizable number
Vaishali	Ahir	11.0
	Koeri, Kewat, Kurmi	5.0 each
	Teli, Kandu	sizable number

Source: The Encyclopaedic District Gazetteers of India, 2000(Bihar), Vol.VIII, Gyan Publishing House, New Delhi.

Note: Some of the districts have been left out due to non-availability of data.

As no census of OBCs have been carried out after 1931, so population of some of these have been mentioned here, district-wise.

Table: 1.4

Castes	Districts	Persons	Males	Females
Dhanuk	Patna	35687	17568	18119
	Gaya	3245	1523	1722
	Saran	19686	9739	9957
	Champaran	12663	6454	6209
	Muzaffarpur	56422	27322	29100
	Darbhanga	147210	70249	76961
	Munger	114133	55834	58499
	Bhagalpur	97315	47956	49329
	Purnea	42255	21645	20610
	Santhal Pragana	12228	6117	6111
	Palamau	3778	1882	1896

Dhobi	Patna	13375	6600	6685
	Gaya	18138	8980	9158
	Saran	20899	10165	10734
	Champaran	23301	11531	11770
	Muzaffarpur	34594	16719	17875
	Darbhanga	25798	12726	13072
	Munger	23277	11459	11818
	Bhagalpur	22588	11491	11097
	Purnea	9240	4943	4297
	Santhal Pragana	8499	4317	4132
	Shahabad	17384	10165	10734
Goala(Ahir, Gopa, Yadav)	Patna	277263	145951	131312
	Gaya	372811	191136	181675
	Saran	332608	167786	184822
	Champaran	209875	179683	174924
	Muzaffarpur	354607	179683	17494
	Darbhanga	400312	202902	197410
	Munger	279407	142689	136718
	Bhagalpur	374677	191310	183367
	Purnea	134934	70610	64324
	Santhal Pragana	123177	62860	60317
	Shahabad	273005	140328	132677
	Hazaribagh	156430	77136	79294
	Ranchi	39486	19974	19512
	Palamau	50268	25656	24613
	Manbhum	40996	22064	18932
	Singbhum	35285	18084	17201

Hajjam(Nai, Napit,				
NaiBrahman)	Patna	30885	15778	15107
	Gaya	44788	21413	23375
	Saran	35794	17434	18360
	Champaran	26105	13162	12943
	Muzaffarpur	45474	21667	23805
	Darbhanga	37279	18179	19100
	Munger	44798	22106	22692
	Bhagalpur	38597	20028	18569
	Purnea	19084	10064	9020
	Santhal Pragana	23497	12097	11400
	Shahabad	28246	13725	14521
	Hazaribagh	33141	16582	16559
	Ranchi	9781	4934	4847
	Palamau	10545	5326	5219
	Manbhum	24936	13028	11908
	Singbhum	3829	2063	1766
Halalkhor(Hindu,				
Muslim)		20742	10251	10491
	Patna	2314	1224	1090
	Gaya	1825	945	880
	Saran	2898	1456	1442
	Champaran	3309	1651	1658
	Muzaffarpur	3964	1929	2035
	Darbhanga	4284	1006	2278
	Shahabad	2525	1247	1278
Mali(Malakar)				
Hindu	Patna	5887	3050	2837
	Gaya	7193	3569	3624

	Saran	6030	2920	3110
	Champaran	5516	2937	2579
	Muzaffarpur	11110	5420	5690
	Darbhanga	6542	3431	3111
	Munger	5719	2914	2805
	Shahabad	5182	2668	2514
	Bhagalpur	3067	1746	1321
	Purnea	5590	2888	2702
	Hazaribagh	1501	801	700
	Singbhum	3202	1956	1346
Tanti(Tatwa)				
Hindu	Patna	13731	6862	6869
	Gaya	3264	1681	1583
	Saran	7588	3630	3958
	Champaran	33576	16559	17017
	Muzaffarpur	56811	26621	30190
	Darbhanga	83941	40067	43874
	Munger	94506	44532	49974
	Shahabad	7698	3769	3929
	Bhagalpur	88745	43472	45273
	Purnea	62582	31462	31120
	Santhal pragana	13146	5675	6571
Koeri(Kushwaha)				
Hindu	Patna	71239	37015	34224
	Gaya	158073	80796	77277
	Shahabad	148653	75838	72821
	Saran	168060	85676	82384
	Champaran	116546	60549	55997
	Muzaffarpur	144877	72607	72270

Darbhanga	147787	74404	73383
Munger	102030	51666	50364
Bhagalpur	90238	45635	44603
Purnea	24694	12820	11874
Santhal pragana	18629	9392	9237
Hazaribagh	63632	31276	32356
Ranchi	9145	4553	4592
Palamau	28124	14033	14091
Manbhum	9740	5289	4451

Source: W.G.Lacey(Rpt.1978) Census of India, 1931 : Bihar & Orissa, Part-11, Usha Publications, N.Delhi.

Subsequently, the projected figures for 1951 of some of these castes are also given.

Table:1.5

Population of Hindu backward castes of Bihar in the census of 1931 & estimated population in 1951

CASTES	1931	1951
Agariya	——	4187
Aghori	——	——
Bagdi	——	9880
Beldar	——	123348
Bediya	——	1581
Barhai(Vishwakarma)	307313	379710
Bari	——	164510
Bhar	——	461
Bind	——	184950
Chain, Chayeen	——	44095
Kahar)	524030	647481

Dhamin	——	1902
Dhanuk	547308	676243
Dhekaru	——	376
Dhimar	——	1417
Dhobi	——	75944
Dhunia	——	269855
Gangai(Ganesh)	——	52475
Gangota, Gangoth	——	78612
Gulgaliya	——	589
Jadupatia	——	57
Kaivartta, Kaviratta	——	108861
Kewat	204881	253147
Hajjam	456779	564387
Kasab(Kasai)	——	19345
Khatik	——	130
Khatwe	——	151539
Khatauri, Khetauri	26787	33097
Kosta, Koshta	——	——
Kurmi(Mahto)	519439	641808
Halalkhor	1599	2181
Mali(Malakar)	72414	89473
Mangar(Magar)	——	1192
Namshudra	——	5178
Nunia, Nonia	——	466950
Mallah	459560	567823
Tanti(Tatwa), Tati, Tatin	524945	648612
Tharu	37338	46134
Tiyar	——	61748
Turha	——	103985

Population of Muslim backward castes in the census of 1931 & estimated population in 1951

Castes	1931	1951
Bhatiara	—	—
Chik	—	—
Dafali	—	—
Dhobi	—	75944
Dhunia	—	269855
Kasab(Kasai)	—	19345
Madari	—	—
Mehtar(lalbegis, halalkhors & bhangis)	1599	2181
Miriasin	—	—
Nat	—	—
Pamaria	—	—

Source: RGI Census Report, GOI, 1954.

To Know the actual situation of OBCs in Bihar a village perspective is must which has been mentioned below:

The vast majority of Bihar's electorate reside in the State's thousands of villages. The village life makes visible the contentions politics of caste empowerment. For many lower caste villagers, electoral politics is more crucially about control of the village and everyday power relations.

An ethnographic account of backward castes of village 'Datiyana' situated in Patna district of Bihar reveals social and political changes resulting from backward class rule during the last 15 years.

Regarding the name of this village, some mythologies prevail, i.e., (a) it derived its name from a Buddhist monk

'Datiyan, (b) 'Datatreya', the grandson of Brahma passed through this region and thus it was named after him; (c) the second coming of Raja Maniyar i.e.; Dutiya anna — became — Datiyana.

Most probably, before 1202 AD this village was inhabited by Muslims and some other castes. After that the king Maniyar of Maner established its rule to protect his people from Muslims. These Bhumihar Brahmins later on settled in this area and for their own convenience divided the whole village in sixteen small blocks, each under one head, from which the present inhabitant derives their descendency. Till date, this village has been dominated by the upper caste Bhumihar but in these 15 years they have lost the previous dominance, due to the emergence of backward caste on economic as well as educational front. Except Yadav and some other upper backward castes, other backward castes inhabit in this village. The social respect traditionally paid to upper caste Bhumihar had ceased, as had the degrading acts of sub- ordination that many lower caste villagers had been forced to endure.

Rise of backward caste to political power in the State offered these lower caste villagers a sense of social-even familiar ownership in the State. They relate themselves to those who are in power through kinship relation. Most of them have also left their traditional occupations and moved to the nearby cities in search of greener pastures. Most of these backward castes are also in government services due to reservation policy of the State Government. To enhance their social status, in different social customs, they are imitating the upper caste, i.e., Bhumihar. They have also benefited from the market economy and some of them have become well to do, having their houses in urban areas, educating their children in public schools and enjoying modern amenities of life.

Recently with the amendment in Panchayati Raj Act, for the first time, seat has been reserved for backward caste to contest election for 'Datiyana Panchayat', which saw a large number of candidates (18 in numbers) contesting for Panchayat seat. This shows their political consciousness. Some of the backward caste members from this village have also joined the Maoist group as most of them are petty landholders or landless labourers and through their militant organisation they strike deal for better farm wages.

Despite all these, the village remain peaceful due to liberal attitude of upper caste towards these backward castes. So, caste conflict do not take place and the village remained peaceful in all these years, as the gap between the oppressors and oppressed has narrowed down to a greater extent.

In the end we can conclude with the remark of Dr. BR Ambedkar who spoke about the moral conflict between Buddhism and Brahminism which is the history of India and to eradicate exploitation of the ruling class i.e., Brahmin culture, caste annihilation is must. But for this a pro-poor and pro-dalit economic policy alone can provide a basis for strengthening the human and market competitive abilities of the oppressed sections, but it cannot erase the glaring inequalities that exist between the SCs and STs and the OBCs on par with the upper castes. So this would again require caste annihilation, which in turn requires a much broader campaign encompassing cultural, social and political aspects as well. We also have to remove economic disparities in this era of globalization and liberalization because it is a serious contributor of social inequalities today. It has changed its shape only due to the existence of market economy, so victims of older forms of discrimination will either continue to be victimized or simply become victims of new forms of discrimination. This village (Datiyana) is an example, how things are changing in favour of OBCs of the State, besides fulfilling Dr. Ambedkar vision.

References

Blair, H. (1980), Rising Kulaks and Backward Classes in Bihar: Social Change in the Late 1970s', Economic and Political Weekly, Vol-XV. No. 2.

Bhatt, SC. (2000), The Encyclopedic District Gazetteers of India(Eastern Zone, Bihar), Vol. VIII, Gyan Publishing House, New Delhi.

Beteille, Andre. Caste in Contemporary India in C.J.Fuller(ed.) Caste Today(1997), Oxford University Press, Delhi.

Basham AL (1990) The Wonder That was India, OUP, Delhi.

W. G. Lacey, 1987 (Rpt) Census of India; 1931, Part-1.Report, Vol: VII (Bihar & Orissa), Usha Publications, Dariya Ganj, New Delhi.

Census Report of OBCs, 1951 (projected), Registrar General of India, GOI, N.Delhi.

Development Conference Report: Bihar, August 21st-22nd, 2005, Development Alternatives-Pricewater House Coopers (P) Ltd, & DFID.

Dirks, Nicholas B. The Original Caste :Power, history and Hierarchy in South Asia, in Mackim Marriott (ed.) 1990, India through Hindu Categories, Sage Publications, New Delhi.

Galanter, Marc(1991) Competing Inequalities: The Law and the Backward Classes in India, Oxford University Press, Delhi.

Ghurye, G.S.(1957) Caste and Class in India, Popular Book Depot, Bombay.

——(1932) Caste and Race in India, Popular Prakashan, Bombay.

Hutton, J.H., Census of India-1931 (1989) Vol.- I & II, Gian Publishing House, Delhi.

Hussain, Majid (1994) Encyclopaedia of India (Bihar), Vol-XXVI, Rima Publishing House, New Delhi.

Report of the Backward Classes Commission (BP Mandal) 1981, Part-1 & 11, Manager of Publication, N.Delhi.

Risley, H.H.(1981) The Tribes & Castes of Bengal, Vol.1, Firma Mukhopadhaya, Calcutta.

Srinivas, M.N.(1972) Social Change in Modern India, Orient Longman, Hyderabad.

The Eastern Anthropologist, April-September, 2002, Vol-55, No. 2-3 Ethnographic & Folk Culture Society, Lucknow.

Working Group on Empowerment of Backward Classes in Tenth Plan (2002-2007), 2001 Chairperson P.S.Krishnan, Ministry of Social Justice & Empowerment, New Delhi.

Yadav, K.C.(1994) India's Unequal Citizens:A Study of OBCs, Manohar, New Delhi.

2

Mobilization of Backward Castes

Mobilization can be defined as the organization of people for the formation of an association, federation or social movement to articulate their needs and demands, values and goals and to accomplish them either through legal or extra legal means (violence). It can be categorized into two types: (a) Instrumental mobilization, which is made for fulfillment of demand like minimum wages, bonus or hours of work etc; by agricultural workers or trade unions or political parties and (b) Symbolic mobilization: which involves mobilization of the members of a collectivity or masses by the leaders or political parties toward the change of values, norms or certain goals of the system. Symbolic mobilization is further divided into (1) intra-systematic and (11) system displacing. Most of the social movements are examples of symbolic mobilization and the movement of the backward castes of Bihar can be seen in this perspective, as Rajni Kothari has pointed out that the institution of caste has played a useful role by providing ready-made traditional channels of mobilization and articulation. But this has its limitation, so backward castes have to find new avenues of social mobility. The traditionally sanctioned avenues of social mobility are virtually closed for them. Also employment and business opportunities are scarce and highly competitive. Moreover, to succeed in business they need capital and in order to gain employment in public or private services, they need higher educational qualifications. These are non-social field and to achieve status in non social fields is not equivalent of achieving social status. Their achievement in non social fields add to their prestige and earn adulation for them in their own group, unless they succeed in weakening or completely destroying the social barriers erected in their path of upward social mobility, they can not hope to succeed in getting themselves socially accepted. This they can achieve only through politics. Politics is a great leveler of social distinctions in as much as by evolving new criteria of selection of leaders; it weakens the traditional bases of social structure and thus affords to the lower caste an opportunity to achieve through politics what they cannot achieve through social instrumentalities. But lacking other instrumentalities of achieving power, they can be effective in politics by their educational achievements. And the best example in context of Bihar is the Kurmi caste, besides other upper backward castes.

Broadly speaking, there are three main theories, which try to explain the structural conditions, and motivational forces which give rise to a movement. These are theories of a) relative deprivation, b) strain and c) revitalization. The theory of relative deprivation has been developed on two different lines: social mobility and social conflict. The former line of development is represented by Merton in relation to reference group in which Runciman has also added problems of inequalities and social justice. Gurr has further provided some clarifications in this concept by including expectations and perceived capabilities which involves three sets of values, i.e; economic condition, political power and social status and gap may arises in it due to decremental deprivation, progressive deprivation and aspirational deprivation.The second theory, i.e; strain theory has been propounded by Smelser's and it is in the form of structural-functional framework.He considers strain as the impairment of relation among parts of a system and includes deprivation under strain.Whereas, looking at both the above approach, Wallace is of the opinion that social movements develop out of a deliberate, organized and conscious effort on the part of members of a society. He further analysed the dynamics of revitalization movement in four phases: period of cultural stability, period of increased individual stress, period of cultural distortation and consequent disillusionment, and period of revitalization.

The participants in a movement, especially among the backward castes in the States view their deprivation in different areas-such as religious, economic, educational and political–as interrelated for they are different manifestations of inequalities and discriminations based on a differential allocation of diverse goods and services.Thus the leader of these movements simultaneously open up multiple fronts to attack the monopoly of the upper castes in various fields.

M.S.A.Rao has also identified four types of such movements : In Madras, Karnataka and Maharashtra, the Brahmin, Non-Brahmin cleavage appeared and the movement had the aim of reducing the dominance of the Brahmin's in politics and professions, the second pattern prevailed in the north, where the cleavage appeared between the general forward and twice- born castes of Brahmin, Bhumihar, Kayastha and Rajput on the one hand and the intermediate castes of Ahir, Kurmi, etc; on the others, the third pattern is that of a conflict between the depressed castes and the forward castes and the tribal movement constitutes the fourth type. A diagrammatic representation of social mobility is given below:

Social mobility—a) Individual : Horizontal : Territorial, religious, political party, family, occupation, and other horizontal shifting without any noticeable change in vertical position

Ascending : Individual infiltration, creation & elevation

b) Social object : Vertical of a whole group

Descending : Individual sinking

Or disintegration of a whole group

a) & b) Economic, occupational, political etc;

Source: Pritim A. Sorokin, Social and Cultural Mobility, p 136

Movement by a particular section of society crop up when it realizes that injustice is being done against them, and it develops a feeling of deprivation and degradation in comparison to other groups. The backward castes movement in Bihar was due to this deprivation and degradation. The main goals of these movements have been getting rights and dignity whatever may be the means to achieve it. The recent evidence of backward caste mobilization suggests that they mobilized themselves for asserting their rights, to have their share in the democratic set up like jobs and positions, fight against atrocities etc. The mobilization is demonstrated in term of organized protests on different occasions for asserting their rights and demonstrating their strength against the powers of atrocities and discrimination. In the democratic set up the organized mobilization appear to act between the State and the people. Increasing awareness among castes is another gain in such movement.

In the process of mobilization, caste came to be used in the electoral process in the Indian as well as the State politics from the first general election. Indeed it had entered the political arena even before. In 1950s and 1960s, the leaders of all political parties condemned in public the use of caste in politics. Politicians freely acknowledged that caste was being extensively used in the politics of post-independence India, but they said that it was being used by other parties, not their own. When it was shown that their party too was using caste, their reply was that they did not start the process but were being forced to accommodate caste in order to survive for in the politics or at least in Indian politics one could not afford to be too idealistic if one wished to remain in business. In other words, they sought to defend the use of caste on tactical rather than ethical grounds. This can be seen in context of recently held election in Bihar before president's rule of 2005.The RJD list of candidates for the second phase includes names of 23 yadavs-koeries, 9 dalits, 5 OBCs, 3 Rajputs, and one each of Bhumihar and Kayasth.The LJP fielded 10 muslim candidates, 7 yadavs candidates while JD(U) had nominated 3 candidates from the minorities, 11 Yadavs, 4 Brahmins, 2 Bhumihars, 6 SCs, 6 Kurmis, 5 Koeries and 2 Rajputs etc;whereas BJP nominated one candidate from it.

Bihar is predominantly an agrarian society. which has its impact on caste–class division. It was a part of the permanent settlement where zamindars were invested with the power of revenue collection by the colonial State. In the initial stage, zamindars also function as the judiciary in the rural areas. In such situation it developed a leisure class with no responsibility in the productive process besides witnessing one of the worst form of de-industrialization and the sufferers were mainly from occupational and artisan class which comprises backward castes in most cases, such as Bania, Nonia or Teli and other similar castes felt handicapped in functioning in Bihar. Also a stigma got associated with their profession with reinforcement of feudalism. A report of Bihar Kisan Sabha has listed forty types of atrocities by the zamindars on the in south Bihar that was later on retaliated by the peasantry. Bulk of these were from other backward castes, but the anti-feudal movement led by the Kisan Sabha before independence, to some extent was successful on its economic agenda but could not absorb the social aspirations of the backward castes tenants. This provided the condition for promotion of cohesion and solidarity among the members of the same caste groups, which resulted in the formation of Triveni Sangh in 1930s and other caste associations. It was due to the aspirations for higher social status which acted as a pressure groups whose aim was to improve their rank in the census. Another important social change that caste associations have achieved, probably, concerns the unity of the caste groups. As Verma (1979) is of the opinion that "the Sabha had amalgamated diverse castes by hyper and hypogamous affiliations and provided an example of how a caste sabha might be deparochialized to certain degree to include various castes which has distinct entities. This process of fusion was also reported by Rao, Kothari, Maru and Myron Weiner. As Kothari has stated that the caste formations were at once aggregative and disaggregative, emphasizing the secular dimension of a plural society. He saw evidence of formation of class configurations out of dispersed and fragmented identities which in ways reflected regional differences and specific political movements.

It is seen that there is a greater solidarity and cohesion between different segments if their interests are common. Though the Kurmi Mahto and Patidar felt a common identity, they preferred to be distinctive in the post-independence era, which has the tendency of "fission after fusion." They have successfully incited the sub-castes to adopt the same name in the census and to break the barrier of endogamy. In the pre-independence era, process of climbing higher in the social ladder was prominent among the backward castes. Each census provided castes with an opportunity to petition the government for getting higher place in the order of precedence and for being recorded under new sanskritised names. In 1911, 16 did so and in 1921, 20 in northern India, including Kurmis, Gadariyas, Kacchi, Lodhs and Ahirs who wanted all to be recognized as Kshatriya. Indeed this move was in keeping with the logic of sanskritization since the objective was not to opt out from the system but to rise within it according to its own rules and values. Keeping in view their move they refused to do begari for the zamindars that brought them in direct confrontation. As discussed above, the formation of caste association and the ethnicisation of caste-two interrelated processes were fostered by the British policy of protective discrimination. It contributed in crystallization of new groups, which resented their non-representation. Caste groups often with low social status were prominent among those who mobilized against the states arbitrary decision. In north India, mobility has been accompanied by the process of sanskritization for granting legitimacy (Koeri, Kurmi, etc; claimed Kshatriya status during the British period). Some studies in this respect has been conducted by social scientists which throw light on social mobility of backward castes, such as, Rowe's study on, The New Chauhans: A Caste Mobility Movement in North India, which uncovers the trends of mobility in the Noniya communities that permit them to reduce the discrepancy between their constrasting positions in the ritual and the economic hierarchies. Another study by Hardgrave's on Nadars of Tamilnadu explains how they have moved from the lower rungs of hierarchy to a position of status and power. His analysis reveals that the process of sanskritization was initially attempted and could not be successful after which they turned to secular strategies through the formation of the Nadar Mahajana Sangam for community integration and mobilization. Similarly G.S.Bhatt's study on the Chamars of Dehradun explains the trends and measures for status mobility to drop their unclean stigma through sanskritization and increased economic opportunities in an urban situation.

While observing the recurrent change through social mobility in Indian society, Mandelbaum opines, individual mobility, by itself is limited and ephemeral and mentioned mobility tactics and modern means for jati improvement through caste associations and federations.

To understand mobilization of Bihar's backward castes, it has been studied under pre and post-independence period.

Pre-independence period:

The first move for mobilization of the backward castes in Bihar could be traced back to 1870, when educated Kurmi elites felt the necessity of social reform(Verma, K.K.:1979). For this purpose two conferences were held respectively at Danapur and Sonepur. This was followed by the formation of the Kurmi Kshatriya Sabha, for which grounds were already prepared in 1901. Similarly the situation of other backward castes were also not good and to improve their lot, some of them formed caste associations like the Yadava Mahasabha, Koeri Sabha (all these communities had an agricultural base), Kewat Sabha, Kushwaha Mahasabha etc.

A list of some of the backward classes associations formed in pre-independence period is given below:

It further got boost from the OBCs census done by the British Govt; as in 1901 the then census commissioner

List of Some backward classes Organisations/Associations functional in 1920

Sr. No.	Name of organisation & District	Place & Estt. Year	Purpose of organisation	chief officials	No. of members
1.	Gope Sabha, Bhagalpur	Murhu, 1911	Dev; of Cowherds	Chairman: A.P. Mandala & J.N. Mandal Secy: G.N. Mandal	50
2.	Sonar Sabha, Gaya	Purani Gowdon 1906	Reform- in caste	Dr. Biharilal, Shyamlal Mokhtar, Ramlal Bhagat	500
3.	Kesarwani Sabha, Gaya	Fatehganj 50yrs back	"	Chamari sao, Kaliram, Sahdeo Ram	1000
4.	Kahar Sabha, Gaya	Chowk, 50yrs Back	"	Sahdeolal, Mahadeo lal, B.Pd. Mokhtar, Gaya Prasad	Amost all
5.	Kahar Sabha, Gaya	Fateh Ganj	"	Baiju Bhagat, Gurucharan Bhagat, Akluram	5000

1.	2	3	4	5	6
6.	Ghamela Kurmi Kshatriya Sabha, Patna	Akangar, 1914	Educational Development,	Babu Guru sahayalal Vakil, Sohan Singh, Brajraj Pd.	250
7.	Rawani sabha, Shahabad	1906	Social Development in Kahar	Mahadeoram guru, Ara	50
8.	Koeri sabha Shahabad	Bholasabid, 31/1/1915	Social reform	Ramchigram, Ara, Sahdeoram Ramsaranram, Motiram	400
9.	Chandvansh Pawan Kurmi Kshatriya Sabha Saran	Salempur, Chhapra, 1915	Reform in Caste	Babulal Kurmi Murlidhar verma, Amirchand Kurmi	25

Source: Bihar special Branch, List of Political and Religious society in Bihar & Orissa, December, 1920.

Herbert Risley decided to give ranking of the jatis in their local context and varnas. This step helped them to improve their ranks in the census along with fulfilling their desire for social mobility, and before 1911 census they mobilized themselves.The first step in this direction was taken by Kurmi and they formed Kurmi Sabha in 1910, which was registered at Patna, and subsequently a constitution was drawn up. Sri Sajivanlal Sinha, who later became the president of the sabha, claimed that the Kurmi was the purest Kshatriya. In 1909 Kurmi Sabha formulated its own draft with following objectives:

a) To foster unity and to promote solidarity among different sections of the community,

b) To promote social, material and general welfare of the community,

c) To make available educational facilities to the kurmi children by opening schools, hostels and libraries,

d) To educate people in new agricultural practices,

e) To publish periodicals and newspapers to keep in touch with the movement,

f) To raise funds by subscription, donation and other means for above objectives.

The Constitution was revised and elaborated during 26th session of the sabha in 1960 but the objectives remained the same.

Later on they organized a sabha in 1929 in which some delegates from the Kurmi Mahto of Chhotanagpur also attended the conference. In this conference, Kurmi Mahto were recognized as akin to other kurmis. This tie up was further strengthened at the 19th session of the sabha held at Purulia, thus enabling the community to gain power in the political field. Apart from politics they opened schools, established hostels and ultimately raised their voice for jobs. Many years later Kurmis tried to play a pivotal role in a similar arrangement. During the 30th session of the All India Kurmi Kshatriya Sabha it was decided to constitute a caste federation with the Koeries. The Kurmi leaders were not planning to create a new caste through intermarriages, but somehow a union was established, known as "Raghav Samaj". The attempt to federate the Koeries and Kurmis was rather inconclusive because of difference in their status and economic activities. The idea behind the federation seems to seek institutional basis and numerical strength in the regional political cleavages. The emergence of Raghava Samaj as a new larger form of consciousness and organization would further break down the dichotomy between tradition and modernity by blurring the line between caste and its modern form of association. However, the attempt to form an effective federation remained in its incipient stage. In the 1930s, some efforts were made on a relatively bigger scale when the yadavas (rearing cattle and selling milk) kurmi (agriculturist) and koeri (vegetable grower) formed a joint front- the Triveni Sangh-to fight for their rights with following objectives, such as, refusal to undertake beggar for the landlords and others upper castes, not to sell their commodities at less than the market price besides others in their agenda. They also began to adopt upper castes name, wear the sacred thread, and so on (Jha, 1977), which has been termed as "Sanskritisation" by M.N. Srinivas. The colonial rulers, thus, by classifying the population had given a new meaning to the Indian Caste system and also provided platform for backward caste/class mobilization.MSA Rao and F.Frankel relates this to the dominance of upper caste on lower castes, which had been sanctified by the religious belief. This trend can be seen in the 1931 census report in which some of the backward castes demanded higher status for them. Some of these are given below:

Table: 2.1

Castes or sub-castes	Designation claimed
Kamar (Lohar), Barhi	Vishwakarma Brahmin
Bhat	Brahman, Bhat Brahman
Hajjam	Nai Brahman, Kulin Brahman
Khati, Sutar	Jangida Brahman
Goala(Ahir, gope)	Yadav
Koeri	Dangi, Kushwaha Kshatriya
Kurmi	Kurmi Kshatriya
Rawani Kahar	Chandrabanshi Kshatriya
Sunri	Shaundik Kshatriya
Jolaha	Sheikh, Sheikh Momin

Source: Census of India-1931, Part 1 Report, Vol-VII, W.G. Lacey, (1987) Usha Publication Delhi.

Besides the above, caste associations struggled against alcoholism, child marriage and some other social evils. For these acts the backward castes were attacked by the upper castes. Accounts of Patna and Gaya districts, the storm centres of this movement, provides many instances of such clashes between them. Introduction of legislative council by British to serve their own interest provided an opportunity to leaders of different castes to contest election and serve the people. Regarding above preferential policy M.N. Srinivas has commented that, "The policy which British adopted of giving a certain amount of power to local self-governing bodies, and preferences and concessions to backward castes provided new opportunities to castes. In order to be able to take advantage of these opportunities caste groups as traditionally understood, entered into alliances with each other to form bigger entities"(seen in formation of Raghava Samaj). The first backward caste leader to grab this opportunity and become a minister in the Bihar Government was Sri Guru Sahaylal, a kurmi advocate from Patna district. He was a member in the interim Ministry headed by Mr. Yunus in 1937 for three months. Another important Kurmi leader was Sri Deo Saran Singh who took an active part in the freedom movement and served as a legislature for a long time. He became minister in the Congress government and later on president of the legislative council. He was also the president of the Backward Class Federation. Triveni Sangh prepared ground on its own for the assertion of its political identity. Previously in Shahabad District Board election, only one member of the backward caste could win the election but after the formation of association they began to win more seats as can be seen from the table given below:

Table: 2.2

Caste division of the members of Shahabad District Board

	Castes	1927	1930	1933	1939	Total
1	Rajputs	18	18	21	11	68
2	Kayastha	5	5	8	2	20
3	Bhumihar	2	3	6	1	12
4	Brahmin	3	2	4	8	17
5	Muslim	1	1	1	1	4
6	Kurmi	1	1	-	2	4
7	Yadav	-	-	-	2	2
8	Koeri	-	-	-	3	3
	Total seats	**30**	**30**	**40**	**30**	**130**

In the year 1933 the total seats in the Board was 40, out of which elections were held for 30 seats and members were nominated for 10 seats.

Source: Prasanna Kumar Chaudhary & Srikanth, : Bahi Dhar Sangh Triveni Ki; Bihar Mein Samajik Nayaya Ka Pehala Sangharsh, Patna, Lok Tantra, 1998.

Similarly the position of the candidates of Triveni Sangh in the 1939 District Board Election was as follows:

Sr. No.	Area	Name	Caste	Won	Defeated
				Voteobtained	
1.	Bhabhua	Ganesh Singh	Kurmi	4796	
2.	Kundra-Mohania	Sakhichand	"		2533
3.	Chainpur	Krishnakant Singh	"		1227
4.	Ramgarh	Ram Pd. Singh	Yadav	1781	
5.	Nawanagar	Maharaj Singh	Koeri		1732
6.	Rajpur	Ramanand	Kanu		1035
7.	Kargahar	Raja Mahto	Kurmi	2516	
8.	Nokha	Shivsundar Pd. Singh	"		1842
9.	Sasaram	Vanshropan Mahto	Koeri		3029
10.	Chenari	Ramvadan	Yadav		2942
11.	Dinara	Ram, Subhag Mahto	Koeri		1374
12.	Bikram Ganj	Gopal Chaudhary	Kurmi	2774	
13.		Shyamlal Sinha	Yadav		2684
14.	Ara	Chhatu Dusadh	Dusadh		045
15.	Jagdishpur	Ramsakal Sinha	Koeri		2888
16.	Sandesh	Devidayal Singh	Yadav		959
17.	Arwal	Lal Bihari Sinha	"		1146
18.		Ramcharan	Koeri		1467
19.	Makhdumpur	Yadunandan	Mahto Dangi		658
20.	Kurtha	Bindeshwari Pd. Sinha	Yadav		901
21.	Ghoshi	Mathura Das	Yadav		687

Source : Election result of District Board, File No. 342/39, 361/39

The party suffered from a serious setback during the 1937 election but in few places where it won- like Ara and Piro-Sahabad district- upper caste landlords retaliated violently. In the year 1939 by capturing some seats in the Board election the Sangh asserted its political power and in turn demanded job reservation for the backwards and dalits.

The caste structure of State Legislature in 1937 & 1945-46 was as follows:

Caste	1937	1945-46
Bhumihars	16	11
Rajput	15	18
Brahmin	11	9
Kayastha	9	10
Kurmi	2	5
Yadav	1	2
Bania	1	2
Koeri	-	3
Marwari	-	2
Bengali	6	4

It also had confrontation with the Bihar Pradesh Kisan Sabha on the issue of exploitation in the freedom struggle against the colonial rule. The Triveni Sangh and the Kisan Sabha also failed to make an alliance because of traditional antagonism between them. Overall the Triveni Sangh played pivotal role in coordinating and consolidating the efforts of the backward castes.The above castes, who through gain of land, trade expansion or army service, had raised their economic position at least to a certain extent, managed to organize themselves through associations and sabhas and discovered new forms of de-brahminized religion and myths of more dignified origins (observed during 1911 & 1931 census of depressed castes, ref; Table:2.1) to challenge the traditional hierarchical Brahminical social order in all the newly emerging arenas of civil society. Similarly Vaishnavite movement among Yadavs, Koeries and Kurmis of Bihar in pre-modern period also had in its root the socio-political message of equality. The (backward) peasant castes were, with few exceptions (Kurmis in part of Patna & Bhabhua thana of Rohtas district and yadava in Saharasa district) raiyats and under - raiyats in the zamindari system. Besides exploitation in the form of malguzari the peasants were also subjected to various forms of beggar and abwabs, illegal cesses etc. The peasants on every conceivable occasions had to pay some amount to the zamindars and others of the feudal hierarchy. The yadavs and koeris had to supply milk and vegetables on lower price than market prices. Even now backward caste peasant performs some beggar for upper castes landlords, except in areas where the tenants have organized and fought against this imposition.—even now, again except where this has been fought out, the front benches in colleges are reserved for upper caste students. All this exploitation and insult certainly do not add up to anything like what the Dalits still faces. But does it not add up to exploitation and psychological and moral injury on account of caste position? To say that this is not of the type suffered by the Dalits is only a way of dodging the question of whether this is exploitation and injury or not?

Establishment of Patna as a State capital, location of Bihar Regimental centre at Danapur, lying of railway line connecting the region to metropolitan centres like Calcutta before Independence, all these created a huge market for the vegetable, milk and other products grown in the region. Support base of the "Triveni Sangh" comprised the main beneficiaries of this market, which triggered agro-capitalism and led to substantial accumulation. The subsequent earth quake of 30s led to a sudden spurt in construction activities which in turn led to fortuitous conditions for brick capitalism, again utilized by the upper backwards, mostly the Kurmis and partly by the Yadavas. With the abolition of the zamindari system large amount of "bakast" land were also transferred to the upper backwards. They in fact, along with the former Bhumihar tenants of the zamindari system, led the green revolution in Bihar. The main beneficiaries were upper backwards, i.e; Yadav, Koeri Kurmi and Bania constituting together 19.0% of population. They strongly began to perceive land as an economic resource which was further strengthened by the introduction of institutional support system. As can be seen from the table given below:

Table 2.3

Detail about aggregate input and output (all crops)in different types of household(Bihar)

Caste	Total value Gross output Per acre	Total cost of Purchased seed per acre	Total cost of Purchased fertilizer per acre	Total cost of Purchased others per acre	Total input cost per acre	Total value of marketed per acre
Brahmin+Kayasta	1624.367	27.949	108.131	49.204	183.625	257.726
Bhumihar+Rajput	1817.490	44.222	117.678	37.297	198.209	201.413
Backward - I	1693.085	37.680	113.370	43.243	193.187	82.090
Yadav	1129.233	14.190	87.174	49.180	120.611	25.445
Koiri	2147.644	72.085	235.858	77.051	354.898	32.241
Kurmi	2727.615	23.904	299.346	108.181	413.811	571.056
Other backwards	1493.264	11.244	76.328	44.394	131.985	59.893
Scheduled castes	1882.070	53.847	121.172	32.320	205.702	120.856
Muslim	1214.280	25.108	86.735	30.372	117.157	135.526

Detail of aggregate input and output of all crops show that Kurmi hold the position in total value marketed, whereas with 201.413(per acre), Bhumihar + Rajput hold third position. The above tables indicate that those peasant castes who themselves are working in the field are in better position than those landholding castes who do not work themselves in the field.

Inspite of all the above achievements, Triveni Sangh never challenged the basic foundations of the socio-economic and political contradictions. However, a great leap was made in the region outside the Hindi heartland, which challenged the domination of the twice-born castes till independence. Social mobilization which took place in the west and south India, helped in economic development after independence. However in the absence of such mobilization, the Hindi heartland lagged behind. It was only after independence that the Constitutional provisions in the shape of reservation in government jobs, educational institutions and other welfare measures brought fruits to BCs and OBCs.

Post-independence Period

After independence two streams were operative within the backward caste segment. One stream was represented by Chandpuri and his co-workers who tried to use the backward castes federation in building up a mass membership in the villages to unite the backward communities and set aside the Harijans. Chandpuri and his workers constituted the Bihar Provincial Backward Caste Association on 10th September, 1947 to fulfill this objective. He started publishing Hindi weekly "Pichada Varga"from Patna since 1949. On 26th January, 1950 in Delhi, this association was converted into All India Backward Caste Association (Chandpuri, 1996). In 1951, Jagjivan Ram, a member of Nehru's cabinet attempted to bring under the control of the congress party the Backward Classes Federation. It was an attempt that Chandpuri foiled. Any how the publication of the Hindi weekly Pichada Varga had to be suspended. But in the same year, he started publishing another weekly Pichada Varga Sandesh (the down-trodden classes newsletter). On 5th December, 1954 Chandpuri submitted on behalf of his federation a memorandum to the Backward Classes Commission (1953-55) headed by Kaka Kalelkar. He met Prime Minister, Nehru as the head of a delegation on 24th October, 1955. In his 50 minutes talk with the delegation Nehru assured to implement the recommendations of the Commission, but this was not implemented in letter. Outside the legislative assembly, the Yadavs, Kurmis and the Koeries leaders conformed to the patterns set by the forward castes and carried out mobilization within their constituencies among their own caste groups. In Bihar the influence of the backward castes had been steadily increasing, Birchand Patel and Shiva Nandan Mandal were influential ministers in the Bihar cabinet in the 1950s and early 60s. During the chief ministership of K.B. Sahay (1963-67) Ramlakhan Singh Yadav was a minister in the government. The backward castes were represented in good strength in the Socialist Communist and the Jan Sangh parties. Under the leadership of the Socialists, in the post-1947 period, movement of backward castes spread to other parts of Bihar. In deed it was an important experiment but could not achieve any success until the attainment of freedom in 1947, when Bihar State Backward Classes Federation was formed. The backward castes (both upper and lower) began to assert their political power around 1948 and held about 14% of the posts in 1960s. As Blair (1980) has showed that the percentage in the Congress legislative party in 1962 of the backwards were just 24.9% an overwhelming bulk of whom were the upper backwards. From 1963 onward in Bihar politics, backward castes began to play a major role with some minor exceptions in this period. The congress debacle of 1967 marks an important stage in the upsurge of the backward castes. In election to the legislative assembly the Bania, Kurmi, Koeri and Yadav candidates returned in big numbers and constituted 31.6 percent of the MLAs. Most of them belonged to Socialist Samajvadi Party. This pattern was repeated in the mid-term polls of

1969 also. Roy argues that in due course of time they became autonomous. Discussing the entry of the peasant castes into politics, he says that most of these castes groups functioned as appendages of the main contenders in the upper castes. Leader from the upper castes co-opted men from the lower castes to leadership position. Congressmen deprived the low caste movement from some of its leaders by co-opting Kurmi leader (eg; Birchand Patel) and Yadavas (Ram Lakhan Singh Yadav). And then they refused to give ticket to Triveni Sangh candiates. Each of the peasant castes entered the Congress divided. In the early 1970s, the All India Kurmi Mahasabha abandoning further the sanskritization logic made an alliance with the Koeries and favoured a merger of all the backward castes. This approach is found among upper backward castes in those regions where the Brahmin did not dominate the modernizing process which was led by powerful peasant castes who were in turn closely associated in vertical ties with other castes. This enabled a cutting short of both the sanskritization and the caste solidarity phases and led straight to inter-caste factional politics as an avenue of social mobility. Bihar provides a good example of rapid succession of various OBCs groups into factional networks of politics for channels of mobilization.

Further, for broadening the base of backward castes, in its 1972 session the main slogan of the above caste Mahasabha was "Pichara Jagao, Desh Bachao", one of the resoulations that allowed other than kurmis to associate with the association.It also asked for the appointment of a Public Service Commission for backward castes besides other welfare measures to be taken for them. In their magazine "Kurmodaya", Vol-1(3)the caste association had published a notice about the forthcoming legislative council election:

"The Sabha appeals to all those graduates residing in Patna district to get themselves registered in the list of electorals by October, 1971; for this they are to fill up the

forms and to enclose an attested true copy of their degrees.It is needless to say that the task for choosing efficient leaders for all the areas rests with us only. If we fail in this task, it would mean that we have disregarded our political rights and further we shall have to suffer a great for its consequences."

Name of some important leaders of Triveni Sangh, who worked for the causes of backward castes is as follows:

(a) Yadunandam Pd. Mehta- (b) 18-2-1911 in village Jitora of lakhan tola. Founder-Triveni Sangh. He wrote a book:- "Triveni Sangh ka Bigual in 1940; besides other books on backward castes.

(b) Sardar Jegdeo singh:(b) 7/4/1886, village: garve of Sahabad Distt.: participated in Janeu Movement and Yadav Mahasabha social reform movement.

(c) Dasu Singh: one of the founder member of Triveni Sangh.

(d) Navdeep Chandra Ghosh: b: (1889) in Bengal presidency (village: Kalatiya). He was an important leader of Yadavs. He also participated in Janaeu movement.

(e) Ganpati Mandal (b: 1902 in Bihpur, Bhagalpur distt.) open school for backward castes in his village and also started social reform movement.

(f) Devgan Pd. Singh (Triveni member, Nalanda Anchal of patna Distt: worked among Kurmi for their betterment.

(g) Nand Kishore singh(b: 1890, Jagdish Puri Tenduni village): Started Social reform movement and asked BCs to append Singh behind their names.(died in 1952).

Even the presidents of early sessions (1926, 1933) of the All India Sabha urged upon the caste people to elect their own candidates in local bodies. The long pending demand of these upper backward castes was ultimately heard by the government and in November 1978, 20.0 percent reservation was provided by the Karpoori Thakur government. By doing this Thakur was only pursuing the Lohia line of further mobilizing the backward castes. He thought that he could successfully graft the Karnataka model on Bihar. The G.O. issued for reservation provoked widespread backlash by the forward castes.Thakur thought that grafting the Karnataka model in Bihar will help in tiding the problem but this did not happened. As Urs had astutely divided the two dominant castes of Lingayats and Vokaligas by putting the former in the forward group and the latter in the backward list. He saw to it that an alliance between them could not take place. Thakur did not resort to any such measures. The forward castes felt that many of the newly rich peasant castes would under report their income. In this way mobilization of backward castes in Bihar has been a belated and fragmented one. In Bihar upsurge of the backward castes meant really the upsurge of the Yadavas. This fact is not likely to enthuse the other weaker landless backward castes. Thakur had no ideology to unite them. In short, Thakur G.O. came without an adequate mobilization and unification of the backward castes. Perhaps he thought that the 1977 election victory represented a viable and durable resurgence of the backward castes, which was not the case. The January, 1980 election proved this. The Scheduled castes and the minor backwards went back to the Congress fold. Further the mobilization of backward castes gather momentum under Laloo Pd. Yadav regime in the initial stage but later on it became weak and another backward leader (Nitish Kumar) with the support from some upper castes grabs the power of the State. In this respect, Rajni Kothari has observed that the "interaction of caste and democratic politics has produced two results: First, the caste system made available to the leadership, structural and ideological basis for political mobilization ....second, the leadership was forced to make concessions to local opinion, take its cue from the consensus that existed as regards claims to power, articulate political competition on traditional lines and in turn, organized castes for economic and political purpose.... Politics and society began moving nearer and a new intra-structure started coming into being". He further states, "Had other avenues of social advancement and status mobility been available to the aspirant caste groups, it is doubtful whether politics would have been so much impressed by caste as it is....Politics affords to the backward castes an opportunity to achieve through it what they cannot through social instrumentalities.

The notion prevailent in Bihar is that, Yadavas, Kurmis and Koeris enjoy more economic power and social freedom because they command large holdings and enjoy Kulak like status, but the facts, however, donot support this position. The OBCs are badly placed even there, for 89.1% of them possess less than 10 acres of land. Out of these, 43.4% have no land of their own. They work mostly as landless labourers, as can be seen from the table given below;

Table: 2.4

Land holdings in Central Bihar (Percent of persons to total in each of the caste group)

Land owing categories (acres) class

Caste	0	0-5	5-10	10+	land lord rich pea-sant	middle pea-sant	poor pea-sant
Upper-	5.7	62.1	17.9	14.3	89.5	2.9	5.5
Backward	43.4	52.0	2.8	10.9	17.7	22.1	52.8
SCs	69.5	30.4	12.1	0.6	2.0	4.4	92.0

Source: Economic & Political Weekly, 17.8.91, Volume XXVI, No.33

The caste status of the tenants indicate that the pure tenants are overwhelmingly drawn from SCs and OBCs whereas owner-cum-tenants have a larger proportion of

OBCs and upper castes as can be seen from the table given below:

Table: 2.5
Percentage Distribution of Tenants by Social Origin, Bihar

Social Origin	Pure Tenants	Owner-cum-Tenants
Scheduled Caste	38.9	20.5
Scheduled Tribes	—	6.7
Depressed Backward Castes	—	2.3
Other Backward Castes	44.4	36.4
Other Castes	16.7	34.1
Total	**100.0**	**100.0**

One of the main reason for this improper distribution of land holding is the pattern of land reform in Bihar which has also affected mobilization of the backward castes into politics. No doubt, the abolition of all intermediaries has definitely helped hard working peasant castes like kurmis, koeris and yadavas but most of the backward castes remained poor. This has led to cleavage and conflict between upper and backward castes in Bihar giving rise to various senas (private armies) to protect the caste interest. If we look at the castes involved in agricultural pursuits, the following scenario emerges:-

Table: 2.6
Agricultural labourers in Bihar

Castes	Percent of agricultural labourer
High castes	00.3
Backward castes	34.2
SCs\STs	51.5
Others(Muslims etc)	14.0

Similarly the Backward Castes and Scheduled Castes do not own land to any significant extent, which increase their dependence for means on livelihood on the land owned by Brahmins and Rajputs. The continuing confinement of lower castes to the ranks of agricultural labourers and the virtual exclusion of upper castes from the ranks of middle and poor peasants and agricultural labourers is well illustrated in the table given below, which shows the class structure of various castes in rural, Central Bihar.

Table: 2.7

Class composition of castes in Central Bihar: Percentage distribution

Category	UC	UBC	OBC	SC
Landlord cum rich peasant	95.70	36.40	4.24	2.67
Middle peasant	1.23	19.79	7.63	2.68
Poor middle peasant	1.23	16.96	3.39	2.01
Agricultural labourers	1.84	26.35	84.74	92.74

Source : Prasad, 1989

With the implementation of liberalization and globalization policy since 1990s, most of the MBCs economic situation has deterioriated, such as with the introduction of modern farm equipment blacksmiths have become irrelevant. Mass scale production of modern kitchenware did the same to potters.Similarly Kahar who once shouldered palanquins has now been replaced by machine driven transport.In this line other MBCs who have been affected are noniyas, telis and other castes. Out of the total OBCs population, 50.0 percent belongs to this category and with the disappearance of their trade, most of them turned to agricultural pursuits as can be seen from the above table where percentage of OBCs agricultural labourers are 84.74 percent, whereas it is 7.63 & 3.39 percent for middle &

poor OBCs peasants. One can see the difference in total percentage of upper backward and most backward castes, given below in the pie diagram:

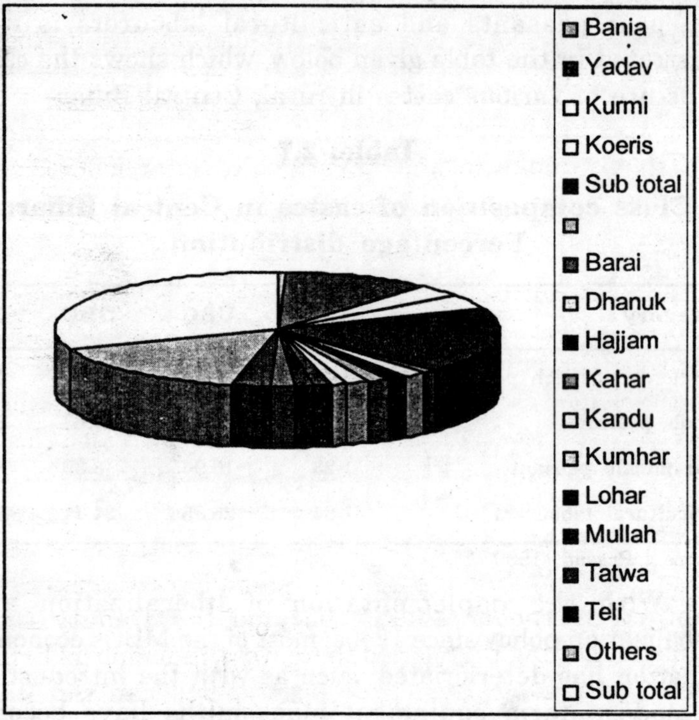

Politicians mobilize caste groups in order to organize their own power. They find in it an extremely well articulated and flexible basis for organization, something that may have been structured in terms of a status hierarchy, but sometimes it is also available for political manipulation-and one that has a basis in consciousness. Commenting on such type of situation, Rajni Kothari said that :

"Once formed on the basis of caste identities go on to acquire non-caste functions, become more flexible in organization, even begin to accept members and leaders from castes other than those with which it started stretches out to new regions, and also makes common cause with voluntary organization, interest groups and political parties. In course of time, the federation becomes a distinctly political group".

This has happened in context of Bihar, since formation of Triveni Sangh by the Kurmi which later merged with Raghav Samaj and later on with All India Backward Classes Association (with branches in different States).

Backward caste mobilization received a shot in the arm with the advent of the socialist party on the political horizon. The party committed itself to secure 60.0 percent in the leadership post in political parties, government services, business and armed forces for the depressed classes. By 1962 the upper backward castes accounted for 22.0 percent of the members of the Congress legislature party, and K.B.Sahay cabinet had 20% representation of these castes in 1963. Similarly in the Mahamaya Prasad Sinha cabinet, Karpoori Thakur became the Deputy Chief Minister. During that period there were 71 members hailing from backward castes in different parties in the Bihar Assembly. The Yadav emerged as the second largest caste group after the Rajput in 1967. If we compare the council of ministers during the tenure of M.P. Sinha and B.P. Mandal, the former being a forward caste chiefminister and later who hailed from backward caste, the following picture emerged, 13 out of 22 members belonged to the upper castes during his ministry whereas during the BP Mandal period only 9 out of 38 belonged to upper castes, which can be seen from the table given below:

Table: 2.8

The social composition of U.F. Minister at the time of M.P. Sinha & B.P. Mandal's Chief Ministership.

Caste of Minister	Number of Ministers during the time of M.P.Sinha	Number of the MLA's at the time of the formation of Soshit Dal
Rajput	5	6
Brahmin	3	—
Bhumihar	4	3
Kayastha	1	—
Banik	—	2
Yadavas	1	6
Kurmi	1	1
Koeri	2	3
Scheduled Castes	1	3
Scheduled Tribes	1	9
Muslims	1	4
Bengalis	1	1
Nai	1	—
Total	**22**	**38**

Source:Dayadhar Jha, State Legislature in India, Abhinav Publication, 1977.

During the next four years, Bihar was plagued by political instability with nine coalition governments and three spells of President's rule. In this period three of them were headed by backward caste leaders like B. P. Mandal, Daroga Prasad Rai and Karpoori Thakur. Chandpuri was instrumental in elevating B.P.Mandal, as the first backward caste chief minister of the State in 1968. The split in the

Congress Party in November 1969 created new opportunities for backward caste. In the Daroga Prasad Rai ministry, the backward castes and the scheduled castes received special attention and were given 53.0 percent ministerial posts. During the Congress ministries between 1972-77 backward class representations in cabinet varied between 20.0 to 28.0 percent.

In May 1972 the All India Kurmi Mahasabha resolved to organize the youth cadre "Bhumi Putra Fauj" to bring internal social reform and mobilization of not only Kurmi but of other Backward Castes people. It also demanded creation of a separate Public Service Commission for the Backward Classes. In the 1977 elections, a large number of backward caste candidates won the elections. The Yadavas alone had 36 members. The issue of reservations for backwards castes came to a head early in 1978. But due to internal conflicts among politicians in Janata Party it took some time in its implementation. After a massive demonstration by backward classes and large scale violence which took place in many parts of Bihar, Government ultimately adopted reservation with some modifications on 21st March 1978. In November, 1978 again reservation policy was revised by the State government and Karpoori Thakur implemented his own formula for reservation purpose. In sociological context he was pursuing "Sponsored Mobility", which takes place on sponsorship or sympathetic disposition of the establishment and becomes a sinequanon. Recruitment of other backward castes to the government service under the Indian Constitution belongs to this category as they enjoy the sponsorship of the State in the form of reservation. Again in order to create an army of supporters at the panchayat level, Karpoori ministry conducted panchayat election in the summer of 1978.These two process initiated by him further gave boost to the social movement. This can be examined in two ways.

Firstly, with all of this manoeuvring capacity he was able to unite backward castes legislators and secondly, it mobilized whole backward community behind him for the time being. This brought some changes in the traditional balance of power relations, altering the social and political relationships.

How the politics of Bihar was affected by the caste based conflict of upper versus backward castes and what are the real sources of strength of different castes, in different elections to the Bihar State Assembly is presented below in tabular form:

Table: 2.9

Percentage of Caste Group

Caste groups	1957	1962	1967	1969	1972	1977
Brahmins	9.54	17.20	13.20	12.30	18.30	7.60
Bhumihars	16.19	12.60	14.80	14.60	14.70	14.80
Rajputs	14.20	23.60	22.20	28.50	19.80	21.70
Kayasthas	4.28	5.40	4.90	3.30	2.00	4.40
Total Upper Castes	44.25	59.00	53.00	53.90	54.80	48.60
Baniks	—	3.30	5.30	6.20	4.60	—
Yadavas	—	11.70	15.20	18.50	11.70	8.24
Kurmis	—	11.70	5.80	4.10	5.60	11.50
Other Upper Shudras	—	6.70	31.60	32.10	27.50	6.40
Lower Shudras including SCs/STs	17.62	1.70	2.90	2.50	2.00	34.9
Total backward castes	22.86	30.50	34.50	34.60	29.50	86.00
Muslims	11.43	8.80	7.40	7.60	13.20	1.00
Bengalis	—	1.70	2.90	3.70	2.50	2.80
Others	3.80	—	—	—	—	—
Total	**100.00**	**100.00**	**99.90**	**100.00**	**100.00**	**100.00**

Source: Economic and Political Weekly, February 14, 1977 & January 19, 1980.

It is clear from the above table that after the election of 1962, the backward castes(including SCs & STs) were gradually increasing their strength in Bihar Assembly going up from 30.50 percent to 86.00 percent in 1977. The corresponding decline of upper castes from 59.0 percent to 48.60 percent is also evident. It is also clear that in the 1967 elections among backward castes, the higher percent went to the yadavas, i.e; from 11.7 percent to 15.2 percent. The table also depicts that in the 1972 elections, the maximum votes went to the Rajputs who secured 19.80 percent of the total votes polled whereas Brahmins polled 18.30 percent in 1972 which reduced to 7.6 percent of the votes polled in 1977. It is also clear that none of the groups was self-reliant and this was the reason why the policy of coaliation, factionalism was brought into practice by both the groups. Some times upper castes leaders like B.N.Jha and K.B.Sahay supported the backward castes and the Scheduled castes and at other junctures reversed their alliances.

Table: 2.10

Cast background of members of the Bihar Assembly

	Upper Caste MLA's	%	OBC MLA's	%
1967	133	41.82	82	25.78
1969	122	38.36	94	29.55
1972	136	42.78	76	23.89
1977	124	38.27	92	28.39
1980	120	37.03	96	29.62
1985	118	36.41	90	27.77
1990	105	32.40	117	36.11
1995	56	17.28	161	49.69

Source: Chaudhary & Srikant, Bihar mein Samajik Parivartan

As above table illustrates, 1990 was the year when OBC members of the legislative assembly (MLAs) first exceeded upper caste members in Bihar, but by a relatively thin margin; the political representation of the upper castes continued to be disproportionate to their population in the state. By 1995, after just five years of Janata Dal rule, OBCs out numbered upper caste MLAs nearly threefold. This dramatic shift in political representation within a very short period of time highlights the changes that Lalu Yadav brought to Bihar, changes with widespread repercussions that influenced everything from local social relations to governance and development.

Another turning point in caste politics came with the rise of autonomous dalit politics during the 1980s.After 1980s, attempts were made in some States, especially in

Bihar and UP, to forge parties mainly on the basis of overwhelming support from certain castes. With the emergence of an urban middle class among the lower castes, largely due to the State policies of land reforms, reservations in education and employment, consolidation of horizontal identities among them and given their numerical strength, elites from these castes broke away from the catch-all parties and formed caste-specific parties to stake their claim for power. The Mandal and the anti-Mandal agitations brought this issue to the fore in the late 1980s.The rise of RJD in Bihar can be understood in this context, which came to power in 1990.The decline of Congress in Bihar was mainly attributed to the walking out of various caste groups from the Congress fold in favour of caste-based parties which stand for strengthening of social justice for these backward castes.

The process of social justice was further strengthened by the Laloo Pd. Yadav government. He gained support of the newly formed – Atyant Pichhra Varg Mahasangh of Bihar-to win the support of extremely backward castes(EBCs). It has expressed its opposition against the exclusion of the creamy layer benefits as per the judicial verdict of the Supreme Court. To please all sections of backward castes, during 1993 the Lalu Government in State assembly brought a bill on Panchayati Raj which was passed by the State Assembly, coupled with the reservation benefits (MBC: 14.0 %, BC: 10.0 % & Women 2.0 %). According to the Bill, the panchayats with majority of people belonging to OBCs will be reserved for them only and in these panchayats upper castes are prohibited even from contesting elections. The result of this and other pro-poor schemes for BCs resulted in winning of Assembly' 2000 by Lalu Prasad.

Table: 2.11

Bihar Assembly Election; 2000: Performance on the basis of caste.

Caste/ party	RJD	INC	BJP	SAM	JD (U)	CPI	CPM	CPI (ML)	BSP	JMM	IND	Total
UC	23	6	23	10	7	2	2	1	0	0	17	91
Yadavas	38	1	8	0	8	-	0	-	-	-	-	55
MBC	19	1	14	18	3	2	0	2	1	2	6	68
Dalits	26	2	8	3	3	2	0	2	3	2	1	50
Tribals	0	6	14	1	0	0	0	0	7	-	1	29
Muslims	17	7	0	2	0	2	0	1	1	1	0	31
Total:	**123**	**23**	**67**	**34**	**21**	**6**	**2**	**6**	**12**	**5**	**25**	**324**

Source: collected from various election reports, documents.

There are 15, 000 Gram Panchayats in the State and except few, most of these Panchayats are numerically dominated by the OBCs. (Mandalisation of politics in reference to Bihar). 2001 panchayat election will go down in the history of Bihar as a turning point for the electoral empowerment of the lower backwards (castes listed in **Annexure- 1**). It can be seen from the result of the panchayat election given below;

Table: 2.12

Percentage distribution of Chairman, Members of Zila Parishad and Mukhiyas by their Caste background.

Caste/Caste Group	Chairmen	Percent of Members	Mukhiyas
1. Upper Caste Hindus of which	35.2	25.3	34.0
i Brahmin	8.2	5.0	7.7
ii Bhumihar	13.5	9.1	12.1
iii Rajput	13.5	10.3	13.4

iv Kayastha	—	0.9	0.8
2. Middle Caste Hindus	45.9	42.1	45.7
A Annexure I castes of which	2.7	3.5	3.9
i Dhanuk	-	0.5	0.6
ii Mallah/Gorhi	-	1.2	2.0
iii others	2.7	1.8	1.3
B Annexure 11 castes of which	43.2	39.6	41.8
i Yadav	35.1	24.2	24.2
ii Kurmi	2.7	4.1	5.8
iii Koeri	-	5.2	6.3
iv Bania/Vaishya	5.4	4.4	3.6
v others	-	1.7	1.9
3. Scheduled Caste Hindus	-	16.9	0.5
4. Scheduled Tribes	-	0.6	15.6
5. Muslims	16.2	13.0	15.6
6. Marwari	2.7	0.3	-
7. Others	-	0.8	2.9
Total	100.0	100.0	100.0
No. of Chairman/Member	37	1160	7120

Notes:

1. Data based on report published in "Prabhat Khabar", June 27, 2001, Patna.Although total number of mukhiyas is 8438, this data relates to 7120 mukhiyas for which caste data was available.
2. (Others)-include-Gangota, Barai, Lohar, Kumahar, Hajjam, Bind, Suryapuri, Mandal, Nonia, Tharu, Cheneu etc.
3. (Others) include- Kalwar, Halwai, Kanu, Surthi, Teli etc.

   Others include Chamar, Dom, and Nat etc.

It further get boost by the Nitish government when the house adopted by voice-vote the Bihar Panchayati Raj Amendment Bill, 2006 under which women would enjoy

50.0 percent reservation in all posts of the three tier Panchayati Raj system, while the people belonging to extremely backward class would get 20.0 percent reservation. Recently(April-May' 06) State Government has held Panchayat election in the State for 8, 452 panchayats and for this 1,30,563 candidates were in fray.

Till recently they were not taken into political or social cognizance in spite of their population being more than 33.0 percent of the total population. With about 108 castes in their ranks, no individual segment had an overwhelming presence as is the case with the Yadavas. In spite of being socially and economically marginalized, they were not given any special attention like dalits or other minorities. There was also no dramatic moment for them to forge a pan-lower backward castes unity. The social and economic positions of castes in this category were not better than that of the dalits. Further in the absence of a pan-backward class movement like that in the south or western India, the possibility of any social mobilization exclusively for them was forestalled. Such was not the case with people from other backward castes.

Protective Discrimination in form of reservation for OBCs which Mandal report allowed them in 1980-were not intended to equalize socio-economic conditions but to empower them. Indeed, it has transformed the OBCs relationship to power: some of their own kind hold office, and psychologically this encourages them to go further.But even more importantly, Mandal enabled the OBCs to win political power. They started to make achievement in political field and the Congress brand of politics simply broke down, which we see in the case of Bihar and the emergence of Janata Dal, which later bifurcated into RJD and JD(U) and at present the later is holding the reign of Bihar.It has also created a sharp polarization of caste in Bihar which can be seen in the voting pattern of forward as well as backward castes in favour of different political parties in Bihar in 1998, presented below in tabular form:

Table : 2.13
Caste and Voting: a sharp polarization in Bihar
(% figure)

Caste	RJD-Cong(I)	BJP-JD(U)
Rajput	8	92
Other upper caste	13	86
Kurmi-Koeri	19	79
Yadav	79	20
Lower OBC	27	55
Dalit	49	43
Muslim	79	19

Sample size for Bihar is 716.

In order to dismantal dominance of .higher castes, Lalu Ministry on the one hand implemented job reservation formula and on the other hand it replaced many higher caste bureaucrats from the main line to the side line by the lower caste bureaucrats.

The Indian Administrative Service (IAS) comprises the highest levels of the state bureucracy. In Bihar in 2002, 143 out of 244 identified officers, or 59.0%, were from four upper caste groups: Brahmins, Kayasths, Rajputs and Bhumihars, while few IAS officers came from the OBCs. As table 2.14 shows, only seven officers came from the three largest OBC groups- Yadav, Kurmi, and Koeri. In addition, all four officers identified as Yadav had entered the IAS through promotion from the Bihar State Administrative Service, an increasingly common practice. IAS officers promoted from the state administrative service are unlikely to occupy any rank above district magistrate. In fact, the situation had changed little from 1985, when there were only three IAS officers from OBC groups in Bihar. Although terms suchs as "Yadavization" and "Yadav Raj" were popularly used to describe RJD rule in Bihar, even after thirteen years of RJD rule, there was not a single directly recruited Yadav officer in the Bihar cadre of the IAS.

Following the implementation of the Mandal Comission's recommendations in 1990 establishing quotas for the recruitment of OBCs in the All India Services, the divide between upper castes and OBC castes within Bihar's political world seeped into the bureaucracy. Since Lalu Yadav's politics revolved around the theme of caste empowerment, and he had the stated intention of displacing the upper castes, the fact that the state administration was run by mostly upper caste bureaucrats created inevitable tension and a lack of administrative co-operation.

Table: 2.14

Caste in the Indian Administrative Service (Bihar Cadre) in 2002

Caste	Total	From Bihar	Other State
Kayasth	54	47	7
Brahmin	60	38	22
Rajput	22	17	5
Bhumihar	7	6	1
Scheduled Castes	25	8	17
Scheduled Tribes	7	0	7
Bania	15	4	11
Muslim	10	9	1
Yadav	4	4	0

Kurmi	3	3	0
Christian	3	0	3
Sikh	2	0	2
Jain	2	0	2
Backward	9	4	5
Unidentified	21		
Total	**244**		

Source: Witsoe, Democracy Against the State, 64

The RJD government exerted control over the bureaucracy through the strategic use of personnel transfers. Transfers of IAS officers formally require recommendation by the chief secretary and approval by the cabinet, but in practice have increasingly come under the discretionary control of chief ministers. Since state governments in India do not have the power to dismiss top-level bureaucrats, and have limited disciplinary options, elected leaders frequently used personnel transfers to control elements of the bureaucracy seen as hostile to the government in power. Key administrative positions in the districts, especially the powerful position of district magistrate, were given to OBC, Muslim, or Scheduled Caste officers. In 1995, thirty out of fifty district magistrates in Bihar were from these group, while 110 out of 113 positions in the State secretariat (where higher level administrative offices are located) were held by officers from upper caste backgrounds.

Political leaders used transfers to punish non compliant officers as well as to position loyal officers in strategic posts. But few IAS officers in Bihar shared a similar political outlook as the RJD leadership. Within such a context, loyalty could be gained only at a price, and this need for the RJD government to secure a loyal cohort of officers from a group which did not necessarily share the RJD's political commitments resulted in increased opportunities for corruption. The emphasis placed on loyality in many cases decreased the government's incentives for monitoring corruption, and decreased incentives within the bureaucracy for achieving higher levels of performance. Schemes such as Charwaha vidyalaya and some other pro poor schemes initiated by Laloo Raj, coupled with restoring of communal harmony(developed M-Y equation) all these had to be carried out by bureaucrats which was done on the order of the Govt; and this made him popular in the initial period and in 2004 Lok Sabha election this equation has successfully worked. Further it was during the 12th Assembly elections, the caste equations came to the fore fully. RJD won 123 out of 298 seats and emerged as the single largest party. It secured second place in 91 constituencies. Among the winners yadavas emerged victorious in 38 seats and thus ensured first place for the RJD (Louis: 2000;980). The RJD alliance remained the most popular choice for Muslim voters. This has been revealed in the study conducted by National Election Study-2004, which is as follows:

Table: 2.15
Party Preference by Castes

Caste	Congress+	BJP+	N
Upper Caste	25	63	213
Yadav	77	16	124
Kurmi+Koeri	18	64	98
Other OBCs	38	36	227
SCs	42	28	125
Muslim	79	9	149

Note: All figures in percentage point. Weighted data set of NES-2004., Economic & Political Weekly.

The above table shows that the huge social groups of Mandal voters remain divided. The numerically dominant backward caste of yadavs (77.0 %) voted for the RJD alliance in very large numbers, while a majority of the Kurmi+Koeri (64.0 %) voted for JD(U) BJP alliance. Since OBCs constitute the largest segments of population, therefore, if casteism gets momentum among them it is the leaders of this segment who are likely to be more and more benefited out of this process (Mishra & Pandey, 1996).

In this context Harry Blair opines about the gradual emergence of the upper backward castes and within this the ascendancy of the yadavas in Bihar politics in the following way. In a State where caste and politics have been mixed in such a strong and often explosive combination for so long, the legislative assembly is a natural place to look for evidence of a change from forward to backward primacy. Other upper backwards grew at the loss of just one caste group, i.e; the yadavas, who by 1977 had become the second largest group in the assembly, next only to Rajputs". This can be seen from the comparative study of caste composition in Bihar under different Government and also the caste/ community background of MPs in different phases. (Table: 2.16 to 2.18)

Caste based polarization has influenced the political and electoral discourse in Bihar over the years and will continue to do so. Similarly, while it will be incorrect to argue that such polarization on the basis of caste is of recent development (specific to Bihar) on the contrary it is pertinent to mention that caste has come to determine the course of election in such a pronounced manner since August 8, 1990- the day when the National Front Government under V.P. Singh decided to implement some of the recommendations of the Mandal Commission.

The politics of backward castes assertion and campaigns on these lines were witnessed in Bihar several years before Lalu Prasad landed on the political scene. Indeed, as one of the leaders of the Sampoorn Kranti Andolan that brought him into the political mainstream, his commitment to the principles of backward castes empowerment was not all that pronounced. After 1990, Lalu Prasad was able to determine the course of Bihar's politics.In this, he achieved what the legendary Karpoori Thakur could not do in Bihar. He constructed a social alliance between the Muslims and the Yadavs (MY).

A significant percentage of the increase in OBC MLAs during the 1990s was actually an increase in the number of Yadav MLAs, who since 1995 constituted 27% of the state assembly Moreover, 40% of the RJD MLAs were Yadavs as compared to only 17% from other OBCs. As the percentage of upper caste representation declined in the last decade and a half, the Yadav caste benefited most in the political arena.

Table 2.16

Caste in the Bihar Assembly in 2002

Caste	RJD	BJP	JD (U)	Samata	LJP	Cong	Other	Ind	Total
Yadav	47	5	9	2	0	0	0	1	64
Kurmi	2	1	1	8	0	1	0	0	13
Koeri	10	1	0	5	0	0	5	1	23
Brahmin	1	4	0	0	0	1	0	2	8
Rajput	6	5	0	6	4	0	1	4	26
Bhumihar	2	4	0	2	0	3	2	6	19

Kayasth	0	2	0	1	0	0	0	0	3
SC	21	6	0	3	2	2	5	0	39
Bania	6	4	0	1	0	0	1	0	12
Muslim	16	0	0	2	0	5	2	0	25
EBC	4	3	2	0	0	0	0	2	11
Total	**115**	**35**	**12**	**30**	**6**	**12**	**16**	**16**	**243**

Source: Witsoe, Democracy Against the State.

Most striking was the lack of representation for Extremely Backward Castes (EBCs). Although an estimated 32% of the population, EBC MLAs made up less than 5% of the Bihar assembly. This unequal representation between different OBC groups made it increasingly difficult for the RJD to claim to represent all lower castes.

The National Election Studies and Bihar Assembly Election Studies conducted by the centre for the study of Developing Societies document the changing support of the RJD. Its strongest and most enduring, support base in Bihar during the last fifteen years has been among Yadav voters, around 80% of whom have consistently voted for the RJD, while around 60% of Muslim voters have voted for the RJD. The continued support that the RJD received from Muslim and Yadav voters provides evidence for the validity of the so-called "M-Y alliance."

From 1995 onwards, upper caste voters leaned toward the NDA alliance, averaging around 60%. As well, in response to Nitish Kumar's break with Lalu Yadav to form his own Samata Party, around 60% of Kurmis and Koeris have voted for the NDA alliance.

Table: 2.17
Caste Composition of major Cabinet Ministries, 1962-97 (full ministers only: figures are in percentages).

Category	BN Jha 1962	KB Sahay 1963	MP Sinha 1967	DP Rai 1970	Kedar Pandey 1972	Abdul Ghafoor 1973	Jagnath Mishra 1975	Karpoori Thakur 1977	RS Das 1979	Jagnath Mishra 1980	Chandra sekhar Singh 1983	Bindesh-wari Dubey 1985	Lalu Yadav 1994	Rabri Devi 1997	Population of each caste groups
Forwards	58	40	67	33	38	38	40	29	50	44	44	62	27	17	13
UB	8	20	20	20	23	23	20	38	20	12	18	25	35	52	19
LB	0	0	7	0	0	5	0	4	0	6	6	12	11	6	31
Muslims & Bengali	8	20	7	13	15	10	13	13	15	19	19	0	11	12	15
SCs & STs	25	20	0	33	23	24	27	17	15	19	12	0	15	13	22
Total	99	100	101	99	99	100	100	101	100	100	99	99	99	100	100

1 Only 16 of 17 full ministers could be identified on this basis of castes. Percentages are therefore an approximation using a base of 16.The figures of upper backwards (UB) may be closer to 18 percent.

2, these calculations are based on complement of 8 full ministers as on 4 April, 1985, and do not account for any expansion of the cabinet after that date.

3. Percentages may not add upto 100 because of rounding.

4. Hindustan Times, dated 30.1.97.

(Figures for 1962 -79 are those from Blair (1980, p.9) for 1980-85 from Frankel(1989, p.118)and for 1994 Assistant Librarian of ANSISS, Patna.

Table: 2.18

Caste /Community background of MPs from Bihar: 1950-99.

	1950	1952	1957	1962	1967	1971	1977	1980	1984	1989	1991	1996	1998	1999
Upper caste	13(43.33)	31(60.78)	33(63.46)	28(52.83)	27(50.0)	22(41.50)	27(50.0)	23(43.39)	26(48.14)	21(39.62)	13(24.52)	15(28.30)	13(24.07)	19(35.18)
OBC	2(6.66)	3(5.88)	2(3.84)	9(16.98)	9(16.66)	15(28.30)	11(20.37)	12(22.64)	9(16.66)	15(28.30)	18(33.96)	20(37.73)	21(38.88)	14(25.92)
SCs	4(3.33)	8(15.68)	10(19.23)	9(16.98)	11(20.37)	7(13.20)	8(14.81)	7(13.20)	8(14.81)	8(15.09)	8(15.09)	8(15.09)	8(14.81)	6(11.11)
STs	3(10.00)	6(11.76)	4(7.69)	5(9.43)	5(9.25)	5(9.43)	5(9.25)	6(11.32)	6(11.11)	5(9.43)	6(11.32)	5(9.43)	5(9.25)	6(11.11)
Muslim/ Bengali, Christian & others	5(16.66)	3(5.88)	2(3.84)	2(3.77)	2(3.70)	4(7.54)	3(5..55)	5(9.43)	5(9.25)	4(7.54)	7(13.20)	5(9.43)	7(12.96)	5(9.25)
Not clear	3(10.00)	-	1(1.92)	-	-	-	-	-	-	-	1(1.88)	-	-	3(5.55)

Table 2.19 Half of RJD's loyal voters in the last decade were Yadavs and Muslims

Caste	Never voted for RJD	Always voted for RJD	Voted for RJD Lok Sabha Election	Voted for RJD Assembly election 2000
All	28	20	26	27
Upper Caste	45	7	9	11
Yadav	2	32	28	27
Muslim	4	26	21	23
Other OBC	26	21	22	20
Dalit	11	13	19	18
Adivasi	12	1	1	1

Source: Sanjay Kumar, The Return of the RJD.

Above table shows, that while there are clear caste-related voting patterns, there is also a crucial distribution of votes cutting across parties and caste categories. The RJD received only 50% of its votes from Yadav and Muslim voters during the 1999 national and 2000 state assembly elections, highlighting the fact that the M-Y alliance alone was not sufficient to win elections. The RJD received 38% of its votes from non-Yadav OBC and Scheduled Caste voters, and even 11% of its share from upper caste voters.

These contradictions within the RJD's claim to be the champion of backward caste empowerment, in particular the disproportionate dominance of Yadavs at the expense of other OBC groups and Scheduled Castes, produced a fragmentation of Bihar's political landscape. The RJD's Scheduled Caste support dropped by half from nearly 50% in 1995 to 22% in 2005, and support from non-Yadav OBCs also declined. This progressive chipping away of the RJD's

Scheduled Caste and non-Yadav OBC support proved to be the decisive factor in the party's slow decline.

Polarization of caste in favour of one caste, i.e; yadavas was seen by other backward castes as well as some portions of muslim communities as denial of social justice to them. Along with this, the demands of peasants as a social class continued to be ignored, and their resentments and agrarian demand were neglected or suppressed. The Times of India(Delhi ed.), dated 23rd November'2005 in its editorial under heading "Vote for Change: Lalu Pd. 15 years raj ends in Bihar" speaks that the people of Bihar has rejected RJD rule who has been in the power for the last 15 years (since 1990). It further says that the political agenda of Lalu and his wife Rabri Devi was limited to the electoral empowerment of some backward castes particularly the yadavas. The RJD failed to use the energy unleashed by ideas like social justice and power to the oppressed to transform Bihar's backward economy. Not surprisingly, social justice in Bihar under the RJD was more on the plane of rhetoric than content. The non-Yadav OBCs and EBCs such as Mallahs, Nais, Kalwars, Kewats, Binds, and Tantis rallied behind Nitish Kumar because there was an overwhelming perception among these castes that the RJDs social empowerment measures were confined to the Yadav community. But that does not mean that they would be ready to revert to the days of upper caste domination. These castes want to have the same socio-economic mobility as that of the backward leaders of Bihar. As highlighted by Professor Kishori Das, Chairperson of the Coordination Committee of Neglected and Extremely Backward Communities, what the EBCs are looking forward to is a renewed and real commitment to the ideology of social justice. "We do not want slogans like the ones that Lalu Pd. gave us repeatedly since 1995, but concrete and meticulous measures that make a fast and effective change". This they saw in Nitish Kumar, the present chief minister of Bihar who himself a product of social justice politics has promised to go beyond the rhetoric and transform Bihar's economy.

So in the election of 2005 Most backward castes with the active help of other backward castes and upper castes dislodged the government of Rabri Devi and another backward leader from Kurmi caste; i.e; Nitish Kumar representing merely 5.0 percent of Kurmi population in Bihar become the next chief minister. This marked a new emerging social combination. The outcome of the 2005 assembly poll is given below in tabular as well as in bar diagram form:

Table: 2.20

Party	Seats won
RJD	75
JD(U)	55
BJP	37
LJP	29
Congress	10
Independent & others	37
Total seats	**243**

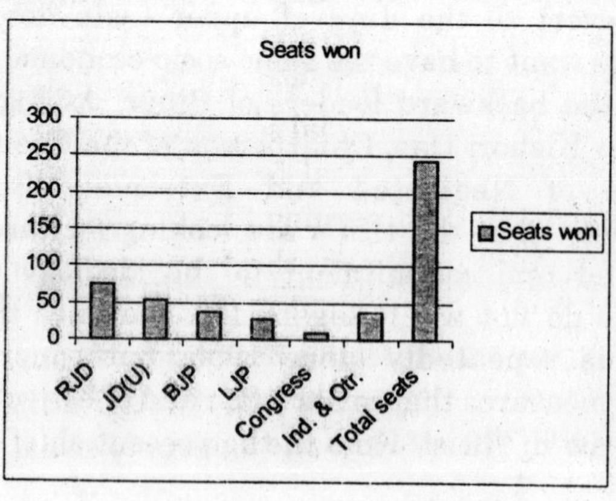

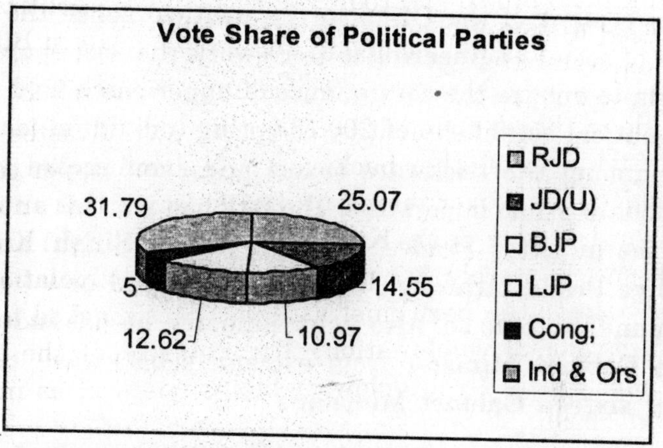

Source: The Times of India, (Delhi edition) October 18, 2005

But this does not mean that the Post-Mandal brand of politics, which has manifested itself in the form of the backward castes dictating political terms in Bihar is about to end with the exit of the RJD. Lalu Pd., espousal of social justice has ensured that Bihar politics will always be guided by Mandal dynamics. It could be a Nitish Kumar or a Sushil Modi or anyone else for that matter, backward castes have acquired a leading role and it is there to stay. Although it is not Lalu Pd., it is only another backward leader who is holding the rein now. According to Shashi Bhushan Rai, the legacy that the RJD leaves is the awakening among backward caste people to the power which gets them social respectability as well. Even social scientists agree with this. According to them, the political hegemony of upper caste people in Bihar has taken a unique turn. They say that if it was not for Nitish Kumar, the National Democratic Alliance(NDA) would have found it difficult to unseat the RJD(Frontline, Nov; 5-18, 2005).In a larger sense, Nitish Kumar had played his role in the social engineering frame work, which is not the same as the agenda of social justice enunciated by Ram Manohar Lohia. Rather than empowerment of the OBCs in the political sense the end game of social engineering is to re-work the socio-political agenda to ensure the continuance of upper caste hold over the political establishment by co-opting individual leaders from among the backward castes and even accord them positions of prime importance. The BJP had put this strategy in place in Uttar Pradesh(through Kalyan Singh) and in Madhya Pradesh(through Uma Bharati). And now he has the mandate to do so. Also in his ministry, he has inducted three Cabinet Minister from extremely backward castes out of sixteen Cabinet Minister.

From the above it can be inferred that the backward caste movement in Bihar can be attributed to numerous social, economic and political factors in the Pre as well as post-independence phase. It threw open the doors of power to the hitherto depressed and backward castes. Being numerically pre-ponderent, they were able to capture the local and provincial source of power. Land reform also paved the way for their economic improvement. The process of economic improvement culminated in the post- green revolution phase. Having gained political and economic power, they also wanted to increase their share in bureaucracy. However, this demand was impelled by other factors also, such as, increased mechanization resulting in increased unemployment in rural areas. Nevertheless, the backward castes urge to enhance their share in the sphere of bureaucracy made them demand reservations in government job.

According to a survey report of 1951, picture has changed little. If we accept the findings of the All India Agricultural labour enquiry, the following outcome will emerge:

Table:2.21

	Brah-mins	Raj-puts	Vaishya	Back-ward castes	SCs & STs	Tribals aboriginal	Others
No. of families	**491**	**429**	**372**	**3639**	**2210**	**207**	**2795**
Percent of total No. of families	5.1	4.5	3.9	38.1	23.2	2.2	23.0
Landowners	81 (71.84)	8.2 (6.32)	1.1 (0.72)	1.1 (7.22)	3.5 (13.90)	—	—
Tenants	—	78.6 (14.07)	31.7 (4.92)	44.0 (66.82)	15.4 (14.19)	—	—
Agricultural workers	—	6.3 (0.95)	18.0 (2.35)	35.2 (44.99)	66.6 (51.71)	—	—
Non agricultural workers	19.0 (6.96)	6.9 (2.25)	49.2 (13.68)	19.5 (53.10)	14.5 (24.01)	—	—
Total	**100.0**	**100.0**	**100.0**	**99.8**	**100.0**		

Source: All India Agriculture Labour Enquiry: Rural Man-Power and Occupation Structure, 1951, pp.55-57.

It is evident from the table that 78.16 percent of land-owners are concentrated in two upper castes. The lower down in the caste hierarchy the greater the extent to which lower castes depend for their living on farm labour.As a result their economic backwardness makes them dependent on the higher castes, such as Brahmins, Bhumihars and Rajputs. Now the situation has changed slightly. Commenting on the politics of culture defined by the middle cultivating castes of eastern U.P. and Bihar in the late 19th and early 20th centuries, the historian William Pinch observes that "the shift from the cultural politics of the early 20th century to the political culture of the 1990s is not one that occurred as a sharp break at independence in 1947 but has been much more gradual, indeed almost imperceptible. The implication of that shift are profound, signaling the demise of a political culture based on an ideology of martial power and the rise of politics based on democratic, demographic realities." Pinch goes on to note that the distinction between the colonial and post-colonial realities had to do with achieving an identifiable measure of social and economic justice in free India. For Kurmi, Yadav, and Kushwaha(Koeri) leader, this would represent a sea-change in Indian political culture crafted around visions of martial grandeur. They also scramble for caste icons in Bihar, as, Kurmi articulated it through the use of Sardar Patel (many Kurmi adopted title of Patel).They also adopted Chhatrapati Shivaji as the tribals of Bihar had done earlier adopting Birsa Munda. Their rivals, the Kushwahas(Koeris) found their leader in Jagdeo Prasad, a trade unionist killed in Gaya a couple of years back, a fit rallying point for social, economic and political assertion. B.P.Mandal was an icon fashioned by the Janata Dal to justify an aggressive pro-social justice political movement even as the Banias of Bihar led by Rajya Sabha MP Prem Kumar Gupta now seek a political icon in Bhamashah-warrior cum advisor of Shivaji's time. These groups came to define themselves in the social democracy of a free India through the mechanism expressed in terms of backward class interest, reservations, and the Mandal phenomenon.In the context of caste in politics, Kothari in his book "Caste in Indian Politics" has argued that casteism in politics was no more or no less than politicization of caste-a political process that played an important role in the facilitation of democracy and growth of social awareness.

In the Post-independence period the pattern of land reform in Bihar is one of the main reasons for the imperfect mobilization of the backward castes into politics. After independence the first Constitutional Amendment Act which inserted clause(4) to Article 15 also amended some other Articles of the Constitution, including Article 31 which relates to removal of intermediaries and land reform. The Patna High Court had invoked the principle of equality before law as provided in Article 14 of the Constitution to block the operation of Article 31. The amendment was carried out to remove this difficulty. While it paved the way to remove intermediaries between the State and the cultivators, it also helped the rich and medium owner-cultivators, mostly belonging to the intermediate castes, as the ceiling laws could not be implemented because of lack of political will.

As mentioned above this section of upper backwards indirectly joined hands with the traditional higher caste big land owners to defeat the laws pertaining to land ceilings, minimum wages and share cropping etc. As these two sections were strong support base of the political party in power, so no serious effort was made by the government to actualizes land reform honestly. Prasad(1991) also support the above views. He observes that the upper stratum of the OBCs in Bihar comprises of yadav, kurmi, and koeri, among whom the well to do sections are prominent in the agrarian economy and politics. He finds that several among these castes were tenants of zamindars (upper castes) and later become landholders following the land reform programme in Bihar. Atul Kohli also identifies three historical factors in this respect, that would have led to the slow conversion of the backward castes from being tenents earlier on to the status of landowners. In the first place zamindari abolition of the 1950s may have led to some land transfers from the twice born castes to their tenents, many of whom were from backward castes. Secondly, the flight of the Muslim zamindars from central Bihar to Pakistan at the time of the partition resulted in some backward castes tenents becoming de-facto landowners. The distress sale of land led to the accumulation of land by the upper backward castes and in many cases they began to emulate like zamindars, which further led to conflict and violence between the upper backward castes and the scheduled castes. After independence, ceiling legislation was passed and led to the pressure on traditional landowners to sell their excess lands to new groups who could afford to buy, many of whom, especially in central Bihar belonged to the backward castes. Kohli estimated that as much as 10.0 percent of the State's agricultural land may have been transferred from the twice-born zamindars to the backward castes. In certain parts of Patna, Nalanda, and Rohtas districts in central Bihar, the zamindars were kurmis. But overall the condition of OBCs remained pathetic in this field, despita Prasad and Kohli support in this regard.

NSS surveys prior to 1999 did not use the OBC category, so no comparison can be made over time to gauge how these patterns may be changing. It is clear, however, that OBC households own less land than households in the "Other" category, and that Scheduled Caste households fare much worse. OBC households own more marginal holdings (less than 0.4 hectares) compared to "Other" category households, but as the size of the land holdings increase, OBC ownership decreases (4.01+it is 0.7%) Only 9% of Scheduled Caste households cultivate land somewhat larger than marginal holdings and 66% do not cultivate, representing the high number of Scheduled Caste households dependent on income from agricultural labor.

Table 2.22

Land possessed (0.00 Hectare)

Social Group	0.00	0.01-0.40	0.41-1.00	1.01-2.00	2.01-4.00	4.01+
Other	6.0%	49.2%	23.0%	12.6%	6.1%	3.1%
OBC	8.8%	58.0%	19.5%	9.5%	3.5%	0.7%
SC	23.8%	67.1%	6.4%	2.1%	0.6%	0.0%

Source: 55th round of NSS (1999-2000) report no. 469.

Table 2.23

Land cultivated (0.00 Hectare)

Social Group	0.00	0.01-0.40	0.41-1.00	1.01-2.00	2.01-4.00	4.01+
Other	33.2%	24.6%	22.6%	11.9%	5.0%	2.6%
OBC	37.8%	32.2%	18.4%	8.6%	2.4%	0.7%
SC	66.1%	26.3%	5.3%	1.8%	0.4%	0.0%

Source: 55th round of NSS (1999-2000) report no. 469.

The average size of cultivated land holdings has decreased significantly, and land being leased out to others has increased. Leasing negatively impacts production because cultivators who rent land (often referred to as "leasing in") are unlikely to make long-term investments: rent cuts into profits, leaving less capital for investment. While leased in land constituted less than 5% of cultivated land in 1992, this increased to nearly 25% by 1998. Households with marginal and small operational holdings cultivate the largest percentage of leased in land.

The graph below displays the percentage of leased-in land by different caste groups. Backward Caste, Scheduled Caste and, to a lesser extent, Muslim cultivators are leasing in a significant portion of their operational holdings, while the percentage of leased in land is marginal for upper caste cultivators. In sum, despite the political empowerment of OBCs in Bihar, land ownership patterns display old patterns of dominance. An increasing percentage of land is being leased out by mostly upper caste landowners to mostly lower caste marginal and small cultivators.

Table 2.24

Leased in land by Caste Groups

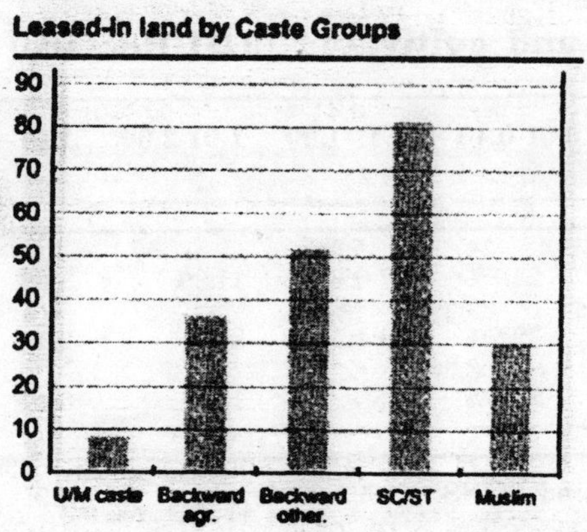

Source: Election Comission of India cited in World Bank, Bihar, 16.

The assertion of intermediate caste took varied forms. In the fifties, they were very few in number, but from the sixties their numbers began to gradually rise and in parliamentary politics, the socialists, the lok dal, the Janata Party and the Janata Dal became their channels of articulation, and from the late sixties they resorted to all sorts of wheeling and dealing. Democracy gave them added

Table: 2.25 Landownership by Caste Absolute Numbers & (in Brackets)Percentage Distribution of Households

caste

Land ownership Group (acres)	Brah-min+ Kayastha	Bhu-mihar+ Rajput	Back-ward	Yadav	Koiri	Kurmi	other Back-ward	SCs	Moslem	Total
0	24 (2.2)	8 (0.7)	251 (23.1)	31 (2.9)	15 (1.4)	8 (0.7)	87 (8.0)	477 (43.8)	487 (17.2)	4087 (43.1)
0-1	38 (5.6)	59 (8.7)	126 (18.4)	70 (10.3)	79 (11.5)	12 (1.7)	61 (8.9)	181 (26.6)	57 (8.3)	682 (27.)
1.25 (18.0)	52 (23.4)	68 (8.6)	26 (6.9)	20 (10.2)	30 (3.6)	11 (7.4)	22 (7.4)	22 (11.5)	36 (11.5)	291
2.5-5.0(36.8)	80 (23.7)	51 (1.6)	3 (8.1)	18 (5.1)	11 (9.4)	20 (3.4)	7 (2.9)	6 (9.1)	20 (8.6)	217
5.0-10.0	77 (52.8)	23 (15.8)	0 (0.0)	3 (2.1)	4 (2.8)	16 (10.7)	7 (5.1)	1 (0.9)	14 (9.8)	145 (5.8)
10.0-20.0	40 (48.5)	24 (29.3)	6 (6.9)	2 (2.1)	1 (1.4)	4 (4.6)	2 (2.1)	0 (0.0)	4 (5.1)	82 (3.2)
20+	8 (41.5)	8 (41.2)	0 (0.0)	0 (0.0)	0 (0.0)	1 (4.1)	2 (8.8)	0 (0.0)	1 (4.4)	20 (0.8)
Total	**319 (12.6)**	**241 (9.6)**	**412 (16.3)**	**144 (5.7)**	**140 (5.5)**	**70 (2.8)**	**188 (7.5)**	**692 (27.4)**	**319 (12.6)**	**2524 (100.0)**

strength due to their numerical superiority. They utilized the benefits of the green revolution package programme to the extent possible and acquired sufficient economic muscle.

They maintained a love-hate relationship with the naxalite movement which was actually the dalit agrarian labourers and poor peasants fight against upper caste landlords. When due to this fight the political power of the old landed gentry was weakened, they moved in to fill the vaccum since they were the only forces able to do that.Thus in the place of the old upper caste dominance the country side became the sight for the domination by a neo-rich pesantary. These new dominant groups, being from the ritually clean castes continued to maintain social distance from the lower castes. These affluent backward castes have been referred to as upper shudras or bullock capitalists.The effort of the government to build networks to aid social advancement among lower castes were thus hijacked by a few politically aware stronger upper backward castes, who also acquired economic and cultural capital. These affluent Castes socially networked among themselves to exclude the others, particularly the dalits.A.Portes and P. Landolt (1996) argued that, if social capital is a resource or gain accumulated through social ties and networks, then we also need to know that some resources people claim come at the expense of others;the same ties that help members of a group often enable it to exclude others.This resource gain led to the feudal ways and values that yield to the temptations of amoral, corrupt and even criminal politics which has brought radical changes in Bihar's social life. The left radical movement in South Bihar inspite of its several limitations greatly assisted in the rise of the backwards in the political arena by mobilizing people belonging to the lower castes-classes cutting across the caste barrier at the middle and lower end of the society in their struggle against the atrocities by erstwhile zamindars and other landlords. Social capital is not only being used in a perverse way but is being accumulated to challenge what Bourdieu calls the *Symbolic Power* of the upper castes which they have acquired through cultural and economic capital.The attributes and benefits of social capital are used to gain legitimacy over other forms of capital which the higher castes have accumulated and gained.

The dalits, the worst off lower castes who are caught between the upper castes and the upwardly mobile newly rich backward castes are left with nothing and formed alliances and network with the extreme left naxalite groups to fight the social hegemony of higher castes in general but more importantly the economic and political hegemony of the affluent backward castes. Although ideologically quite different, the attempt of the radical peasant movements that also utilized caste sentiment to further their struggle, gave rise to private armies (senas). Most of these private armies emerged in late 1970s and 1980s as a feudal response to the growth of naxalite groups. Since then, an estimated 15 private armies have existed at various points of time in the State including prominently: Kuer Sena, Bhumi Sena, Lorik Sena, Sunlight Sena, Bramharshi Sena, Kisan Sangh, Gram Suraksha Parishad, Ranvir Sena, Ganga Sena etc; In many cases these senas attacks on their own brethren; i.e; upper backward castes senas attack on lower backward castes and in most of the cases the former castes has upper hand in it. So as to say that from 90s onward, it is the upper backward castes that have benefited more out of the backward class assertion and specially yadav during Rabri Devi government; (1997), out of 39 ministers from the upper backwards, 24 were from yadav caste alone. Some of the important Boards/ Corporations were also handed over to the OBCs especially yadavas. By and large the lower or middle ring of backward classes is facing problems of unemployment. Though they constitute the middle order of the caste structure, their assertion in the last seven decades point to the social change being introduced in Bihar. The upper castes had their hegemony and dominance unchallenged for centuries. In the post-independence period, it is the upper backward castes that have come to the centre stage of Bihar's politics. The status of lower backward castes during all these years had, however, remained unaltered. While economic empowerment had touched a fraction of the upper backward castes, the large segments of the lower backward castes remained economically disadvantaged. Politically also they were marginalized. Karpoori Thakur brought them to the centre stage by implementing Mungerilal Commission, which ensured separate reservation for them.They also had to bear the brunt of the anti-reservation agitation along with the upper backward castes. During the early part of the tenure of Lalu Pd. Chief ministership, he found them to be his natural ally, specially during his conflict with the other segments of the upper backwards led by Nitish Kumar. Like ShriKrishna Sinha, Lalu had also out-maneuvered his powerful opponents by promoting several lower backward caste leaders, like Rameshwar Rai(Amat), Puncham Mandal(Dhanuk), Ravindra Kumar(Tanti), Ramdev Bhandari(Kewat), Ram Karan Pall(Gaderia) and Jai Narain Nishad(Mallah).Even after the rise of Karpoori Thakur or Dhanik Lal Mandal, the lower backwards did not acquire a separate identity which Lalu had done but later on Yadavisation of politics led him to debacle in state poll. It is not out of context to cite here the view of C. Jaffrelot (2003) who states that the :

> Power is now being transferred on the whole peacefully, from the upper caste elites to the subaltern groups. While riots did take place during the Mandal affair such transfers of power are generally accompanied by large scale violence. The relative calm of the Indian experience is primarily due to the fact that the whole process is incremental: the upper castes are still in command, with the OBCs forming a second line of leadership, a new

> generation in waiting. The educational backwardness of the lower castes is such that they will probably not be able to dislodge the elites for several decades. Second, the rise of power of the lower castes is very uneven. They have taken over in Bihar but remain in a subordinate position in Rajasthan. Third, the conflict is not based on a clear cut political opposition since the upper caste dominated parties have low caste members in their ranks and vice versa. Fourth, the upper castes are loosing ground in the political sphere and in administration but the liberalization of the economy-which coincided with the implementation of the Mandal Report-has opened new opportunities for the upper castes in the private sectors; and hence they may no longer regret their traditional monopoly over bureaucracy being challenged. Fifth, and more importantly, the rise to power of the lower castes is not irreversible and linear. There is a trend but they will have to overcome several handicaps in pursuing it. The lower castes suffer from a structural lack of unity. The scheduled castes and the other backward classes do not comprise discrete categories. They are divided along caste lines according to gradual inequality principle that Ambedkar described even before independence.

Because of the exclusion they face, it has been easier for them to form an all India dalit identity but there was hardly any change in the economic and social positioning of the lower castes in the rural areas.

Inspite this, another major reasons for the imperfect mobilization of the backward castes into politics could be found in the social and political economy of the rural Bihar, for example the Jajmani system which consists of two main units- Jajman who are economically powerful and are generally from the upper castes and the Kamins who(except of Brahmins) are from the lower castes and are usually poor. The Kamins provide various kinds of customary services to their Jajmans in return for various kinds of entitlements, the whole arrangement, ie; an unequal social system, is based on the ritual and secular hierarchies of the caste system. Though this form of arrangement is found all over India under different names, its ideal typical forms are found in north Indian villages inhabited by other upper castes.

The recent evidence on backward caste mobilization suggests that the backward castes mobilized for asserting their rights what they ought to have their share in the democratic setup like jobs and positions, fight against atrocities. Their sphere of operation might be secular, democratic, and power element is inherent in it.The mobilization is demonstrated in terms of organized protests on different occasions for asserting their rights and demonstrating their strength against the powers of atrocities and discrimination.The recent mobilization and protests appear to achieve the substantive gains in positions, land and assertion through democratic means.

In the light of the above and other factors that are influencing the OBCs political as well as social life, it is of great interest to see, what shape it will take in future in Bihar and it also posses questions before social scientists to ponder over it.

References

- Aloysius, G. (1997) Nationalism Without A Nation in India, Oxford University Press, Delhi.
- Blair, H.(1980) "Rising Kulaks and Backward Classes in Bihar: Social Change in the Late 1970s" Economic and Political Weekly, Vol-XV, No, -2
- Bourdieu, P(1986) Distinction: A Social Critique of the Judgment of Taste, London
- Conference on State Politics in India in the1990s; Political Mobilization and Political Competition.
- Chandapuri, Second Freedom Struggle, Mission Prakashan, Saraswati Bhavan, Mandiri, Patna.

- Choudhary, Prasanna, K. Land Reform in Bihar:Need for a Fresh Appraisal, & Iyer, K. Gopal. Concealed Tenancy: Dilemmas of Share-Croppers in Bihar in yugandhar BN & Iyer, K. Gopal(ed.) (1993), Land Reform in India, Bihar: Institutional Constraints, Vol-1, Sage Publications, New Delhi.
- Chaudhary, Prasana Kumar & Srikant(2001), "Bihar Mein Samajik Parivartan ke Kuch Aayam (1912-1990), Vani Prakashan, New Delhi-110002
- Das A.N. (1992) The Republic of Bihar,, Penguin Books India(p) Ltd; New Delhi
- Das, A.N.(1983) Agrarian Unrest and Socio-Economic Change in Bihar:1900-1980, Manohar, New Delhi.
- Encyclopaedia of India and Her States, (1998) Shyam Nandan Singh. Politics of Job Reservation for Backward Castes in Bihar: 1977-79, Vol:7, Deep Publications, New Delhi.
- Frankel, Francine & Rao, M.S.A (eds.)1989-90, Dominance and State Power in Modern India, Vol.2, Oxford University Press, Delhi.
- F. Francise (ed.) 2006, Social Justice & Stalled Development: Caste Empowerment and the Breakdown of Governance in Bihar. CASI, Philadelphia.
- Gupta Shaibal(January, 2002) Subaltern Resurgence: A Reconnaissance of Panchayat Election in Bihar; ADRI, Patna, (working paper no:8), Economic & Political Weekly.
- Gupta Shaibal "Emergence of New Social Elites in Bihar Crisis or Change" Economic & Political Weekly.
- Gupta, Shaibal (5/12/05) Between the facts and a hard place, The Bihar Times, Patna.
- Gupta Shaibal (Dec, 2004) Nature of Elite Formation in the Hindi Heartland: A Comparative Assessment of Bihar and M.P, ADRI, Patna.
- Goyal, Santosh. Social Background of Officers in the Indian Administrative Service; in Dominance & State Power in Modern India, Vol I (ed.) F. Frankel & MSA Rao, 1989 OUP, Delhi.

- Express News Service, Zero Growth During Lalu-Rabri Regime: Nitish White Paper, Indian Express, April 4, 2006.
- Hasan, Zoya(1998), Quest for Power:Oppositional Movements and Post-Congress Politics in UP, Oxford University Press, Delhi.
- J. Prabhash (2001) Affirmative Action and Social Change: Social Mobility of Dalits, Anmol Publications Pvt; Ltd; New Delhi.
- Jaffrelot, Christophe "Positive Discrimination and the transformation of Caste in India.
- ....(2003) India's Silent Revolution : The Rise of the Low Castes in North Indian Politics, Permanent Black.
- Jha, PK (1994) Changing Conditions of Agriculture Labourers in Post-Independence India: A Case Study from Bihar, Ph.D. dissertion, JNU, Centre for Economic Studies and Planning, School of Social Sciences, New Delhi.
- K.C. Yadav (1994) India's unequal Citizens: A Study of the Backward Caste, Manohar, New Delhi.
- Kohli, Atul (1990) Democracy and Discontent: India's Growing Crisis of Govern-ability, Cambridge University Press, Cambridge.
- Kothari, Rajni(ed.) 1995, Caste in Indian Politics, Orient Longman Limited, Hyderabad.
- Kumar Suresh "Dalit Discontent and the pattern of Mobilisation: The experience of Bihar" Lal, A.K "Other Backward Classes in Bihar" in Bhosale, BV (2004)(ed) "Mobilisation of Backward Communities in India."
- Kumar, Anand.(29-30th Sept;'2005), Seminar paper "Some aspects of post- conflict face of poverty: A Study of 4 villages of Musahari Block, Muzaffapur(Draft) IIPA, New Delhi.
- Kumar, Dr. Ravi, Failure to Translate Social Justice into Development-Exploring Backward Castes Politics in Bihar, Nov-December 2005, Council for Social Development, New Delhi.
- Kumar, Sanjay. A Shift Across the Social Divide, The Hindu, March 10, 2005.

- ....Janata Regionalized: Contrasting Bases of Electoral Support in Bihar & Orissa in Regional Reflections: Comparing Politics Across India's States (ed.) Rob Jenkins (2004) OUP, Oxford.
- ....New Phases in Backward Caste Politics of Bihar in Caste and Democratic Politics in India, (ed.) Ghanshyam Shah (2004), Anthem Press, London.
- Louis, Prakash. Caste, Politics and Dominance: Assertion of the Backward Castes of Bihar, in H.S.Verma(ed.)2005, The OBCs and the Dynamics of Social Exclusion in India, Serials Publications, New Delhi
- Mohanty, N R(29th-30th Sept) "Chronic Poverty and Social Conflict in Bihar"(Draft) IIPA, New Delhi.
- Mohanty, K.K.(1993) Social Mobility and Caste Dynamics, Rawat Publications, Delhi/Jaipur.
- Mammen Mathew "Scramble for Caste icons in Bihar, The Hindustan Times, New Delhi 28 April, 1998.
- Panadiker, V.A.Pai(1997)(ed.) The Politics of Backwardness: Reservation Policy in India, Reservation and After;The case of Bihar by Sachchidananda, Konark Publishers Pvt; Ltd;, New Delhi.
- Prasad, P.H.(1989) Poor-Peasant Movement in Central Bihar, Unpublished.
- Purnima S. Tripathi "A Vote for change" Frontline, Vol:22A issue 25, November 5-18, 2005
- Ramashray Roy, Caste and Political Recruitment in Bihar in Rajni Kothari(ed.) 1970 "Caste in Indian Politics., Orient Longman, New Delhi.
- Dayadhar Jha, State Legislature in India, Abhinav Publication, 1977
- Radhakrishna, R. & Sharma, Alakh.N.(ed.)1998, Empowering Rural Labour in India, Institute of Human Development, New Delhi.
- Rao, MSA(1987) Social Movements and Social Transformation, " Manohar, New Delhi.
- Runciman, W.C.(1966) Relative Deprivation and Social Justice, Routledge & Kegan Paul, London.

- Report of the Backward Classes Commission, 1980 (Vol: 1& 11), Government of India.
- Sharma Premlata (2002)" The Problems of Dalits and OBCs, Book Enclave, Jaipur.
- Sathyamurthy T V (1996)(ed.) Class Formation and Political Transformation in Post-Colonial India" Agricultural labour and the Poor Peasant Movement in Bihar, Oxford University Press, New Delhi.
- Shukla, Kiran(1987) Castes Politics in India, Mittal Publication, New Delhi.
- Sinha S.K., 2004, The Bhumihars: Caste of Eastern India, Raj Publications, New Delhi.
- The Eastern Anthropologist, Vol;-55, No.-2-3, April-September'2002
- Verma H.S, (2005) The OBCs and the Dynamics of social exclusion in India, Serials Publications, New Delhi.
- Verma K.K.(1979) Changing Role of Caste Association, National Publishing House, New Delhi.
- Verma Binoy N(1993) Agrarian Relation in Transition, Vol-1, Ashish Publishing House, New Delhi.
- Venkitesh Ramakrishan, "A New Era in Bihar", Frontline, Vol: 22A, issue 25, November 5-18, 2005.
- V.K.Krishna Ananth, "Shifting Alliances in Bihar", Economic & Political Weekly, January 1, 2005
- W. G. Lacey, 1987 (Rpt) Census of India; 1931, Part-1.Report, Vol: VII (Bihar & Orissa). Usha Publications, Darya Ganj, New Delhi.
- Walter Hauser (February, 1997)" Bihar Changing Images of Caste and Politics, in the State of Bihar, Seminar#450
- Weiner, M(2001) The Struggle for Equality:Caste in Indian Politics in Atul Kohli(ed.) The Success of India's Democracy, Cambridge University Press, Cambridge.
- Yadav Muneshwar, Politics from Below & Cyril Robin, Bihar Elections: Laloo against Who?, Economic & Political Weekly, Vol-39, No.51 December 18-24, 2004.

3

Mungeri Lal Commission And After

Social aspirations of backward castes to establish their social as well as political identity was aroused due to the census of 1910 and later on this led to the formation of "Triveni Sangh" in 1930s in Bihar which in several ways marked the beginning of an era for them because through this association they strived for their social and political emancipation. The question of reservation, in general, was discussed in the round table conference and provisions were made in the communal award of 1932, known as Poona Pact. The provision under this Act was as follows:

1. There shall be seats reserved for the depressed classes out of the general electorates seats in the provincial legislatives as given below in the table:

Table : 3.1

Province	No. of Seats
Madras	30
Bombay & Sindh	15
Punjab	8
Bihar & Orissa	18
Central Province	20
Assam	7
Bengal	30
United Provinces	20
Total	**148**

2. Election to these seats shall be by joint electorates, subject to certain conditions laid down in the Poona Pact.

As against 78 seats allotted to the depressed classes in the State legislative, the Poona pact gave 148 seats. However, untouchables lost the right to elect their own representatives and this right was transferred to the Hindus. It had some lacuna but somehow it paved the future course of action.

Montague-Chelmsford Reforms also recognized caste as an indicator of social backwardness.and welfare measures were suggested accordingly to some castes identified as depressed castes. The 1935 Act later on developed these welfare measures into reservation for those identified as socially backward.

After independence, in 1951, the Bihar government issued a G.O. listing the OBCs in two Annexures i.e; Annexure-1 consisting of 79 castes who were deemed to be more backward than the 30 castes that were in Scheduled-2 (**Annexure-II**). Way back in 1953 Baijnath Singh had introduced in the Bihar Assembly a non-official bill seeking to reserve 25.0 percent of the State jobs to OBCs, but under the pressure from the party leaders it was withdrawn. The Backward Classes Federation and particularly leaders like Dev Saran Singh, a kurmi, represented for job reservations in the State for the OBCs. This was not seriously entertained by the Congress. The State Government, Recruitment Department, vide its circular **2 N-173/49-7079 of 25th July, 1957** issued to various departments a list of other backward castes who were socially and educationally backward for their information and guidelines to be followed by them. As far as question of reservation in government services is concerned, Memorandum **No. 111-3L-6/50A-9909 of 13th November, 1953** issued by the State government stated that during appointment in class 111 & IV government services, OBCs belonging to Annexure-1 should be considered. In 1953 the Central Government under Article 340 of the Constitution of India appointed a Commission under the chairmanship of Kaka Kalelkar to look into various aspects of backward classes and to give suggestions to the Government. Different State Governments as well as publics provided their valuable comments/suggestions to the Commission. In this context, on 5th December, 1954, Chandpuri, the then president of the Bihar State Backward Classes Federations submitted a memorandum to the Backward Classes Commission (1953-1955) He also met prime minister, Nehru as the head of a delegation on 24th October, 1955. In his 50 minutes talk with the delegation, Nehru assured to implement the recommendations of the Commission; but he never did what he said in this regard. The first Backward Class Commission prepared a list of OBCs which consists 126 OBCs of Bihar.

On August 14, 1961 the Ministry of Home Affairs on this issue addressed to all the State government stating "while the State government have the discretion to choose their own criteria for defining backwardness in the view of the Government of India, it would be better to apply economic test and then to go by caste." Regarding the preparation of lists of backward classes it was observed "even if the Central Government were to specify under article 338(3) certain groups of people as belonging to OBC's. It will still be open to every State government to draw up it's own lists for the purpose of Articles 15 & 16. Therefore, the State government may adhere to their own lists. Any all India list drawn up by the Central government, would have no practical utility. Following the Balaji decision of 1963 in the Supreme Court, the Patna High Court held in 1964, these two lists unconstitutional. In view of this, the State Government decided that the current educational benefits should be given only to such students of OBCs mentioned in the 1951 order whose family monthly income was below Rupees 500. For admission to medical colleges, the income limit was fixed at Rupees 250 per month. It was also decided not to make any distinction between the two annexures. In the meantime, a ministerial sub-committee was constituted by the State Government to prepare a list of backward castes and also to frame the parameters for determining backwardness.This sub-committee prepared a list of 112 castes which were considered as backward. Subsequently, State Government vide its office order **1980-S of 29th July, 1966** issued a list of 112 backward castes who were entitled for scholarships in colleges and reservation in government services. Again on 12th April, 1968, the State Government constituted a Commission to frame criteria for determining backwardness and also to prepare a list of such castes. On the basis of social and educational backwardness the Commission prepared a list of backward castes to meet the obligation under Article 15(4) of the Indian Constitution. This list was also challenged before the High Court on certain technical ground and thereafter the Court quashed the Government order. Thus the field was open for appointment of a new Commission to look into different aspects of backward castes and subsequently to prepare a list of these castes.

Meanwhile the Indian political system in 1967 witnessed the emergence of coalition Governments resulting in downfall of monolithic Congress rule in North India. The Congress government under the leadership of Indira Gandhi had taken note of it and a number of populist measures were taken in Central and different State governments to win back poor and backward castes. In Bihar also, with the emerging trend of caste and class conflict in rural areas, lower caste workers were sympathetic to the naxalite movement. Rural rich peasantry of backward castes was voters of the socialist party. The Communist party of India also broadened its political base among them. All these phenomena were taking place and moving towards the emergence of class consciousness among the rural and urban poor masses. It was an unpalatable trend for the Congress and other non leftist parties. Their interest was based on caste stratification of society. Coupled with this, the failure the of first Backward Class left the State government to appoint Commission on its own to draw up the list of backward communities and to look into certain other ancillary tasks. In Bihar a Commission was constituted at the instance of Karpoori Thakur, the then chief minister with seven members under the chairmanship of Mungeri Lal, a former Congress minister in December, 1971(Annexure-3). Unlike Devraj Urs of Karnataka, he was not from the dominant caste of Bihar. The term of references of the Commission were as follows:

a) to examine the extent to which the orders issued by the State government in regard to the reservation of posts and services for scheduled castes and tribes have been implemented by various departments and to explore the circumstances in which some of the orders were not implemented,

b) to examine whether the different departments have considered the claims of candidates belonging to the other backward classes in making appointments;

c) to examine the extent of representation of scheduled castes and scheduled tribes in various State government undertakings;

d) to evaluate different welfare programmes being inplemented for the scheduled tribes/castes and other backward classes;

e) to assess whether the steps taken for the progress of other backward classes are adequate.

Mungeri lal Commission adopted the following criteria in its report:

- Low social status in the traditional caste hierarchy of Hindu society.
- Number of people who Lack general education in any caste or community.
- Inadequate representation or absence of representation in government services.
- Inadequate representation in the area of trade, commerce and industries.

Mungeri lal Commission submitted its report in February, 1976, during the hey day of emergency. It prepared a list of other backward classes and most backward classes, keeping in view the following facts:

a) Only economic criterion cannot be adopted for determining backwardness to any class of citizens, because Article 15(4) of the Indian Constitution speaks of "Any class of citizen who are socially and educationally backward",

b) For inclusion in the OBCs list only caste criteria of the said caste cannot be taken into consideration, this criterion can be applied when any caste group is socially and educationally backward.

c) While determining social backwardness of any class of citizen, its occupation, poverty, representation in government services and public sector undertakings, their participation in political and social fields should be taken into consideration.

d) For determining educational backwardness of any class of citizen, percent of literacy should be kept in mind

e) On the basis of Balaji case, preparation of two lists i.e; Annexure-1 & Annexure-11 for backward and most backward castes is not necessary.

In nutshell, for preparation of OBCs list the Commission took into consideration the social status, educational backwardness, adequacy of representation in government services and adequacy of share in trade, commerce, industry etc. of the concerned castes. The first list prepared by the Commission included 128 other backward classes in the State; and the second list comprises 94 most backward castes. The main recommendations of the Commission were:

> Reservation of 20.0 percent vacancies in all Government Departments, local bodies and State Government Undertakings for the candidates of other backward castes. In addition, 3.0 percent of such vacancies were recommended to be reserved for women and the same percentage for economically weaker sections. Only those

candidates should be given the benefit whose family income was below the minimum income-tax limit. It also recommended that in Government and Local bodies services at least the following representation of OBCs be maintained:

Group 1 —— 25.0 % reservation of total vacancies

Group 2 —— 33.1/3 % " " " "

Group 3 —— 40.0 % " " " "

Group 4 —— 40.0% " " " "

Besides the above, the Commission has strongly recommended that in case of appointment in Judiciary, steps should be taken to provide benefits to SCs, STs and OBCs in accordance with the Article 335 & 16(4) of the Constitution. The Commission arrived at this conclusion on the basis of memorandum submitted by the Bihar State Backward Class Association, which shows the representation of backward classes in judiciary:

Table: 3.2

	Total No. of Judges	Backward Class
Patna High Court	20	Nil
District Judge	18	1
Addt; District & Sub-Judge	50	Nil
Munsif, Addt; Munsif	300	30
Advocate	12, 000	800

Reservation of 24.0 percent seats in engineering, medical and other professional institutions for students of other backward castes; and

Grant of various other benefits like allotment of house sites, grant of scholarships, reimbursement of tution fees etc; to OBCs.

On educational front the report found the following position in respect of educational concessions. Some reservation was given to those applicants belonging to either Annexure-1 or Annexure-2, whose annual income was less than Rs. 300. The social welfare department gave fee concessions etc; to the OBC students. There was no reservation for them in industrial training institutes. The OBCs had no reservation in the jobs. However, the Commission did not examine the conditions of neglected social groups in detail but accepted the list prepared in 1951 for granting scholarship to backward and more backward caste students of Bihar.

The following table reflects the educational conditions of the backward caste students to a certain extent: (information provided to the Mungerilal Commission)

Table: 3.3

Educational condition of OBCs and others

Number of High Schools in Bihar—— 2800

Data collected for class Xth of 380 High Schools.

Sl.No.	Caste	No. of schools admitting students of these castes	Total number of students	Total No. of OBCs students	Students of these castes
1	Kumhar	58	3610	1561	92
2	Koeri	86	5053	1950	408
3	Kurmi	190	14169	4212	815
4	Teli	118	6813	2540	381
5	Bania	46	2697	1125	161

6	Badhai	61	3925	1548	110
7	Hajjam	196	13141	4613	300
8	Mallah	48	3022	1150	74
9	Yadav	270	15805	5375	1508
10	Ansari	6	358	150	10
11	Kandu	23	1339	586	24
12	Kahar	48	2713	1101	97
13	Lohar	26	1680	681	44
14	Tanti	19	1394	476	21
15	Turha	4	356	150	3
16	Tamoli	3	337	93	5
17	Bind	1	40	30	2
18	Beldar	3	204	97	4
19	Bherihar	14	683	311	16
20	Halwai	33	2119	809	43
21	Mali	9	544	203	12
22	Nonia	23	1183	468	28
23	Sudi	31	2154	858	102
24	Modi	3	111	48	5
25	Thathera	3	167	48	3
26	Kalwar	24	1472	597	61
27	Momin	13	914	410	70
28	Kunjara	3	202	69	5
29	Marwari	1	160	73	1
30	Dhanuk	32	2217	827	76
31	Kasera	2	284	122	2
32	Kamar	6	181	95	4
33	Deohar	3	251	56	11
34	Amat	6	442	125	7
35	Barnwal	7	324	154	11
36	Sonar	27	1797	647	30
37	Khatwe	3	247	66	2
38	Banpar	2	66	24	5
39	Sanyasi	1	106	26	0
40	Dhunia	7	399	182	10
41	Churihaar	1	50	11	0
42	Julaha	7	505	207	20

43	Kewat	10	455	207	18
44	Musalman	15	699	254	30
45	Bhuniya	1	55	2	2
46	Poddar	1	117	48	5
47	Suraak	1	117	43	1

Source: Mungerilal Commission Report, part 111, pp 111-113

From the above, it can be inferred that the backward castes are far behind in the field of education except neo-forward (yadav, kurmi, koeri, bania), represented in proportion to their population. In comparison with the traditional forward castes they are certainly behind as they are late comers in the field of education. In higher education it is found that the number of backward class students is less than that found in the schools. This is because the drop-out rate at the school stage used to be more from backward castes. Earlier they were denied access to the educational institutions, by the dominant castes of the villages. In 1858 the government had announced that all schools maintained at the cost of government shall be open to all classes without any distinction. After independence, their case has been taken up for educational advancement. Educational backwardness of the backward castes cannot be seen as economic backwardness in general. Earlier they were pre-occupied with their hereditary occupation or cultivation. We can see this difference is narrowing down as they are moving in the field of education and putting challenges to the upper castes in the field of jobs also.

The fifth report of the Bihar Backward Classes Commission, 1976 deals with the denotified groups in Bihar, most of them belongs to backward castes. While the Commission has shown much concern about their problems, the most important part of the report seems to be their introduction. The main occupations of these castes are ironsmithy, hunting, jugglery and acrobactics, snake charming etc. They were subjects of humiliation and subjugation at that time as well as today. Some corrective measures have been taken by the State government to ameliorate their conditions but a lot more is required to be done for this sections of society to bring them in mainstream of society.

The Mungerilal Commission has raised very valid ground for reservation that is, adequate representation under Article 16(4). The Commission has given table of number of employees of OBCs in different departments in comparison to SCs & STs and others.

Table : 3.4

Forest Department, 1st January, 1972, Representation of OBCs

Name of service	Total No. of employees	S.Cs Total	%	S.Ts Total	%	B.Cs Total	%	Others Total	%
Class 1	52	—	—	1	2	5	10	46	51
Class 11	40	—	—	5	13	2	5	33	82
Class 111	4821	285	6	854	18	540	11	3142	65
Total	**4913**					**547**	**11.13**		

Rural Engineering Organisation, 1st January, 1972, Representation of OBCs

Name of service	Total No. of employees2	S.Cs Total	%	S.Ts Total	%	B.Cs Total	%	Others Total	%
Class 1	42	—	—	—	—	—	—	—	—
Class 11	60	—	—	—	—	—	—	—	—
Class 111	927	40	4	22	2	83	28.6	148	49.8
Total	**1029**					**83**	**28.06**		

Revenue & Land Reform Department, 1st January, 1972, Representation of OBCs.

Name of service	Total No. of employees	S.Cs Total	%	S.Ts Total	%	B.Cs Total	%	Others Total	%
Class 1	8	—	—	—	—	—	—	—	—
Class 11	21	—	—	—	—	—	—	—	—
Class 111	150	3	2	2	13	14	8.3	131	87.3
Total	**179**					**14**	**8.3**		

Education Department, 1st January, 1972, Representation of OBCs.

Name of service	Total No. of employees	S.Cs Total	%	S.Ts Total	%	B.Cs Total	%	Others Total	%
Class 1	114	1	0.1	1	0.1	2	1.0	110	96.7
Class 11	414	3	0.8	6	1.5	4	0.9	401	96.8
Class 111	9215	259	2.8	98	1.0	742	8.1	8121	88.1
Total	**9743**	**263**	**3.7**			**748**	**7.6**		

Supply & Commerce Department, 1st January, 1972, Representation of OBCs

Name of service	Total No. of employees	S.Cs Total	%	S.Ts Total	%	B.Cs Total	%	Others Total	%
Class 1	8	1	12.5	—	—	—	—	7	87.5
Class 11	16	—	—	—	—	1	6	15	9.4
Class 111	128	2	1.56	2	1.56	18	14	186	82.88
District Hqr	1513	75	4.9	28	1.7	—	—	—	—
Total	**1665**					**19**	**10.0**		

Source: Mungerilal Commission Report part 111, pp 120-124.

In other departments like forest 11.3 percent, in rural engineering 28.06 percent, in revenue & land reform 8.3 percent, and in supply & commerce Deptt; 10.0 percent were from OBCs. When all the job seekers are not able to get employment, the OBCs leaders found its remedies in job reservation and not in the job for all. OBCs' reservation was opposed on different grounds by different political and social groups of Bihar. Janata MLAs and leaders were divided in two camps. First camp was totally against reservation as it restricted the merit and brought inefficiency in administration. In their view, programme of preferential treatment to the backward castes is against equality among individuals. Others were opposed to the criteria of implementation of reservation. They agreed in favour of Annexure-1(MBCs), but were against the Annexure-2(BCs). The radicals were also against it. They believed that piecemeal changes could not ameliorate the condition of the poor. They favoured structural changes which could create enough jobs and educational opportunities. Reservation, they agreed, ignited revolutionary spirit of the have-nots. Janata party MLAs belonging to anti-reservationist group sent a letter to Shanti Bhushan Committee. In that, they made the following arguments:

a) Announcement of proposal for job reservation was politically motivated,

b) Economic condition rather than caste should be the criterion of backwardness,

c) 50.0 percent reservation in government posts would adversely affect in the long run the administrative efficiency in the State.

They were also of the opinion that it might result in perpetuation of backwardness as vested interests of the affluent stratum of the group, listed as backward, will be the immediate beneficiaries of the policy of protective discrimination policies.

In November, 1978 against the backdrop of anti-reservationist protests and suggestions of Central leaders, Karpoori Thakur government issued G.O. accepting the classification of the Commission and announced the following reservation scheme:

Backward Classes	8.0 percent
Most Backward Classes	12.0 percent
Scheduled Castes	14.0 percent
Scheduled Tribes	10.0 percent
Women	3.0 percent
Economically Backward	3.0 percent

According to the then chief minister, the reservation decision would benefit the following sections of the society:

1) Socially and educationally backwards,

2) Socially and educationally backwards Muslims,

3) Women belonging to all castes and community;

4) Poor people other than backwards.

Under category OBCs persons having income less than Rs. 8000 were included. Backward Castes share was fixed at 8.0 percent where as 12.0 percent remained with MBCs. Of the remaining 6.0 percent, 3.0 percent each were reserved for women and economically backward castes whose income did not exceed Rs. 3000 a year. The notification of the reservation policy by the Karpoori Thakur Government was more a dangerous deception than clear enough to symbolize its real concern for the upliftment of the backward classes. According to this notification, the process of reservation for backward classes was to remain the same as in the case of Scheduled Castes and others i.e; 20.0 percent of reservation comprised even those who edged out general candidates on the basis of their merit. This meant that the candidates qualifying for the jobs on the basis of their proven eligibilities which out distanced them even among the general candidates had to be clubbed within the 20.0 percent ceiling, simply because they hailed from these socially and educationally disadvantaged sections. Karpoori Thakur government could hardly realize the magnitude of this malicious blunder which robbed the backward classes of their fundamental rights rather than providing them succor and solace even after centuries of social segregation and economic exploitation. As a matter of fact, this camouflaged mischief in the notification itself, was the glaring example of how anti-reservationist lobby succeded in dominating and even distorting a government decision of crucial importance which was to embody the spirit of Indian constitution in this regard. Basically the problem of reservation is due to unemployment. In the existing system government is not able to provide jobs for all.

In this context Shaibal Gupta (2002) observes that the status of lower backward castes during all those years had, however, remained unaltered. While economic empowerment had touched a fraction of the upper backward castes, the larger segments of the lower backward castes remained economically disadvantaged. Politically also they were marginalized. Karpoori Thakur brought them to the centre stage by implementing Mungeri lal Commission, which ensured separate reservation for them. This process gain momentum under Lalu Yadav Government, when he enhanced the 10.0 percent reservation to 14.0 percent and after the vivisection of the State, to 18.0 percent. Some observations made by the Mandal Commission Report in context of implementation of reservation by the State is as follows:

- In Bihar, the job and seat reservation schemes came as a bolt from the blue for the forward castes. Had they been covered by the reservation schemes earlier and slowly shunted off to the open competition pool, it would have been a different matter.
- The reservation of 3.0 percent for the economically weaker section is just a drop in the ocean for the Bihar forward castes. Had this share been larger, probably, the forward castes would have found themselves divided and too weak to resort to backlash.
- Karpoori Thakur got his famous G.O. issued in 1978 without preparing ground for organizational movement of OBCs in the corridors of power, as had been done by Devraj Urs in Karnataka. Thakur and Yadav G.Os. were planted from above and due to this they were unable to create a strong base for political mobilization and empowerment of the backward castes.
- The classifications of castes do not permit any falsification, as the classification is based on the broad caste lines, and not on sub-caste lines. A Rajput cannot pass off as a Kurmi or Koeri and remain undetected for a long time.

Before preparing the list of backward castes of Bihar, Mandal Commission itself surveyed many blocks and villages to get first hand information about it, which was later on used by the NCBC for preparing its Central List of OBCs.The following is the list of villages and urban blocks surveyed by Mandal Commission:

Table: 3.5

Sr. No.	Name of the District	Name of the Village	Name of the Urban Block
1	Purnea	Siktihar, Chehwacha	Purnea
2	Kathiar	Rataniya Khurd, Madani	Mavihari
3	Saharsha	Beldara, Laukahi	Madhepura
4	Bhagalpur	Paharpur, Garawadhinilk	Bhagalpur
5	Munger	Khajuria, Kharar	Jamalpur
6	Begusarai	Chak Muzaffar, Sankhu	Reghara
7	Santhal Pragana	Bahadur chuh, Barua	Dumka
8	Darbhanga	Gadari, Kiratpur	Alinagar
9	Samastipur	Kharihara, Itmasnagar	Samastipur
10	Madhubani	Gangoli, Durgapalli	Madhubani
11	Muzaffarpur	Paraswaninath, Jagadish Kantal	Gannipur
12	Vaishali	Akhtarpur, Rampur Jhariya	Mahnar
13	Sitamarhi	Barawejia, Singrahiya	Sitamarhi
14	East Champaran	Mahua, Rupdih	Motehari
15	West Champaran	Hardiya, Patalenhauli	Nayatola
16	Saran	Parmanand Chapra, Mamupur	Ravalganj
17	Gopalganj	Dewanpurtola, Mohar singh, Ballahadra	Barali
18	Siwan	Hariharpur, Beraso	Mahrajganj
19	Patna	Chainpur, Fatehpur	Danapur
20	Nalanda	Eshakpur, Basawan	Biharsharif
21	Gaya	Amora, Dariyapur	Gaya
22	Aurangabad	Narsharamba, Hemla	Aurangabad
23	Nawada	Manjhila, Rajmadh	Nawada
24	Bhojpur	Kusamba, Baruna	Dumraon

25	Rohtas	Kusahi, Sonbarsa	Dehri
26	Palamu	Khap.Dulhar	Daltonganj
27	Hazaribagh	Ambadih, Jharia	Ramgarh Cantt
28	Giridih	Godi, Jardewagi	Garangdih
29	Dhanbad	Koradih, Nayadih	Karkend
30	Ranchi	Kunburdaga, Gone	Khinjar
31	Singbhum	Jargo, Bagrai Sai	Chaibasa

In an article in economic and political weekly, James manor has compared the achievements of Devraj Urs and Karpoori Thakur as follows:

"Thakur proclaimed his policy of preferment for 'backward classes' soon after taking office. He did so in order to signify "that the backward had displaced the forwards as the dominant force in Bihar politics that the old days of dominance in the public affairs from village to state legislation by the twice born were gone forever." But he made this announcement before he had either consolidated backward classes control in the State level political arena or developed programmes to provide backward classes with new economic and political resources in the form of substantive patronage from Government. His early offer of preferment inflamed feelings among both forward castes and scheduled castes who felt threatened by it and led to the collapse of his government before it had time to achieve its major goals. It was replaced by a government which was dominated by Forwards and Jan Sanghis. In the words of Devraj Urs, Karpoori climbed into the ring before he learned how to box".

Harry W. Blair (1980) observes that the Karpoori Thakur's reservation policy changed Bihar's political economy and initiated the process of replacing the forward castes by the backward castes as the dominant stratum in the system of social stratification. The upper strata of OBCs

(Bania, Yadav, kurmi, Kahar, Kandu, Kumhar, Mallah, Tatwa, Teli); i.e; 19.3 percent of the total population in Bihar dominated their political economy and improved their social status remarkably. Some of the conclusions of Blair's study are as under:

a) The transfer of power to the upper strata of the OBCs might be expected to continue at the local level along political lines,

b) Noticeable transfer of economic power in the country side to the backwards as the forward are not able to face the fury and aggressiveness of the upper strata of OBCs,

c) There is a continuing struggle between the forwards and the backwards,

d) The condition of landless agricultural labour is weakened and would be weakening further because of inroads of capitalism in Bihar's economy.

The Congress ministry under the chief ministership of Dr. Jagannath Mishra did not take any serious action on it. Dr. Mishra considered the main problem before these castes to be economic backwardness, not the social backwardness. Keeping this in mind he constituted a cabinet sub-committee to study the full report and on the basis of its recommendations constituted a financial corporation exclusively for the members of these communities. However, Bindeshwari Dubey did it. But his action in amending the reservation rules in the secretariat, commissionerate and district level employment faced sharp opposition. Due to this Karpoori reservations formula was not implemented in 17 districts. The situation was expected to improve after the State passed under the Janata Dal rule in 1989, specially when V.P. Singh implemented the Mandal Commission Report on 13 August, 1990 and the chief minister Lalu Pd. Yadav announced to follow the suit at the State level. But the high castes stood in the way.

Supported by the Congress, BJP and others, they rose up in almost an open revolt.In spite of this, the Bihar Governor issued Bihar Reservation in Posts and Services Vacancies(for SCs, STs & OBCs) Ordinance, 1991, stipulating imprisonment and Rs.1000.00 fine on the appointing officer who ignores provisions of the ordinance, on September 26, 1991.It needs mention that the Government of Bihar already implemented reservation for backward castes basing on Karpuri's formula in 1978.

The announcement led to an open confrontation between forward castes and backward castes in the whole State, which erupted often into clashes, arson, and destruction. It was a caste based movement dominated by the students of middle class categories. To some extent it provided courage to OBCs to fight the dominance of upper castes. In 1977 Forward Caste Leauge and Backward Caste Federation were formed to fight job reservation. In their fight they find leadership respectively from upper castes legislators and backward castes legislators dominated by yadavs and kurmi. They mobilized people for their causes. Even before this declaration, State legislators in Bihar were divided on the basis of former constituents of the Janta Party, and also on lines of caste and region. Karpoori Thakur lost many of his supporters of forward caste (excluding socialists) as they thought it as injustice to their caste or community. In case of Mandal Report, the first bugle of agitation against it was blared in Patna. The students of the university and colleges came out to fight the great menance. But for want of a centralised leadership, the stir could not spread far and wide. It remained confined mostly to the north Bihar where the forward castes, still dominant, made a bid to overcome stiff resistance from backward castes like yadavs and kurmis. After a week or so, some sparks reached some districts of central and south Bihar but these too, could not have the desired impact there.Unlike in 1978, when the Rajputs took the lead in central Bihar, this time they were reticent. The Bihar State Anti-Reservation Morcha tried to make it a mass movement in other regions with the help of political parties, specially the Congress, but it could not take off and the agitation died down after some time.

On seeing that it was extremely difficult to counter Lalu Pd. Yadav in this manner, the high castes moved to the Supreme Court to get the Yadav order stayed. The apex court helped them for a while but eventually the apex court too, walked out of Lalu Pd. way. He won the battle for social justice on 13 November, 1991. The OBCs had reason to feel joyous. But not the high castes, who were a great deal annoyed. Yet they could not turn violent to express their displeasure for the reasons listed by Prof. Bachan Singh of Patna University who saw things from close quarters in Bihar:

The fact is that the anti-reservationist now do not dare to face the administration of Lalu Pd. Yadav on the controversial issue. The students who had launched the agitation in 1990 were ruthlessly suppressed by the police at Dharna Chowk....Elsewhere, too, the police acted ruthlessly against those opposing the reservations.The tacit support and patronage which they enjoyed in 1978-79 from the bureaucrats is also missing as no official want to invite wrath of Mr. Yadav. The Congress and the BJP, which were instrumental in sustaining the agitation in 1990 are silent. The Congress leaders like Rajendra Singh Bismil, Ramjatan Sinha, and Mahachandra Prasad Singh, who were active in the agitation two years back, are maintaining a low profile.

Pro and anti-reservation movement came to be articulated in terms of the backwards versus the forwards, as reservation further narrowed the job opportunities for the job seekers belonging to upper castes. Both the social groups had put forward for and against the theory and practice of reservations. In general the backward caste spokesmen favoured and upper castes opposed it.

Pro-reservationists had given argument that Hindu mythology and scriptures established the superiority of Brahmin (upper castes) and the low social ranking of the backward castes and shudras. Till now social status is determined by this notion. A poor Brahmin has better social status than a rich from backward castes. So, the caste criterion of reservation is permissible on this basis. Dr. Shah considers it as the cultural domination of upper castes. It will be neutralized only when they will get benefit for their historical disadvantage.

It is true that caste based reservation had been enjoyed by the the upper strata (elite) of the S.C./, S.T. and the same will be the case with the backward castes. Some scholars are in favour of continuation of reservation for the sons and daughters of the SCs and STs, IAS and other senior officials. They consider that it will give moral support to the downtrodden. In the same circumstances beneficiaries are not in favour of excluding some developed backward castes from the benefit of job reservation of OBC's, which is provoking upper castes youth. The Gujarat government has not excluded the highest income group of backward castes from the benefits of reservation. This was also the motive of Bihar government but it failed to implement it in view of anti-reservationist movement.

Further OBC's leader claim adequate representation for their community as they find 85% of State government jobs in the hands of upper castes, which constitute 15% of the State population. In Bihar, social prestige and recognition goes with a government job. According to one survey, 83% of the bureaucrats at different levels in Bihar belong to the upper castes. Therefore, reservationists opined that poor Brahmins and Harijans cannot be put on the same footing. Poor Brahmins have good access to job, education and have relations to help them. They are brought up in a culturally superior family and social environment conducive to the development of their self confidence. These facilities are not available to OBCs, so they deserve reservation It will solve to some extent rising unemployment problems among backward castes.

The main motive behind reservation is to bring the downtrodden in the national mainstream. Government job gives status and power that are more valuable than economic benefits. In their view, the problem of backwardness is social, not economic.

As a result of reservation policies, other backward castes have privileged access to education as well as government and public sector jobs. These caste groups have become increasingly assertive and their political leaders have started demanding a greater share of the pie. This increased representation (job reservation, etc.) has been analysed by Bardhan (1998) as essentially anti-market. It means that efficiency and merit considerations are valued less than group equity and caste rights. The inevitable result of this "drift towards the backward and lower castes" (Bardhan, 1998:132) is that the traditionally privileged access of the upper castes to the state is getting constrained, and, as Bardhan suggests, this could be one of the reasons why the upper castes tend to support the pro-market policies - they seek for greener pastures outside the state, now their traditional state pastures become dryer and less accessible.

This hypothesis is supported by Milner and Sahay (1997) in their interpretation of 'the irony of backward caste politics in a liberalising economy'. According to Milner and Sahay (1997) the lower caste groups have increasingly succeeded in gaining control of the Indian State, but the question is whether these caste groups will be able to convert this political power into economic power. Given the higher levels of education among the upper castes, the lower caste groups are seriously disadvantaged. This leads Milner and Sahay to conclude that "even if there is no current discrimination based on caste, it is unlikely that most Backward caste members are going to be able to effectively compete in the new liberal economy".

The liberalisation of the economy thus fits the upper caste interests very well. And also the emergence of Hindu nationalism, according to Milner and Sahay, can be interpreted as an attempt to regain some of the privileges.

It is not accidental that paralleling the political take over of the Backward castes has been the emergence of a Hindu Nationalism led by, and primarily supported by, the upper castes. The resurgence of Hindu nationalism in the face of Backward caste political control and a liberalization of the economy may sound like an upper caste conspiracy to maintain their dominance and hegemony! While certainly some members of the upper castes have been important actors in key events, a look at some of the details suggests the overall changes are not masterminded by anyone or any group, though the outcome may be close to what the upper castes could have hoped for, given their demographics. (Milner and Sahay, 1997:13)

Both Bardhan and Milner and Sahay raise interesting points, but there is little empirical evidence when it comes to this point of the tension and/or relationship between the increasing political power of the backward castes on the one hand and the shift to a market economy on the other. Further investigation of why different categories of people are supporting the reforms would be necessary to show the extent to which Bardhan's greener pastures hypothesis bears some truth.

Criticizing the merit theory they said that intellectual merit and efficiency should not be the only basis of job. It is used to exploit weaker sections and deprive them of their share. There must be competition among equals and not among unequal. It leads to disproportional representation of different castes and communities. They also regard merit as the product of socio-economic condition. The children of socially superior and prosperous parents are doing well in education and job market. The backward castes have not been in better socio-economic conditions; therefore they are entitled for reservation. It will not lead to decline of administration and efficiency but integrate the political and social systems. They opine that reservation in jobs and educational institutions also ensure social equality.

After land reforms, most of the neo-forward castes became small and medium farmers and acquired property and wealth, which enabled them to snap links with money lenders. The only challenge they posed to the upper castes was in the sphere of jobs over which the upper castes still had their hegemony by virtue of their superior education. Anti-reservationist regarded it as a long term politically motivated strategy to weaken the status of upper castes and enhance their own.

Table: 3.6

Total number of vacancies per year

Name of agencies	No. of jobs every year
State Government Department	2, 000
State Public Sector Undertakings	4, 000
Local Bodies	2, 000
Central Government Undertakings	15, 000
Total	**23, 000**

Source: Ishwari Prasad, "Job Reservation for Backward in Bihar", Janata, New Delhi, April 23, 1978.

In a bigger State like Bihar 23000 jobs is only a drop in the ocean. Even in this small number when 50.0 percent became reserved, upper castes youth get frustrated. They thought it would aggravate unemployment problem. But the picture is slightly different than it appears. Only about two percent of jobs have so far been filled by the Scheduled Castes and Scheduled Tribes candidates. The rest of the quota has been grabbed by upper castes under the seemingly plausible plea of non-availability of suitable candidates from these categories. This position was bound to continue even in the case of reservation for backwards as very few candidates, especially among the extremely backward castes were there to aspire for these jobs. In the social ladder they are certainly below the upper castes, but they acquired better social position in a few districts. It is true that a certain proportion of candidates who could benefit from the reservation hailed from relatively better off middle castes, such as, yadavs, kurmis, koeiris and vaishyas. For instance, Brahmins and other forward castes in Nalanda, Patna, Nawada, Rohtas, Saharsa, Madhepura, Khagaria and few other districts are dominated by neo-forward castes. Their economic and educational superiority is declining. They have lost power and just their ritual superiority is continuing. Backwardness in Bihar is not only of caste but of region also. But it is absolutely mischievous to say that all of these candidates belonged to wealthy families of these castes and that majority of people of these castes are prosperous and powerful like feudal lords of upper castes. In fact, the proportion of land rich and economically well-off persons among these castes is almost the same as the proportion of land-poor and impoverished among castes. The case of even vaishyas does not make an exception, because if we exclude Marwaris, Agarwals and some affluent sections of Rauniyars and Kesarvanis, their position will be identical to other backwards castes. Even the bulk of Kurmis and Koeris with the exception of land-rich Dangis and Awadhiyas, respectively, constitute the rural-poor in the villages. Likewise except a slander proportion of land-rich and educated families, the majority of yadavs live in extremely impoverished conditions in the villages. It is these people who have been constrained to sell or mortgage their small possessions of land and have become landless agricultural labourers over years. Conditions of these people are similar to those of the Harijans from the view point of segregation and exploitation. Those who have had a close look at the pattern of land ownership, income, and caste can easily realize that the majority of these middle castes still lag behind on different social index parameters.In the absence of land reform and some kind of land protection policy for these most backward castes, mainly engaged in agriculture sector, the fruits of reservation will not be reaped by these peoples (MBCs). But the real culprit is our social structure itself, as Indian society has been organized on the principles of heredity and ascriptions.

If we apply Article 15(4) of the Constitution of India, i.e; socially and educationally backwardness, on these intermediate castes in Bihar one can inferred that these castes people never suffered the humiliation as the Harijans had to suffer. Similar view has been echoed by sociologist, Dipankar Gupta in a paper entitled" Caste Based Reservations and the Issues of Citizenship", where he writes, "The backward castes are agrarian communities who never suffered discrimination in villages like SCs did........After independence and the abolition of landlordism, this so called castes of backwards rose in the rural economic and political hierarchy and many of them became substantial landowners.....In villages, today they are politically the most strident castes and are well represented in many elected bodies as well as in the local administration."

Another objection to social backwardness of few backward castes is that they got better political participation in State and Central government politics due to their numerical superiority.

So far the identification of backward classes into backward and most backward classes was done with a view to give separate percentage of reservations among them so as to ensure justice. Second point in this context was that the issue of reservation to backward classes related to reservation in State services and not in national services wherein no scheme of reservation was applicable for OBCs. It was Mandal Commission which confronted with the issue of dividing backwards among backwards and most backwards on the plea of anti-reservationist that the benefit of reservation will be cornered by forwards among the backwards. Neo-forward castes of OBCs have also objected to the division of OBCs in backward and more backward. They referred to the 1964 judgments of Patna High Court which called this division illegal. 80% respondents of sample from OBCs have raised this point. A few of the MLAs quite agreed to the division of OBCs. But on certain ground Mandal Commission refused to divide backwards into different categories. The issue of division of backward classes again rose in Mandal Case. The majority of them were of the opinion that there is no constitutional or legal bar to a State in categorizing the backward classes. It did not suggest that it ought to be done. It only said that if State Government chose to do so that would not be invalid. Such a division was approved on two grounds:

a) On Mandal criteria itself the division is approved, as any caste, group or class which scored eleven or more points was treated as backward class. It is not as if all the several thousands of castes/groups/classes scored identical points.There may be some castes/groups/classes which have score points between 20 to 22 and there may be some who have scored points between 11 to 13. It cannot reasonably be denied that there is no difference between these two sets of castes/groups/classes (Mandal case. P 434, para 802)

b) Article 16(4) recognizes only one class, i.e; "backward class of citizens" and does not speak of SCs & STs separately as does Article 15(4). Even SCs/STs are included in "backward class of citizens" and separate reservation is made for them. The logic behind it is that if SCs/STs and OBCs are lumped together, OBCs will take away all the vacancies leaving SCs and STs high and dry. The same logic also warrants categorization as between more backward and backward(Ibid, para 803).

Broadly speaking seven Judges agreed to classification of backward classes and two judges did not allow any sub-classification. The purpose of division may be served better if it is taken in a spirit in which Karpoori Thakur adopted it or which was devised by Chinnappa Reddy. The main objective must be to ensure representation to all sections of backward classes and not to isolate some by giving preference to most backward or poorer sections as Thommen, J. wished in Mandal case or the OM dated 25.9.91 speaks.

With Mandal and other State Commission determining different criteria for identification of OBCs, the above uncertainties appeared. Also there appeared to be a majority of Judges who favoured a bundle of criteria including caste, economic condition, occupations and comparability to deconditioned of SCs and STs, but the exact criteria was far from clear. As Bihar Government(1976) adopted caste-cum-communities –occupation as one of the criteria for identifying backwardness. Again in 1981-83, it suggested low economic status for this purpose. In 1979, it adopted income criteria and prepared a list of 128 castes/communities whose annual income was less than rupees 12, 000/- per annum. This shows a lot of discripencies in identification criteria for backward classes. This can also be seen in the list prepared by the Mandal Commission for backward classes and State Commission where there is no consistency. On the basis of both, a common list of OBCs for Bihar was prepared (Annexure-6) alongwith other states.

Subsequent additions/alterations in the list can be seen at Annexure - 7 & 8.

Castes listed as the backward communities by the Bihar Government, but not by the Mandal Commission:

Badawar,	(in the Siwan and Rohtas District),	Banjara,	Bhuiya,	
Christian (Harijan),	Christian (Other Backward Castes),		Chain,	Daphali (Muslim)
Dhobi (Muslim),	Gorhi (Chhabi)		Jadupatia,	Kewat
Kamar (Lohar, Karmkar)	Khond,		Moriari,	Naiya,
Pandi, Vedia	Pingania,		Sukiyar,	Sutradhar

Castes listed by the Mandal Commission as Other Backward Castes, but not by the Bihar Government:-

Aphale,	Banatkar,	Bansphod,	Beldiya,	Bhadbhuja,
Bojana,	Chain,	Dangi,	Daphali,	Dhanwar
Dhari,	Gadawa,	Gadihar (Muslim),	Ganda,	Godi (Chhabi),
Godra,	Gokha,	Gonahar/ Gorah/ Gothaham,	Gusuriya,	Godhi
Nima/Karanjia/Kasar (Muslim),		Irika,	Jadup,	Juang
Julaha, Kabadi, Kahar				
Chandrabarai/ Chatrapati/ Chotaravanshi Ramani/ Rawani/ Paneri, Kali				
Kalwar,	Kamakar,	Kandra	Kanjara,	Kela
Khandwar,	Khistar,	Koli,	Kritiria,	Karw
Lodha,	Lohar,	Mahto,	Mahishya,	Mahur
Mamagam,	Morio,	Nav-Bauddha/Neo-Buddhist, Pahira,		
Panri,	Patnayak,	Patwa,	Pathar/ Kut/ Bachigolia	
Phutdhar,	Shiyal,	Sodhar/ Noyar,	Sunari,	Tamboli,
Tapoli,	Thakurai (Muslim),	Thathera		

All these have its impact including Mandal Commission report on the masses, which formed the basis for writ petition. The failure of the five Judges bench in Vasant Kumar case to agree on a single approach led to the rare formation of a nine Judge Bench of the Supreme Court in 1992 to decide this and several related issues known as Mandal Commission .case (Indira Sawhney & Others Vs. Union of India & Ors.). In this case the Supreme Court reached a 6-3 decision largely approving the report and its recommendation and issued a long set of judicial opinions. Which are as follows:

1. Establishment, empowerment, equipping and bringing the National and State Commissions for backward classes to an operational position.

1.1 There ought to be a permanent body in the nature of a commission or a tribunal to which complaints of wrong inclusion or non-inclusion of groups, classes and sections in the lists of OBCs can be made.

1.2 Even if any new class/group was proposed to be included among the OBCs, such matters must be referred to the said body in the first instance and action taken on the basis of its recommendation.

1.3 The body so created can also be consulted in the matter of periodic revision of lists of OBCs. As suggested by Chandrachud, CJ in Vasanth Kumar case, there should be periodic revision of these lists to exclude those who have ceased to be backward or for inclusion of new classes, as the case may be.

1.4 Such a body must be constituted both at the central and at the level of States within four months from the date of judgment.

1.5 Such a body must be empowered to examine requests/ complaints of the said nature and pass appropriate orders.

Its advice/opinion should ordinarily be binding upon the government. Where, however, the government did not agree with its recommendations, it must record its reasons.

1.6 The body must be composed of experts in the field, both official and non-official, and must be vested with necessary powers to make a proper and effective inquiry.

1.7 It was equally desirable that each state should constitute such a body which will go a long way in redressing genuine grievance. Such a body can be created under Article 16(4)-as a concomitant of the power to identify and specify backward class of citizens, in whose favour reservations is to be made.

1.8 Strictly speaking, appointment of a commission under Article 340 was not necessary to identify the OBCs. Article 340 does not say so. According to it, the commission was to investigate the condition of the SEBCs and difficulties under which they laboured and to make recommendations as to the steps that should be taken by the union or any state to remove such difficulties.

1.9 They should become immediately operational and be in a position to entertain and examine forthwith complaints and matters of the nature aforementioned, if any.

1.10 It should be open to the government of India and the respective state governments to devise procedures to be followed by such a body.

2. Correction and updating of OBC list;

3. Specification of the bases of the creamy layer: This direction shall not, however, apply to the states where reservations in favour of the backward classes were already in operation. They can continue to operate them. Such states shall, however, evolve the said criteria within six months from the date of the judgment and apply the same

to exclude the socially advanced persons/sections from designated OBCs(para 861(B).

4. Litigation regarding classification among the backward classes, creamy layer and implementation of the OMs only before the Supreme Court.

One important aspect was identification of backwardness as ever continuing process of inclusion and exclusion of classes of citizens entitled to the constitutional protection of reservation. For exclusion, mean test should be applied and this should also be revised periodically keeping in view the change in rupees value. For this at the national level in 1993 National Commission for Backward Classes was constituted and it was open for different State governments to constitute their own Commission where it does not exist.

For the above purpose, State Legislator passed a bill which was approved by the State Governor on 19th August, 1993 and notified by the Government in the Bihar Gazette on 21st August, 1993. The (Bihar Act 12, of 1993) said bill is known as The State Commission For Backward Classes Bill, 1993, to constitute a State Commission for Backward Classes other than the Scheduled Castes and Scheduled Tribes and to provide for matters connected therewith or incidental thereto.(see Annexure-4 for BSCBC, 1993).

Section 9(1) of the Act of State Commission for Backward Classes-1993 provides that it shall "examine the request for inclusion of any class of citizens as a backward class in the lists and hear complaints of over-inclusion or under-inclusion of any backward class in such lists and tender such advice to the State Government as it deems appropriate. Since its inception in 1993 till date (2006), the State Backward Class Commission has included 49 Castes/ communities in the State list, which is given below:

अनुसूची-1 में नया समावेशन	अनुसूची-2 में नया समावेशन	अनुसूची-2 से अनुसूची-1 में स्थानांतरण	अभ्यावेदन पर विचारोपरांत यथावत रखी गई, जातियां, अनुसूची-2
1. (कमर) चंद्रवंशी (कहार) के साथ क्र0-30 में)	मोदक/मायरा	सिन्दुरिया	वैश्य पोद्धार
2. ईटफरोश/ईटाफरोश/गढेहेरी/ ईटपज इब्राहिमी (मु0)	सामरी वैश्य	कुम्हार (प्रजापति) चुड़ीहार (मु0)	स्वर्णकार देवहर
3. फकीर, दीवान एवं मदार (क्र0-93 के साथ)	सुरजापुरी (मु0)	राईन (मु0)	कलाल/एराकी (मु0)
4. मोमिन (मु0) क्र0-94 के साथ जुलाहा/अंसारी	कुल्हैया (मु0) कसौधन	अमात इदरिशी (दर्जी)(मु0)	बरई (चौरसिया) हलवाई
5. ठकुराई(मु0)	लक्ष्मीनारायण गोला	रंगरेज (मु0)	ठठेरा
6. सोयर	दांगी	मुकेरी(मु0)	पटवा
7. कुर्मी (महतो)	वियाहुत कलवार	--------	--------
8. वक्खो(मु0)	गंद्यवनिक	8(आठ)	8(आठ)
9. छीपी(मु0)	दोनवार		
	गोलदार		
10. अदरखी (मु0)	कथबनिया		
11. तिलि	मंडरिया (मु0)		
12. सैकलगर (सिकलगर)	सदगोप		
	जट (हिन्दू)		
13. शेरशा-हवादी (मु0)	जट(मु0)		
	भाट (हिन्दू)		
14. नागर	बाथम वैश्य		
	कलाल/एराकी (मु०)		
-------------	-----------		
14 (चौदह)	19 (उन्नीस)		

Under section 9(2) of the Act, the advice of the commission shall ordinarily be binding upon the State Government.Section 11 provides for periodic revision of list by the State Government as under:

1) The State Government may at any time, and shall at the expiration of 10 years from the coming into force of this Act and every succeeding period of 10 years thereafter, undertake revision of the lists with a view to exclude from such lists those classes who have ceased to be backward classes or for including in such lists new backward classes; and

2) The State Government shall while undertaking any revision referred to in sub-section(1), consult the Commission.

For inclusion and exclusion of backward classes in the State List, the State Commission has adopted the criteria/indicators followed by the NCBC(with some modifications wherever it is required), which is as follows:

A. Social:

1. Castes and communities generally considered as socially backward;

2 (a) Castes and communities, which, for their livelihood mainly depends on agricultural and/or other manual labour for wage and are lacking any significant resource base.

(b) Castes and communities, the women of which, as a general practice, are for family livelihood or for supplementing family's low income, mainly engaged in agricultural and/or manual labour for wage.

(c) Castes and communities, the children of which, as a general practice are for family's livehood or for supplementing family's low income, mainly engaged in agricultural and manual labour.

(d) Castes and communities, which in terms of the caste system, are identified with traditional crafts or traditional or hereditary occupations considered to be lowly or undignified, unclean or stigmatized.

(e) Nomadic and semi-nomadic castes and communities.

(f) Denotified or Vimukta jati castes and communities.

3. Castes and communities, having no representation or poor representation in the state legislative assembly and district level panchayati Raj institutions during the ten years preceeding the date of the application.

B. Educational

1. Castes and communities, whose literacy rate is at least 8 % less than the state or district average.
2. Castes and communities, which the proportion of matriculates is at least 20 % less than the district or state average.
3. Castes and communities, which the proportion of graduates is at least 20 % less than the district or state average.

C. Economic

1. Castes and communities, a significant proportion of whose members reside only in Kaccha houses.
2. Castes and communities, the share of whose members in number of cases and in extent of agricultural lands surrendered under the agricultural Land ceiling Act of the state, is nil or significantly low.
3. Castes and communities, the share of whose members in State Government posts and services of Group A and B/ class 1 and 2, is not equal to the population-equivalent proportion of the caste/community.

On the basis of above criteria Bihar Govt; has included 49 castes/Commumities and NCBC has included/rejected the request of following castes/communities for inclusion in the Central List of OBCs for Bihar.

Table: 3.7

Castes/Communities considered by NCBC for inclusion in the Central List of OBCs for Bihar since 1993 onwards.

Advice No. & Date	Caste/ Community	Inclusion	Rejection
Bihar/1/96 6.2.96	Shekhra (from Bekhra)	Correction	
Bihar/4/96 25.6.96	Pangi	1	
Bihar/5-6/98 15.4.98	Kalal, Eraqui,	2	
Bihar/5-6/98, 15.4.98	Jaisawal		1
Bihar/7-18/98 13.8.98	Kasaudhan/Kardhodhan, Barhi, Tomar, Rashtogi, Lohani, Ayodhayavasi, Baig Vaishya, Jain Vaishya, Gaud Vaishya, Bais Vaisya, Kath Bania and/or Kaithal Vaishya, Bangiya Vaishya (Bangali Bania)		12
Bihar/19/98, 2.9.98	Saifi		1
Bihar/20/98 3.9.98	Gangai(Ganesh)	1	
Bihar/21/98 3.9.98	Kewat, Murawari	2	
Bihar/22/98 28.9.98	Kulahiya	1	
Bihar/23/98 8.10.98	Shershahbadi	1	
Bihar/24/98 22.10.98	Sukiyar	1	

Bihar/25-27/99	16.4.99	Buranwal, Kamlapuri Vaishya, Poddar		3
Bihar/28/99	21.4.99	Musahar(Christians)		1
Bihar 29/99,	7.5.99	Newar(Christians)		1
Bihar/30/99	17.5.99	Tili		1
Bihar/31/99	17.5.99	Nagar	1	
Bihar/32/99	17.5.99	Adarakhi		1
Bihar/33/99	21.5.99	Gandhbanik		1
Bihar/34/01	4.7.2002	Sadgope as a synonym of Yadav	1	
Bihar/35/01	4.7.2002	Saikalagar(Sikligar)(Muslim)	1	
Bihar/36/04		*Deletion of Mahto from Kurmi(Mahto) only Kurmi	1	
Bihar/37/04		*Bakho(Muslim)	1	
Bihar/38/04		*Thakurai(Muslim)	1	
				22

* Notification in respect of these castes has been appended in appendices. (Annexure-8)

In the third National Conference of Chairpersons of State Backward Classes Commission held on July'05 in New Delhi, one of the major issues taken up in the conference was to bring similarity between State List and Central List, because due to this gap in both the lists, OBCs candidates are facing lots of problems.In the light of the decision taken up in the conference, NCBC has requested the State Governments to send the list of those castes/communities not included in the Central List but they do exist in the State List. A list of such castes/ communities send by the State Government of Bihar with a request for inclusion in the Central List is as follows:

Table: 3.8

S.No.	Castes/Communities in the State list but not in the Central List	Entry No. in the State List
1	Kewarth	11
2	Bhat(Muslim)	88
3	....Faquir/Diwan/Madar(Muslim)	93
4	..../Julaha/Ansari	94
5	Chippi	105
6	Itfarosh/Itfarosh/Gadheri/itpaj/ibrahimi(Muslim)	112
7	Jadupathiya	10
8	Pardha	17
9	Badhai	18
10	Bania(....Modak/Mayara, Bihayut Kalwar, Barnawal, Batham Vaishya, Gonadar	20
11	Sutradhar	30
12	Jat(Hindu)Saharsa, Supaul, Madhepura and Arariya Distts.	39
13	Jat(Muslim)Madhubani, Darbhanga, Sitamarhi, Khagaria and Arariya Distts.	40
14	Gadaria(Muslim)	41
15	Donwar	42
16	Surajpuri(Muslim)	43

The Commission for Backward Classes was constituted by the Act of the State Government for a noble cause; i.e; for their welfare, emancipation and empowerment. But in practice, on the following grounds it is facing lots of constraints in doing its own job, such as;

a) On the basis of creation: The State Commission has been created through Acts of the legislatures and is more prone to frequent changes in their structure and functions. Quite often, the Acts contain such provisions, as the State Government may prescribe. These prescriptions can be made through a notification under reference to clause in the parent Act. Most probably, there are chances of creeping irregularities in it.

b) Functionaries: The composition of the Commission and its tenure is most important. As the Commission has a fixed tenure and its members, chairperson and other functionaries are appointed by the State Government who comes from different background. Some of them having political background. So many a times there is lack of co-ordination among themselves. As these political appointees gives preference to their own vocation. In case of Bihar, the post of members have been filled after a long gap during the president rule (September' 2005 one social scientist and two social activist) but the post of other regular functionaries are lying vacant for some years, including Member-Secretary. This has its negative impact on the functioning of the Commission. Also, many a times they do not get salaries, TA/DA on time. No training programmes have been designed to train the officers and employees as it is evident from their skills. Also there is lack of qualified professionals, such as Research Officers, /Research Investigators etc; who can either be appointed on deputation or on regular basis as the case may be for smooth functioning of the Commission, but the Bihar Backward Classes Commission lacks all these facilities at present.

c) Functions: Within the comity of the permanent mechanism created after Indra Sawhney verdict at the State/UTs levels, two types of models have emerged. One of these copied and patterned after the NCBC, is mere inclusion/exclusion entity, whereas the UP and MP models are total empowerment models. Their Acts actually use the language of amended Article 338 replacing the words SC and ST with OBC or BC. And they have wide ranges of power under the above Article. This in fact has caused a few problems in the relationship of these Commissions with their respective government departments. The total overlap of jurisdiction and the power of civil court in terms of collecting evidence and recommending corrective action is cause of this friction. Although total empowerment model of the commission have not performed all their functions equally well, but the successive national conference of the NCBC and the SCBCs, the latest one held on July, 2005 at New Delhi, recommended its adoption by all other States and the Bihar BCC is no exception. During my official visit to Patna in October, 2004(in connection with PH of some castes/communities), I came to know that the State Commission is moving a draft based on these States to the State Government for delegation of more powers. But till date the Commission has not been successful in its efforts.

d) Funds: The Bihar State BCC needs funds for carrying out surveys to determine the castes/communities to be retained in the list of OBCs in the State. But the State Government has not sanctioned any fund for this purpose. Yet, the Government expect to finalize their recommendation about deletion of OBCs communities from the existing list. Thus the very purpose of the Act 12, 1993 of BSCBC is defeated whose section 11(1) & (2) speaks about the periodic revision of the list by the State Government and for this Commission has to be consulted. Even the release of funds to meet salary and allowances of the members and the staff of the commission do not come in time on many occasions. So, it is the need of the time to strengthen the financial condition of the Commission for effective functioning.

e) Facilitation: The central issue with respect to facilitation of the Backward Class Commission is the kind of treatment being given to their identity, work, help and assistance provided to them in carrying out their mandate, and the seriousness/urgency/importance given to their recommendations. On this account the situation of the State Commission is not very good. It has not been given that importance which it deserves. This depend on the ruling class, how it treats the Commission and here the situation is not so well. Also the backward classes themselves are fragmented. Therefore, they have not succeeded in forcing the ruling coalitions in the State to address to serious tasks of their emancipation and empowerment.

References

- Article by James Manor on K. Thakur, Economic and Political Weekly, Annual Number, 1980.
- Bharti, Indu Politics of Anti-Reservation Stir in Bihar, Economic & Political Weekly, (Feb.10, 1990)
- Das, Bhagwan, Moments in a History of Reservations, Economic & Political Weekly, October 28, 2000.
- Mungeri lal Commission Report, 1976 Part-III & IV, Government Publication, Patna.
- Milner, Murray Jr. and Sukirti Sahay (1997)"Victory without the spoils? The irony of backward caste politics in a liberalizing economy". Paper presented at a Conference of the American Sociological Association, Toronto, Canada, 9-13 August, 1997.
- Ishwari Prasad, April 23, 1978, "Job Reservation for Backward in Bihar", Janata, New Delhi.
- National Commission for Backward Classes Annual Report, 2004-05, Minto Government Press, Minto Road, N.Delhi
- Mandal Judgement, Writ Petition(Civil, 930 of 1990), Vol-1 to 111, Ministry of Social Welfare, Government of India, N.Delhi.

- K.C.Yadav (1994) India's Unequal Citizens: A Study of the Backward Caste, Manohar, New Delhi.
- Kumar BB (2004), Backward Classes Movement in India, Omsons Publications, New Delhi.
- Rajni Kothari (ed.) 1970 "Caste in Indian Politics. Caste and Political Recruitment in Bihar by Ramashray Roy, Orient Longman, New Delhi.
- Ramaiah, A (1991) "Mandal Commission Recommendations:A Critical view" in A.A.Engineer(ed.) Mandal Commission Controversy, Ajanta Publications, Delhi.
- Verma, HS (ed.) 2005, The OBCs and the Ruling Classes in India, Rawat Publications, Jaipur/New Delhi.

4

Protective Discrimination

Basically any reservation is discriminatory, for reservation means that as between two candidates of equal merits, the candidate belonging to the reserve quota is preferred to the one having no reserve quota.

The Constitution of India ensured equality of opportunity to all irrespective of caste, gender, religion and one's social location.It provided opportunity to equal access in the public domain. It was a major achievement of the dispensation of democratic political order in independent India.However, the formal disjunction between one's social location and opening up of the opportunity structure in public/political domain did not guarantee the equality and social justice to the deprived groups of the society. In the case of Indian society, which is defined by structured inequality, the social location of individuals and groups has a strong bearing on his/her circumstances and consequent unequal access to opportunity structure of the public domain.Since social location of an individual has been a major source of privileges and deprivations and determinant of individual circumstances in India, the deliverance of social and economic justice cannot be based only on the principle of merit and equality of opportunity in the public domain.

If we look at the position of backward castes of Bihar in different occupations during pre-independence period, the following pictures emerges, which indicates that overall their positions were very low.

Govt. of India officials (1901)

Caste	Patna Com.	Bhagalpur Com.	Chhota nagpur Com.
Ahir	1	3	1
Bhabhan	-	3	-
Vaid	4	-	1
Bania	1	-	-
Brahman	52	15	10
Kayastha	33	28	3
Koeri	1	2	-
Rajput	-	7	-
Tanti/Tatwa	-	1	-
Others	2	1	1

Professor & Teachers (1901)

Caste	Patna Com.	Bhagalpur Com.	Chhota-nagpur Com.
Ahir	11	41	63
Bhabhan	254	120	27
Brahman	670	804	127
Kayastha	2542	977	249
Koeri	154	24	4
Rajput	288	247	48
Kurmi	136	30	8
Teli	52	36	14

Advocate & Law Agent (1901)

Caste	Patna Com.	Bhagalpur Com.	Chhota-nagpur Com.
Ahir	2	-	53
Bhabhan	186	13	8
Brahman	179	145	51
Kayastha	902	258	129
Koeri	4	11	3

Source: Census of India, 1901, Vol-1A Bengal, Part-II Table-from (502).

Medical (1901)

Caste	Patna Com.	Bhagalpur Com.	Chhota-nagpur Com.
Ahir	6	9	15
Bhabhan	70	65	34
Bania	13	3	16
Brahman	830	432	69
Chamar	1	-	-
Hajjam	41	12	-
Kahar	13	1	2
Lohar	-	1	28
Kandu	23	-	-
Kayastha	488	158	112
Koeri	21	3	-
Kurmi	22	1	17
Rajput	63	29	10

Clerk, Inspector & Others (1901)

Caste	Patna Com.	Bhagalpur Com.	Chhota-nagpur Com.
Ahir	66	19	1
Bhabhan	352	95	4
Bania	25	20	-
Brahman	294	299	80
Kalwar	25	1	14
Kandu	28	-	-
Kayastha	2772	1172	277
Koeri	25	6	-
Kurmi	55	22	-
Rajput	103	91	25

(Source: As above)

In the Post-independence period, however, the set of policies of protective discrimination were adopted as a measure of social engineering and for the upliftment of weaker and deprived sections of our society and for the purpose of redressing the ills of the past and ushering in an egalitarian social order.

Protective discrimination programmes can be divided into three broad categories: a) Reservation which allot or facilitate access to valued positions or resources such as reservation in legislatures, reservation in government services and in educational institutions, b) protective measures are employed though less frequently in land allotment, housing and other scarce resources like scholarships, grants, loans and health care etc; c) protective measures are specific kinds of action plans for removal of untouchability, prohibition of forced labour etc.

Under category (a) seats have been reserved in panchayat election in Bihar for backward castes. For reservation in government services Article 16(4) has been incorporated in the Indian Constitution. This particular provision fall under the head "Right to Equality". In order to give effect to general right to equality under Article 14, the Constitution secures all citizens a freedom from discrimination on grounds of religion, race and caste. In specific application of this equality guarantee; the State is further forbidden to discriminate against any citizen on grounds of place of birth, residence, descent, class, language and sex. Articles 16(1) & 16(2) also protect their right of reservation in public appointment. It is noteworthy that under Article 16(4) reservation in government services can be made not only at the initial stage of recruitment but even in the matter of promotion from a lower to a higher post or cadre. Thus, selection posts can also be reserved for backward classes. Article 15(4) on the other hand lay down that the State is not prevented from making any special provision for the advancement of any socially and educationally backward classes. The expression "making any special provision" is evidently an open ended provision and government can really go on providing a whole array of facilities for promoting the interest of socially and educationally backward classes, for example waiving of fees, age, special coachings, scholarships, grants, loans etc. Interestingly, however, the use of Article 15(4) has exclusively been made so far for providing reservation in educational institutions.

Under category (b) one can refer to Article 46 of the Indian Constitution which states about the obligation of the State towards the weaker sections and SCs and STs in promoting their educational and economic interests with utmost care, and also to protect them from social injustice and all forms of exploitation. In pursuance of the directives of the above article, various land re-distribution and allotment programmes have been initiated. In fact so great was the enthusiasm of the government in this particular respect that hundred of land reforms were passed in the first five years after independence. This ensued a spate of litigation in the courts, as the land reforms laws infringed the right to property of the land owners. However the government was so determined to affect land reforms that the right to property which was provided under Article 31 of the Constitution was modified six times and finally done away with, for the purpose of avoiding litigation in land reforms measures of the Government.

(C) Preferential policies aimed at protective discrimination, are various action plans, for the removal of incapabilities on the part of the unprivileged groups. Constitution itself talks about prohibition of forced labours under Article 23, in pursuance of which bonded labour abolition act was passed in 1976. In recent years there have been strenuous efforts to release the victims of debt bondage, who are mostly from scheduled castes and scheduled tribes. Anti-untouchability programme is another area of governmental concern. Constitution itself abolished untouchability vide Article 17 which lays down that "Untouchability is abolished and its practice in any form is forbidden. The enforcement of any disability arising out of untouchability shall be an offence, punishable in accordance with law.

Besides the above, the law also permits reservations to 12 other species of backward classes under Article 15(1) & 16(1), (i.e; physically and mentally impaired, remote/ inaccessible areas, ex-serviceman, dependents of freedom fighters etc ;). The point involved is elaborated in Indra Sawhney Vs. Union of India (Mallik, 1992):

.........all reservations are not of the same nature. There are two types of reservation, which may for the sake of convenience, be referred to as 'vertical reservations' and 'horizontal reservations'. The reservations in favour of SCs, STs and OBCs under Article 16(4) may be called vertical reservations whereas reservations in favour of physically handicapped [under clause I of Article 16] can be referred to as horizontal reservations. Horizontal reservations cut across the vertical reservations, known as inter locking reservations. To be precise, say 3 % of vacancies are reserved for physically handicapped persons; this would be reservation related to clause (1) of article 16. The persons selected under this quota will be placed in appropriate category; if he belongs to SC category he will be placed in the quota by making necessary adjustments; similarly if he belongs to the open competition category he will be placed in that category by making necessary adjustments. The State Government in 2006 approved an ordinance seeking to replace the Reservation Act, 1991, reducing reservation to the Scheduled Tribes to one percent and enhancing quotas for Scheduled Castes from 14 to 15 percent, for EBC from 14 percent to 18 percent, for OBC from 10 to 13 percent and for women among the OBC from 2 to 3 percent.

Apart from the above Articles, other Articles of the Constitution which advances the goal of social justice is Articles 330, 332, 335, 338, 340, 341, and 342. These constitutional provisions have been made after a thoughtful consideration by the members of the Constituent assembly who were quite conscious and aware about the dynamics of socio-economic order of Indian society.Besides these provisions, those who have achieved certain position in the society from the underpriviledged classes or at par with the upper sections, there is also provision of their exclusion from the purview of protective discrimination (i.e; creamy layer).

The genesis of creamy layer can be traced back from the schemes of educational scholarships that were framed in the pre-independence period for the purpose of giving financial support to the students of weaker sections of the society including the OBCs. The general criterion was to fix some income limit/occupational status of the parents of students to be eligible for getting these scholarships. The first such step was taken by the then Madras government in 1885 by introducing supportive grants-in-aid code for educational institutions so that financial assistance to these institutions may be regulated for the purpose of providing special facilities including financial assistance to the students of the weaker sections of the society (Government of India 1980:4). After this, generally, income criterion was adopted by different States for sanctioning scholarships to the weaker sections of the society that is evident from the table below:

Table: 4.1

Income limits for weaker sections for obtaining scholarships etc;

State	Year	Per annum income limit fixed for the family of the weaker sections for getting scholarships and other facilities
Andhra Pradesh	1970	Less than Rs.6000.00
Bihar	**1951**	**Less than Rs.6000.00**
Gujarat	1976	Less than Rs.7200.00
Jammu & Kashmir	1977	Less than Rs.3000.00
Karnataka	1975	No income limit was fixed, lower economic housing and occupational status was taken into account
Kerala	1966	Less than Rs. 4200.00
Uttar Pradesh	1977	Preference given to poor families of weaker sections

With the advent of industrial revolution in the west and later on its spread in the whole world was looked upon by proliteriants as a means for achievement of economic freedom and later on political and social equality. It was believed that industrialization will lead to capital accumulation which will ultimately "lead to making available to masses goods and services that will raise their standards of living, and thus in the end narrow inequalities, eradicate poverty and lead to an era of prosperity" (Kothari:1997:37).

The persistent poverty, stagnant educational status and inequalities raised concern about the achievement of social justice. By now it has been universally accepted that social justice implies " a political and structural commitment by society to direct the resources of modern civilization to benefit all people" especially those at the margins of society(Swartz:2004:153). Amartya Sen's capabilities approach redefined the idea of social justice in terms of capabilities and opportunities and linked it to the idea of freedom.Describing freedom as the central to the process of development, he argued that "development can be seen ... as a process of expanding the real freedom that people enjoy" (Sen). He further argued that development should eliminate sources of unfreedom such as "poverty as well as tyranny, poor economic opportunities as well as systematic deprivation, neglect of public facilities as well as intolerance or over-activity of voices of repressive States"(ibid).Social justice theorists and practitioners have been demanding the same by saying that the discrimination on basis of social identities must be eliminated in order to bring every citizen at par in terms of development.

Bihar has not made any progress as far as furthering the agenda of social justice in terms of development is concerned.Absence of infrastructure, employment opportunities and tremendous resource wastage in the State still persists. Not only the overall situation in the State has been dismal but the condition of the section which constituted the agenda of the government, the backward castes, has also not shown much improvement. The Mungerilal Commission had pointed out that out of available data received from some of the Departments of Bihar Government, the total percent of reservation availed by the OBCs in services was very low as compared to their percentage in the total population of the State and proposed to hike it, so that they can get social justice.It has been shown by bar chart given below:

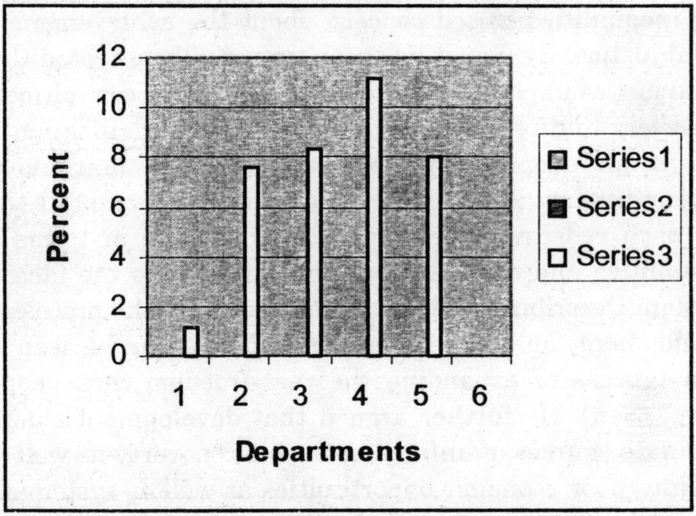

Source: Mungerilal Commission, Part III, 1976, Govt; of Bihar.

1. Supply & Commerce Deptt.
2. Education Deptt.
3. Revenue & Land Reform
4. Forest Deptt.
5. R.E.O.Deptt.

For providing social justice and in turn freedom to the backward castes to a greater extent, State Government later on modified its reservation policy to serve the purpose of backward communities in better ways which has definitely benefited them in facilitating entry into educational institutions and in government service.The Mungerilal Commission also recommended that to be successful in the competitive examination relaxation of 10.0 percent marks required by the OBCs candidates should be granted, besides age relaxation of 5 years.This has been implemented in modified form, which has given them security, status and wealth. Many families have moved to the middle class category and they are all the time striving for moving up the social ladder. Unfortunately, however, the benefits have tended to cluster around some castes and also in some families. This is perfectly natural. Because of some pre-intervention, endowments or opportunities, certain sections of the population take time by the forelock and reap the benefits. It is therefore, necessary not to leave this to natural process. Those in charge of distribution of benefits must take special care to see that the most deserving people get it and the distribution is more equitable. The more backward castes among them must be identified. The income criterion may be used to block certain families enjoying higher incomes from getting benefits. This step would also blunt the resentment of the non-scheduled caste poor. This income criterion comes under the purview of creamy layer. So, it would be not out of context to mention here about creamy layer to know the exact nature of it. Literally, 'creamy layer' means a fat and strong layer of cream formed in milk that can be separated from the milk very easily and clearly without any dispersal. It is also noteworthy that creamy layer is related to the formation and determination of layer but not the strata. In case of OBCs, creamy layer is the forward part of backward classes that should be identified on the basis of its social advancement (such advancement as renders them misfits in the backward classes). The forwardness of forwards among backward classes cannot be measured in terms of the backwardness of the backward sections of these social classes. It has to be judged on the basis of social capacities gained by them to compete with the forward classes.

The issue of determination of creamy layer among OBCs adopting means test for the purpose of divesting such classes of reservational benefit arose in Mandal case.The first and foremost issue in this respect to be decided would have been whether the philosophy of creamy layerisation would be limited to OBCs only or SCs and STs too for whom reservational benefit had been given since long and there have been eyebrow of elitists since long as the issue of reservation in central services for OBCs was not in contemplation. The second question was: who were the opponents of giving benefits to all OBCs including their upper crust and was it advisable and realistic outlook to declare the upper crust of OBCs outside the purview of reservation side by side the vacation of stay order against the union policy. As a matter of fact, while dealing with the issue of reservation of SCs/STs in State of Kerala Vs. N.M. Thomas, Krishna Iyer, J. pointed out one of the dangers of reservation to be that "its benefits, by and large, are snatched away by the top creamy layer of the backward castes or classes keeping away the fortunate layer to consume to the whole cake". He cited the revealing fact based on research conducted by A.N. Sinha Institute of Social Sciences, Patna that, there exist a dual society among Harijans-a tiny elite gobbling up the benefits and the darker layers sleeping distance away from the special concession". The illiteracy and ignorance as well as poverty among the non-creamy OBCs is still larger and the posts for OBCs will remain vacant after the mean test which will reduce the entire exercise to a farce. Therefore, it is observed that the removal of the creamy layer class would render the OBCs into a position like a ship without a captain and the backward class movement would suffer a serious setback. The highest castes, powerful and privileged, will continue to rule the most. Likewise, the mean test would not be workable in the sense that a lakhpati can easily become an OBC by concealing his income and a landlord by transferring his land to benami owners. Therefore, Lalu Pd. Yadav has rightly termed it "fraud on the Constitution" the centre decision to exclude the creamy layer from the purvicw of job reservations.It is viewed as a conspiracy aimed at presenting the OBCs from taking their rightful place in the government services. A hosts of other social scientists have also criticised this concept on one ground or the other. Some of the Hon'ble Judges in the Mandal case has also pointed out at the adoption of some types of criteria for excluding well off sections from amongst the OBCs.According to Sawant, J. "what is more, it will lead to perverting the objectives of the special constitutional provisions.Hence, taking out forwards from among the backward classes is not ony permissible but obligatory under the constitution". Similarly, R.M. Sahai, J. pointed out that creamy layer amongst backward class of citizens must be excluded by fixation of proper income, property and status criteria. Following the Supreme Court direction's on creamy layer, Central Government appointed an expert committee to frame guidelines and to provide suggestions. In the light of the direction, the report on creamy layer was prepared by the expert committee headed by Justice (Retd.) R.N. Prásad who issued a long set of guidelines in this regard (Annexure-9). Later on it was adopted by the Bihar Government in respect of separating well off sections from among OBCs. Table 4.2 reveals different parameters on creamy layers.

In the State of Bihar, the Bihar reservation of vacancies in posts and services (Scheduled castes, scheduled tribes and other backward classes)[Amendment] ordinance, 1995 was promulgated on January 27, 1995 amendeding Section 4 of the Bihar Act, 1992 and after the second provision, the following provision was added : "Provided

Table: 4.2

Juxtaposition of the recommendation of the Prasad committee regarding the criteria of identification of creamy layer

Among OBCs in Relation to the Parameters given by the Supreme court in Indira Sawhney Case

Category of Exclusion from Ambit of Reservation	Parameters of Exclusion from Availing of the Benefit of Reservation as given by Apex Court											
	Purely single criterion							Consideration of local condition	Adequate representation	power sharing	capacity to compete with higher classes	As an exception
	position	income	wealth	land holding	occupation	plantation	vacant land/ building in urban agglomerant					
1. Constitutional post	[	×	×	×	×	×	×	×	×	×	×	×
2. Service Category	×	×	×	×	×	×	×	×	×	×	×	×
a) Group A/class I officers of All India Central & State services (direct recruits)	[	×	×	×	×	×	×	×	×	×	×	×
b). Group B/class II officers of the Central & State services (direct recruit)	[	×	×	×	×	×	×	×	×	×	×	×

	c) Employees in public sector undertakings etc. equivalent posts of above mentioned categories, income criteria till the determination of equivalent of posts.	[	×	×	×	×	×	×	×	×	×	×	×
3.	Armed Forces including paramilitary forces.	[	×	×	×	×	×	×	×	×	×	×	×
4.	Persons engaged in professions	[	×	×	×	×	×	×	×	×	×	×	×
5.	Property owners a) Agricultural holdings	--	×	×	×	×	×	×	×	×	×	×	×
	b) Plantations	×	×	×	[	×	×	×	×	[	[	×	×
	c) Vacant land &/or building in urban agglomerations	×	×	×	×	×	×	×	×	×	×	×	×
6.	Income/Wealth	×	×	×	×	×	×	×	×	×	×	×	×

{ = Applicable
X = Not applicable.

also that reservation under clause 9(d) shall not apply to the category of backward classes specified in Schedule III", which is as follows:

Schedule III

(1) The son or daughter of the president of India, the vice-president of India, the chief justice and judges of Supreme court of India, the chief justice and judges of high courts, the chairman and members of the union public service commission and the chief Election commissioner.

(2) The son or daughters of such officers who have been directly recruited in class I services of the central government or a state government or an undertaking or an institution fully or partially financed by them :

(a) whose income from salary is Rs. 10, 000 or more per mensum

(b) whose wife or husband, as the case may be, is at least a graduate;

(c) who or his wife or her husband, as the case may be, owns a house in an urban area; and

(d) whose mother or father has also been directly recruited to class 1 services.

Explanation: Class 1 means the pay bracket fixed by the State government from time to time for class 1.

(3) The son or daughter of such persons engaged as doctor, advocate, chartered accountant, tax consultant, financial consultant, management consultant, architect or other professionals;

a) whose average income from all sources for three consecutive financial years is not less than rupees ten lakh per annum,

b) whose wife or husband, as the case may be is at least a graduate and

c) whose family owns immovable property at least of rupees twenty lakh

(4) The son or daughter of such persons engaged in trade or commerce,

a) whose average income from all sources for three consecutive financial years is not less than rupees ten lakh per annum

b) whose wife or husband, as the case may be, is at least a graduate ;and

c) whose family owns immovable property at least rupees twenty lakh.

(5) The son or daughter of such industrialist

a) whose level of investment in running unit or units is more than rupees ten crores

b) such unit or units are engaged in commercial production for at least five years; and

c) whose wife or husband, as the case may be, is at least a graduate

(6) The son or daughter of such agricultural land holders

a) whose average income from all sources other than agriculture for three consecutive financial years is not less than rupees 10 lakh per annum.

b) whose wife or husband, as the case may be, is at least a graduate; and

c) whose wife or husband, as the case may be, owns house at least of rupees 20 lakh in an urban area.

(7) the son or daughter of a person other than the persons

specified in serial numbers 1 to 6 of this schedule:

a) whose main source of income is other than animal husbandry, poultry, fisheries, weaving, craftsmanship, handicraft and artisanship;

b) whose average income from all sources for three consecutive financial year is not less than 10 lakh per annum;

c) whose wife or husband, as the case may be, is at least a graduate ; and

d) whose family owns immovable property at least of rupees 20 lakhs.

(8) If a person, included in serial numbers 1 to 7 of this schedule performs inter-caste marriage with a backward class person other than the categories under serial numbers 1 to 7 of this schedule, his/her son or daughter shall not be excluded.

Note: The level of income and the value of the mother of the candidate himself shall be deemed to be decisive in respect of income, value of property and educational qualification.

Additional conditions for Exclusion in Bihar

A close scrutiny of the identification of creamy layer among OBCs in Bihar brings out that the State has put some additional conditions for exclusion than what has been prescribed in the guidelines in Indra Sawhney judgment. The details are as follows:

a) In case of service category including IAS, IPS or any other all India service, the additional requirements put is that such person should draw a salary more than rupees 10,000 or more per mensum, the spouse be graduate and wife or husband owns house in urban area.

b) In case of professionals, an income of rupees 10 lakh per mensum was fixed as criterion and the wife or husband is at least graduate and also the family owns immovable property of the value of at least rupees 20 lakh.

c) For industrialists, the requirement was the investment of rupees 10 crore for at least five years and spouse was at least graduate; for agriculturists, an income of rupees 10 lakh in year from the sources other than agriculture and graduation of spouse was essential; and for any other persons not mention in the above categories, the income from all sources required for continuously three years was fixed at not less than rupees 10 lakh, graduation of spouse and immovable property worth rupees 10 lakh.

Consequent upon the Supreme Court Judgment in Ashok Kumar Thakur Vs. State of Bihar and Others, Constitutional validity of the criteria for determining the creamy layer for the purpose of exclusion from backward classes, laid down by the State of Bihar was challenged under Article 32 of the India Constitution. Pronouncing the judgment, Justice Kuldeep Singh(on behalf of himself and Justice Saghir Ahmed) held that the criteria laid down by the State of Bihar for identification of creamy layer among OBCs was violative of Article 16(4), wholly arbitrary- violative of Article 14 and against the law laid down by this court in Indra Sawhney case. The Court further directed that for the academic year 1995-96 the state of Bihar shall follow the criteria laid down by the Government of India in its office memorandum of September 8, 1993. However, it was open to the state to lay down fresh criteria for the subsequent years in accordance with law.

The apex court emphasized that the protective discrimination in the shape of reservation under Article 16(4) had to be programmed in such a manner that the most deserving section of the backward class benefited and it is only at the lowest level of backward classes where standard of deprivation and the extent of backwardness may be uniform. It further stated that the jobs are very few in comparison to the population to give adequate representation in the state services. It was, therefore, necessary that the benefit of reservation must reach the poorer and weaker section of backward classes. Economic ceiling to cut off the backward classes for the purpose of job reservations was necessary to benefit the needy section of the class. The mean test was, therefore, imperative to skim off the affluent sections of the backward class.

The main objections of the Supreme Court in this case against the creamy layer formula of the State of Bihar was :

a) in the context of Article 14, it was objected that the attachment of the conditions in almost all categories like graduation degree of spouse and holding property in urban area was such that they had no nexus with the object sought to be achieved and due to inservability of such conditions the whole exercise was struck down; and

b) in the context of arbitrariness, Justice Kuldeep Singh pointed out, "It was difficult to accept that in India where the per capita national income is rupees 6, 929(1993-94), a person who is a member of the IAS and professional, earning less than rupees 10 lakh per annum, is socially and educationally backward".

Thus in a nutshell, it can be concluded that in this case the emphasis was laid down for skimming off affluent section (based on economic criterion) from the OBCs for getting benefits of reservation under article 16(4) of Indian Constitution.

Errors Made in Ashok Kumar Thakur's case

The judgments, given by Justice Kuldeep Singh (on behalf of himself and Justice Saghir Ahmed) made certain omissions, which are against the letter and spirit of judgment in Indra Sawhney case.

(1) The implementation of the principles of affluence to include a backward class person in the creamy layer without taking into account the social disabilities they suffer in is against the spirit of judgment in Indra Sawhney case. Indra Sawhney cited only a case of economic exception and, in point of fact, precluded application of only economic criterion. (In Indra Sawhney case, writing the majority judgment, Justice Jeevan Reddy examined the case of a backward class carpenter going to middle east and working there as a carpenter. He stated that the income of this carpenter would be high by Indian standards but because of disabilities he suffers, his sons and daughters cannot be excluded from the reservation quota. But, the situation of the carpenter would be different if he rises so high and becomes a Factory owner and employs people in his factory. In this case, his special status had been rising and he would not be eligible for reservation benefits. Only the later part was taken into consideration in Ashok Kumar Thakur's case, not the whole contextual interpretation given by learned judge, Mr. Jeevan Reddy.)

(2) In this judgment, observations made by Justice Sawant were also quoted but his main thrust was on social backwardness. According to him, economic criteria by itself will not identify the OBCs under article 16(4). It is to be based on social backwardness that is caused on account of educational and economic backwardness.

(3) Justice Sawant also stated that the purpose of reservations to OBCs is not to alleviate poverty but to

give an adequate share in power. Thus, means test should ensure capacity to compete with forward classes and that too in higher level services. No such precautions have been given in this judgment.

(4) This judgment also omitted the issue of chewing of benefits by affluent persons (creamy layer) of upper castes in non reserved categories (the issue raised by Justice Chinnapa Reddy in Vasanth Kumar case and relied upon by justice Pandian in the Indra Sawhney case).

(5) The judgment also did not consider the problem of non fulfillment of Quota of OBCs after skimming off creamy layer.

(6) On the one hand, the judgment accepted the criteria fixed by Prasad committee for identifying creamy layer among OBCs, but at the same time it did not pay any attention to observation of this committee about the reservation in the central services for the OBCs for the first time and non implementation of such scheme by some of the state government's by that time.

(7) The judgments ignored the role and competence of family, particularly, mother in socializing the child because sociologically it is the competence of the mother to handle the child at an early age that makes him/her competent enough to face the reality of life.

(8) The other criterion was that of ownership of house in urban areas. This also makes difference in the development of personality of individuals because it provides a healthy environment to develop a child in family.

However, due to this judgment, the criterion fixed by the Government of India vide OM No.36012/22/93-estt.(SCT), dated 8.9.1993 for the identification of the creamy layer among OBCs is applicable to Bihar also.

Description of category	To whom rule of exclusion will apply
I. Constitutional posts	Son(s)/daughter(s) of (a) President of India: (b) Vice president of India: (c) Judges of the Supreme Court and High courts (d) Chairman and members of UPSC and of the state public services commission, chief election commissioner, Comptroller & Auditor General of India. (e) Persons holding constitutional positions of like nature.
II. Service category	
A. GroupA/class I officers of the All India Central & State Services (direct recruits)	Son(s)/daughter(s) of (a) Parents both of whom are class I officers, (b) Parents either of whom are class I officers, (c) Parents both of whom are class I officers, but one of them dies or suffers permanent incapacitation (d) Parents either of whom are class I officers, and such parent dies or suffers permanent incapacitation has had the benefit of employment in any international organizations like UN, IMF, World bank, e.t.c. for a period of not less than 5 years. (e) Parents both of whom are class I officers, dies or suffers permanent incapacitation has had the benefit of employment in any international organizations like UN, IMF, World bank, etc; for a period of not less than 5 years. Provided that the rule of exclusion

	shall not apply in the following cases: (a) Sons and daughters of parents either of whom are both class I officers and such parent dies or suffer permanent incapacitation. (b) A lady belonging to OBC category has got married to a class I officer, and may herself like to apply for a job.
B. Group B/class II officers of the Central and State services (direct recruitment)	Son(s)/Daughter(s) of (a) Parents both of whom are class II officers. (b) Parents of whom the husband is a class II officer and he gets into class I at the age of 40 or earlier. (c) Parents either of whom are class II officers, and such parent dies or suffers permanent incapacitation has had the benefit of employment in any international organizations like UN, IMF, World bank, e.t.c. for a period of not less than 5 years before such death or permanent incapacitation. (d) Parents of whom the husband is a class I officers (direct recruit or pre forty promoted) and the wife dies or suffers permanent incapacitation and (e) Parents of whom the wife is a class I officer (direct recruit or pre forty promoted) and the husband is a class II officer and the husband dies or suffers permanent incapacitation. Provided that the rule of exclusion shall not apply in the following cases: Son(s) and daughter(s) of (a) Parents both of whom are class II officers and one of them dies or suffers permanent incapacitation.

	(b) Parents both of whom are class II officers and one of them dies or suffers permanent incapacitation, even though either of them has had the benefit of employment in any international organizations like UN, IMF, World bank, etc; for a period of not less than 5 years before such death or permanent incapacitation.
C. Employees in public sector undertakings etc.	The criteria enumerated in A & B above in this category mutatis mutandi to officers holding equivalent or comparable posts in PSUs, banks, insurance Organisations, Universities, etc; and also to equivalent or comparable posts and positions under private employment. Pending the evaluation of the posts on equivalent or comparable basis in these Institutions, the criteria specified in category VI below will apply to the officers in these institutions.
III. Armed Forces including Paramilitary Forces (Persons holding Civil Posts are not included)	Son(s) and daughter(s) of parent either or both of whom is or are in the rank of colonel and above in the Army and to equivalent posts in the Navy and the Air Forces and the Paramilitary Forces; provided that- (i) if the wife of an Armed Forces Officer is herself in the Armed Forces(the category under consideration) the rule of exclusion will apply only when she herself has reached the rank of colonel; (ii) the service ranks below colonel of husband and wife shall not be clubbed together; (iii) if the wife of an officer in the Armed Forces is in the civil employment, this will not be taken into account for applying the rule of exclusion unless she

	falls in the service category under item No.11 in which case the criteria and conditions enumerated therein will apply to her independently.
IV. Professional Class and those engaged in trade and industry.	Criteria specified against category VI will apply.
(i) Persons engaged in profession as doctor, lawyer, charted Accountant, Income tax Consultant, financial or management consultant, Dental Surgeon, Engineer, Architect, Computer Specialist, Film Artists and Other Film Professionals, Author, Playwright, Sportspersons, /or Professionals, Media Professionals or any other vacations of like status	
(ii) Persons engaged in trade, business and industry.	
	Explanation: (1) where the husband is in some profession and the wife is in class II or lower grade employment, the income/ wealth test will apply only on the basis of the husband's income. (ii) if the wife is in any profession and the husband is in a employment in a class II or lower rank post, then the income/ wealth criterion will apply on the basis of the wife's income and the husband's income will not be clubbed with it.
V. Property Owners.	
A. Agricultural holdings	Son(s) and daughter(s) of Persons belonging to a family (father, mother, minor children) Which owns

	(a) only irrigated land which is equal to or more than 85.0 percent of the statutory ceiling area, or (b) both irrigated and unirrigated land, as follows: (i) The rule of exclusion where the precondition exist that the irrigated area (having been brought to a single type under a common denominator) 40 % or more of the statutory ceiling limit for irrigated land (these being calculated by excluding the unirrigated portion). If this precondition of not less than 40 %, then only the area of unirrigated land will be taken into account. This will be done by converting the unirrigated land on the basis of the conversion formulae existing, into the irrigated type. The irrigated area so computed from unirrigated land shall be added to the actual area of irrigated land and if after such clubbing together the total area in terms of area is 85 %or more of the statutory ceiling limit for irrigated land, then the rule of exclusion will apply and disentitlement will occur. (ii) The rule of exclusion will not apply if the land holding of a family is excusively unirrigated.
B. Plantations : (i) coffee, tea, rubber, etc;	(i) Criteria of income/wealth specified in the category VI below will Apply
(ii) Mango, citrus, apple plantations etc.	deemed as agricultural holdings and hence criteria at A above under this category will apply. Criteria specified in Category VI below will apply.
C. Vacant land and/or buildings in urban areas or urban agglomerations.	Explanation : Building may be used for residential, industrial or

	commercial purpose and the like two or more such purposes.
VI. Income/wealth test	Son(s) and daughter(s) of (a) persons having gross annual income of 1 lakh or above or possessing wealth above the exumtion limit has prescribed in the wealth tax act for a period of three consecutive years. (b). Persons in categories 1, II, III and VA who are not disentitled to the benefit of reservation but have income from other sources of wealth which will bring them within the income/ wealth criteria mentioned in (a) above Explanations (i) Income from salaries or agricultural land shall not be clubbed (ii) The income criteria in term of rupees will be modified taking into account the change in its value every three years. If the situation, however, so demands, the interregnum may be less.

Explanation: wherever the expression "Permanent" occur in this schedule, it shall mean incapacitation which results in putting an officer out of service.

The issue of creamy layer formula is one which relates to evaluation of protective discrimination involving inherently contradictory efforts, i.e; pursuing equality in the land of hierarchy. Protective discrimination policies are argued to entail systematic departure from norms of equality such as merit, evenhandedness and indifference to ascriptive characteristics. There are many justifications for it but the question arises that should creamy layer

Note: (i) Clarifications regarding creamy layer amongst OBCs have been dealt in details by DOP&T in their offfice order no. 36033/5/2004-Estt. (Res.) dated 14.10.2004

(ii) Now it has been increased to Rs. 2.50 Lakh per annum. (Annexure-5) formula be adopted to make protective discrimination more effective is an open issue depending on its assessment as beneficial or deleterious effect. Every scheme of protective discrimination has to be evaluated in terms of costs and benefits. Marc Galanter has very aptly put each claimed benefit paired with the opposite claim of cost, which is mentioned below:

Table: 4.3

Benefits and Costs of Protective Discrimination

	Benefits	Costs
1.	RE-DISTRIBUTION Vs Prefences provide a direct flow of valuable resources to the beneficiaries in larger measure than they would otherwise enjoy.	DIVERSION These resources are enjoyed by a small segment of the intended beneficiaries and do not benefit the group as a whole.
2.	REPRESENTATION Vs. Preference provide for participation in decision making by those who effectively represent the interests of the beneficiaries, interests that would otherwise be under-represented or neglected.	MISREPRESENTATION By creating new interests which diverge from those of the beneficiaries preferences obstruct accurate representation of their interests.
3.	INTEGRATION Vs. By affording opportunities for participation and well being, preferences promote feelings of belonging and loyalty among the beneficiaries, thereby promoting the social and political integration of these groups in into Indian society.	ALIENATION By emphasizing the separateness of these groups, preferences reduce their opportunities for (and feelings of) common participation.
4.	ACCEPTANCE Vs Preferences induce in others awareness that the beneficiary groups are participants in Indian life whose interests and views have to be taken into account and adjusted to.	REJECTION Preferences frustrate others by what they consider unfair favouritism and educate them to regard the beneficiaries as separate elements who enjoy their own facilities and have no claim on general public facilities.
5.	INTEGRITY Vs Preferences permit forms of	MANIPULATION Preferences subject these groups to manipulation by other,

	action that promote pride, self-respect, sense of achievement and personal efficacy that enable the beneficiaries to contribute to national development as willing partner.	aggravate their dependency, and undermine their sense of dignity, pride, self-sufficiency and personal efficacy.
6.	INCUBATION Vs	OVER-PROTECTION
	By broadening opportunities preferences stimulate the acquisition of skills and resources needed to compete successfully in open competition.	Preferences provide artificial protection which blunts the development of the skills and resources needed to succeed without them.
7.	MOBILIZATION Vs	ENERVATION
	By cultivating talents, providing opportunities and incentives and promoting their awareness and self- conciousness, preferences enhance the capacity of the beneficiary groups to undertake organized collective action.	By making them dependent, blunting the development of talent, undermining self-respect, preferences lessen the capacity for organized effort on their own behalf.
8.	STIMULATION Vs	SEDATION
	By increasing the visibility of the beneficiary groups, promoting their placement in strategic locations, and emphasizing the national commitment to remedy their condition,preferences serve as a stimulas and catalyst of enlarged efforts for their uplift and inclusion.	By projecting an image of comprehensive governmental protection and preferment, preferences stir the resentment of others,allaying their concern and undermining initiatives for measures on behalf of the beneficiary groups.
9.	SELF-LIQUIDATION Vs.	SELF-PERPETUATION
	The benefits of preferential treatment are mutually reinforcing and will eventually render any special treatment.	This arrangement created vested interest in their continuation, while discouraging the development of skills, resources and attitudes that would enable the beneficiaries to prosper without special treatment.
10.	FAIRNESS Vs.	UNFAIRNESS
	Preferences compensate for and help to offset the accumulated disablements resulting from past deprivation of advantages and opportunities.	Preferences place an unfair handicap on individual who are deprived of opportunities they deserve on merit.

11.	SECULARISM	Vs.	COMMUNALISM
	By reducing tangible disparities among groups and directing attention to mundane rather than ritual standing, preferences promote the development of a secular society.		By recognizing and stimulating group identity, preferences perpetuate invidious distinctions, thereby undermining secularism.
12.	DEVELOPMENT	Vs.	STAGNATION
	Preferences contribute to national development by providing incentives opportunities and resources to utilize neglected talent.		Preferences·impede development by misallocation of resources, lowering of morale and incentive, and waste of talent.

Out of all cost- benefits assessment, the effort of creamy layerisation is based on sedation i.e, preferences stir the resentment of others on this issue one has to be most objective and empirical in evaluation of aspirations of compensatory discrimination through reservational justice and its performance. There is much force and reality that redistribution of reservational benefits is not spread evenly throughout the beneficiary groups-OBCs. In the very nature of the scheme it can never be ensured. In utilization of preferential treatment substantial clustering develops which reflects the structural factors (e.g. the greater urbanization of some groups) more than deliberate group aggrendisement, as often charged. It is but natural that the better situated among beneficiaries enjoy a disproportionate share of preferential programme benefits.It is aggravated by passive administration and by the concentration of high echelon of benefits. It is also convicting to argue that "where the list of beneficiaries spans groups of very disparate condition- as with the most expansive lists of other backward classes—the "creamy effect" is probably even more pronounced.The general view is that the creamy layer formula ought to have been applied to all the beneficiaries of protective discrimination-SCs/STs/OBCs. One may find force in the argument of Mr. V.M. Tarkunde, a noted lawyer, that by the concept of creamy layer the charge of casteism, which has often been leveled against the reservation policy will lose much of its force.

The real issue is: what is main guiding spirit behind the adoption of "creamy layer formula". The obvious object are two- fold - first, to ensure (in principle) that the benefit of reservation reaches to really deserving section of OBCs, and second, to cool down impatient anti-reservationists and cure their heart burning against enrichment of affluent section of backwards. Will skimming off of creamy layer of OBCs ensure the reaching of benefits to the non creamy layer of OBCs? The Mandal case was decided on 16.11.1992 after more than four decade functioning of our constitutional scheme. Objections have been raised from time to time against snatching of reservational benefits by developed strata of backwards including SCs. But no empirical study has ever been produced before the Supreme Court to establish the case that creamy layer of backwards has taken away all the benefits. The hard reality is that the desired percentage of reservation for SCs/STs has still not been filled in. In class one services their representation has reached upto 5.68% as against their 22.5% quota and in all class (II, IIIand IV also) it has reached upto 18.72%. This percentage of reservation is inclusive of the creamy layer. What will be result if creamy layer is taken away from reservational benefit? Will it not tender the representation to a poor zero from 5.68% in class I?. The same analogy applies with equal force to OBCs. (the Supreme Court itself has left SCs/STs unaffected by creamy layer formula.)* The representation of OBCs with 52% Population and 27% reservation of seats had only meager number of representation to class I in Central as well as State services. The situation is some what well off in lower services in the State. The moot question is that, if creamy layer is taken away, will the non-creamy layer be able to compete and fill 27.0 percent job vacancies?. Will it not amount to a circuitous deprivation of reservational justice to backward castes in collectivity? Thus in absence of data of community –wise representation the whole exercise becomes impressionistic: Mandal himself has

* Now it has advocated creamy layer for SCs & STs and has left to the Govt; to evolve formula for it.)

lamented in his report that the commission did not even receive replies to the information sought by it from various Government Departments and Organisations on the caste-wise composition of their services.The Supreme Court was not feeded with any data of such type.In the case of Bihar more or less similar situation prevails and without sufficient data on OBCs representation, it will be difficult to chalk out any plan in this respect. In the third National Conference of the States Chairpersons of Backward Classes Commissions held in New Delhi in July' 2005, it was suggested and approved that the States will provide data of its OBCs population to the NCBC for creating data bank as well as it will be helpful in chalking out programmes and policies for the welfare of OBCs. But the data from Bihar has not been received till date in the Commission.This indicates that how sincere is the State Government in this respect.

Besides these, income criterion was applied in allocating seats to the wards of weaker sections in the hostels of educational institutions in Andhra Pradesh, in local bodies in Maharashtra, in medical education in Bihar, for providing fee concessions in educational institutions in Rajasthan, Orissa and Delhi (Government of India 1980:4-10) The State of Bihar had fixed reservation in the post-graduate medical courses for different categories as follows:

SCs	—	14.0 %
STs	—	10.0 %*
Extremely backward classes	—	14.0 %
Backward classes	—	9.0 %
Ladies	—	3.0 %
Total		**50.0 %**

* After Creation of Jharkhand, it has been fixed at 1.0%.

Against the above reservation of Bihar Government in medical courses a case was filed by Ajay Kumar and Others and this case is known as Ajay Kumar Singh and others Vs. State of Bihar and others, SCC 401, which is as follows:

The State of Bihar has established and maintains certain medical colleges in the State. The basic course in medicine in India is MBBS. After a student completes this course, he is entitled to pursue post graduate medical courses, known as MS/MD. Seats in post graduate medical courses are few and there is acute competition therefore. The State of Bihar had provided for reservation of seats in post graduate medical courses in favour of backward classes to the extent of 50%. This was contrary to the recommendation of the Medical Council of India, which is established under a parliamentary statute–(the 'Medical Council Act'). The recommendation of the medical council was that so far as post graduate medical courses are concerned, the rule of reservation should not be applied and that all admissions thereto should be made only on the basis of merit alone. The rule of reservation made by the State of Bihar was challenged by some students. The Supreme Court conceded the power of State government to pursue admission policy consistent with Article 14 in relation to those institutions which are maintained out of public fund.The regulation of Medical Council was held to be advisory in nature and not a binding direction. The Supreme Court tried to reach the regulation consistently with Article 15(4) which is constitutional power and cannot be overridden or superseded by a regulation by Medical Council under the Medical Council Act, 1956. State power was conceded under entry 25 of list III and was declared consistent with Union power under entry 66 of the Union List.The regulation revised upto 1988 recommending admissions to post-graduate medical education for students being selected strictly on merit judged on the basis of academic record in the undergraduate courses was interpreted to mean that the student shall be admitted to post-graduate training strictly on the basis of merit in each of the relevant classes or categories as the case may be.

The validity of 50.0 percent reservation of seats for SCs/STs/OBCs/Women candidate in the post graduate courses was challenged on the ground that it would be detrimental to the interest of the society, as the society would be saddlcd with less competent and less efficient doctors to the extent of half the number available. Speaking for himself and on behalf of SC Agarwal and MK Mukherjee, JJ; Jeevan Reddy, J repelled the contention on the following grounds:

1. Such a submission is premised on the assumption that reservations are basically anti-meritarian. Jeevan Reddy, J. repelled this assumption and pointed out that, reservation is provided only at the stage of entry and not at the stage of exit.In the matter of passing the examination, no concession is shown to members of reserved classes. The pass marks are uniform for all. This mean that even if a less meritorious student is admitted under a reserved category, he has to improve his standard and has to acquire the same proficiency as any other candidate while passing the examination."

2. No empirical study has been brought to the notice of the Court to establish that candidates admitted under reserved quotas generally lagged behind in the matter of marks or proficiency in the final examinations. To quote Jeevan Reddy, J., They may enter under different categories but they come out as one single class".

3. The academic performance is no guarantee of efficiency in practice. It is, therefore, wrong to presume that a doctor with good academic record is bound to prove a

better doctor in practice.The argument that reservation would be detrimental to the society has no force.

On this point the Supreme Court explained its decision in Mandal Case citing excerpts from the case at p.751 of SCC, Para 856 where in the Court had repelled argument as to anti-meritarianism of reservation and had added that reserved category candidates are endowed with that much merit as the candidates of general category and in given opportunity they may prove their worth by overcoming initial deficiency.

The Supreme Court had to clarify Mandal Judgment on other points of reservational benefit's claim at two stages and in promotion.

1. It was argued that the candidates seeking admission to post-graduate medical courses had already enjoyed the benefit of reservation at the time of admission in MBBS and are supposed to improve, therefore, reservation at the stage of admission to the post-graduate courses again is uncalled for and contrary to public interest. The Court rejected it on two grounds: (a) the argument is not based on proved evidences. The candidates seeking reservational benefit at the post-graduate level might not have availed the benefit of reservation at the stage of admission to MBBS. He might have been admitted on his own right through the general quota.Due to the competition at the level of the post-graduate medical courses which is extremely acute, he may have to seek the benefit of reservation; (b) there is nothing in Article 15(4) to convey that a student cannot be given the benefit of reservation at more than one stage during the course of his educational career. The Supreme Court clarified its earlier observations in Mandal case declaring certain posts and research courses to be treated as unreserved to be found in paras 838-839 at p.752 of SCC.The Court pointed at that(i)the observation was made

with reference to Article 16(4) which was qualified by Article 335, whereas no such condition is stipulated under Article 15(4).

(ii) while making the said observations, the Court was speaking about posts in research and development organizations in specialities and superspecialities in medicines, engineering and such other courses. The Court was not speaking of admission to specialities and superspecialities,

(iii) The MS/MD were not superspecialities.The clarification of Court was that in any event, this Court did not say that they were not permissible;the government was asked to consider the advisability of providing for reservation in those posts having regard to the nature and level of those posts.

The Supreme Court also rejected the argument of petitioners on the ground that in as much as substantial amount is paid by way of stipened to post graduate students, admission to post graduate course is in effect an appointment to a post. Relying on Mandal case judgement that no reservation is permissible in the matter of promotional post for doctors who had completed MBBS course. The Court rejected it on the basis that irrespective of stipend, admission to medical courses cannot be equated with appointment to a post and certainly not to an appointment by promotion.

Ajay Kumar case is very significant in the area of reservational justice to OBCs because of its reinterpretation of Mandal case. It attaches much flexibility leaving to the judgment of the government to take policy decisions whether to reserve seats in superspecialites or not.

No reservation formula is given flexible interpretation by the Court. It may not hold much of force due to the following reasons:

(i) It cannot be said that reservation is anti-meritarian and therefore to avoid representation of backwards in very important services will not be in accordance with the mandate of Article 16(4) stipulating adequate representation not only in few services but in all types of services.

(ii) Open posts are not always filled on consideration of the merit and merit alone.Most of the times worst candidates are choosen against open posts and nothing is possible againt beneficiaries of unwritten reservation appointed on considerations other than merit, if he possesses minimum prescribed qualifications.This is so more in educational institutions where less meritorious are inducted against open posts.

The flexibility of Ajay Kumar's case appears to find expression in other cases also.

The only justification for denial to the creamy layer of the reservational benefit is the cooling down of the heart burning among status quoits. The main reason behind this tendency is not any love affair with really backward and depressed castes but the hard reality of Indian social life that upper castes cannot tolerate the political power slipping out of their hands. If the reaction of upper castes is so motivated, there is no justification of denying reservational benefits to the creamy layer of OBCs which will not benefit their depressed brethren. That is the reason why Mandal report especially knocked down such reasons. It observed, "it is certainly true that reservation for OBCs will cause a lot of heart burning to others, but should the mere fact of this heart-burning be allowed to operate as a moral veto against social reform?". In case of Bihar, this heart burning of the upper castes has been discussed above in this chapter.

Besides heart-buring reservation policy has divided the society into forward and backward.It perpetuates the menance of casteism and sub-casteism in a new shape.Today, we have divided the people not only into major castes but also in sub-castes for reservations, while raising the bogey of social justice and development which has proved to be detrimental to their all –round development as citizens of a free India.The emergence of the SP-BSP in UP is the first classic example of fight not only for power but also of reserve discrimination against upper castes for prevailing on the Manuvadi system over their progency.

It is often stated that the elite among the backward classes are no more really backward. These people have made remarkable progress both educationally and economically and in politics they are now a force to be reckoned with because of their numerical preponderance. Of course, there has emerged a section of elites in several lower castes during the post-independence period, but they are in a microscopic minority. It cannot belie the fact that a vast majority of them still have not been able to make much headway in their life for various reasons. One should not ignore the fact that many of the OBCs are socially and educationally in no way better off than SCs. In terms of different aspects of backwardness there is a great deal of empirical overlap between the OBCs and the dalits. The moot question is: Why should the majority of the OBCs people continue to suffer for better lifestyle of a few within the OBCs or the depressed section of the society?. Professor Arvind Sharma says that it is morally and ethically justified to temporiraly favour certain groups if it can be demonstrated that they were discriminated against as such. But there are two points to be considered.One, whether the historically wronged group is a caste, class or some other entity like a gender based group, should be defined historically and empirically and not assumed theoretically.

And two, one should accord priority to those groups who have suffered more systematically and pervasively than the others". Another most acute assessment of the Mandal reservation policy came from the sociologist Andre Beteille. He argued that reservation for SCs and STs was undeniably motivated by the imperatives of social justice. For centuries these communities had been stigmatized, discriminated against, and condescended to. The move to reserve 22.5 percent of government jobs for them was an acknowledgement of the need to redress a historical injustice. On the other hand, reservation for OBCs was motivated by the imperatives of power. These castes had benefited substantially from the agrarian reforms undertaken after independence. Once a tenants –at-will, they had now become owner-cultivators themselves.At the same time, since they were also numerous, they had become influential in electoral politics. Through the sixties and seventies, more and more OBCs became legislators and parliamentarians, State ministers and chief ministers. Economically and politically, the real beneficiaries of the Indian democracy had been these upper OBCs in many States including Bihar. What they lacked was administrative power. By virtue of the privileges granted in form of reservation they had begun to enter in the government services and the rest that is reservation in higher educational institutions is in the offing, thus they have come to a full circle. Moreover, in the post-reform period where the government jobs are shrinking, the need of the hour is reservation in the private sector. The market lays emphasis on merit and efficiency and donot pay any attention to the distinction of purity and pollution. So the State government has to frame policy for this keeping in view the changing scenario to suit the needs of market economy, as protective discrimination has its own limitations. Therefore, social intervention and action may help us to achieve the goal of social justice in the true sense of term.

This social action may be in the form of health care, poverty allevation programmes, access to education etc; unless it will have its impact on the socio-economic infrastructure and ultimately in the field of politics. Social justice is being used in the present scenario as a slogan to perpetuate the justice of power in a growing environment of social insecurity. Development has come to mean distribution of grants, loans and subsidies to win votes. In such situation social intervention is must to achieve the goal of social justice.

References

- Burman, BK Roy, (1992) Beyond Mandal and After: Backward Classes in Perspective, Mittal Publications, New Delhi
- Bihar Backward Classes Commission Report (Mungerilal), part III, 1976, Patna.
- Chaudhary, Samrat "Mandalocracy", Sunday Hindustan Times, 9th April 2006, New Delhi.
- Galanter, Marc, Who are the Other Backward classes? An Introduction to a Constitutional Puzzle, Economic and Political Weekly, October, 1978, Bombay.
- Galanter, Marc(1984) Competing Equalities:Law and the Backward Classes in India, Oxford University Press, Delhi.
- Gehlot, N.S.(1999) India at fifty: Facing Stresses and Strains, National Publishing House, Jaipur/Delhi.
- Hooda, Sagar Preet(2001) Contesting Reservations, Rawat Publications, New Delhi.
- Kumar, Subodh. Reservation: A Panacea for all Ills, Mainstream, Vol-XLIV, No.18, April 22, 2006.
- Maheshwari, S.R.(1993), The Mandal Commission and Mandalization: A Critique, Concept, New Delhi.
- National Commission for Backward Classes Annual Report;2005-06, Government Press, Minto Road, New Delhi.

- Prasad, A(1997) Reservational Justice to OBCs: Theoretical and Practical Issues, Deep & Deep Publications, New Delhi.
- Roy, R; Caste and Political Development in Bihar, in R.Kothari(ed.), 1970, Caste in Indian Politics, Orient Longman, New Delhi.
- Sachchidananda, Reservation and After: "The Case of Bihar, in Panandiker V.A.Pai, (ed), 1997, 'The Politics of Backwardness, Reservation Policy in India," Konark Publishers Pvt. Ltd, Delhi.
- Singh, Parmanand (1985), Equality, Reservation and Discrimination in India, Deep & Deep Publications, New Delhi.
- Sachchidananda (1977) Harijan Elite, Thomson Press, Faridabad.
- Sharma, Premlata.(2002) The Problems of Dalits and OBCs, Book Enclave, Jaipur.
- Sinha, Anil Kumar (Compiler) Aarakshan, Eastern Book Agency, 305, Buddha Plaza, Buddh Marg, Patna-1.
- Seth, L. "Reservation and Changes in Elites Perceptions, Financial Express, 24th December, 1986.
- Singh, S.N.(1987) Reservation:Problems and Prospects, Uppal Publishing House, New Delhi.
- Verma, H.S (2005) The OBCs and the Ruling Classes in India, Rawat Publications, Jaipur/New Delhi.

5

Welfare Measures for Backward Castes

Articles 15(4), 16(4), 38, 46 and a sets of Articles in part XVI, clause (i) of Article 38 makes it obligatory for the State to "Strive to promote the welfare of the people by securing and protecting as effectively as it may, in which justice Social, economic and political shall inform all the institutions of the national life". Article 46 further contains a very significant directive regarding promotion of educational and economic interest of other weaker sections and to protect them from social injustice in all forms of exploitation.

Keeping in view the upliftment and welfare of the backward castes, different provincial government enunciated special measures for them before independence especially in the field of education (Grants-in-Aids to schools).After independence some of these welfare measures continued in one form or the others, for example the educational scholarship provided by the Bihar government during 1949-50 is the testimony of it, which is presented below:

Table: 5.1

Backward Classes Scholarship for Bihar: 1949-50

Course	**No. of Seats**
Medicine	35
Engineering	18
Agriculture	2
Technology	1
Science	4
Education	—
Commerce	5
Law	—
Arts	3
Ladies	4
Total	**72**

Similarly Bihar Government at that time spend Rs. 2, 40, 396 on primary & secondary education and Rs. 96, 840 for post-matric education.This process continued after 1950 and it is pertinent to mention here that for this purpose State government prepared a list of backward castes in 1951(Annexure-2).

The Mungerilal Commission also went into the causes of educational backwardness as well as looked into various aspects to improve their economic conditions.No doubt, in the State Government Schools, there was provision for free education upto middle level however they find it difficult to buy books and stationery. Mostly children of these backward communities are also an earning member for their families, therefore some of them start earning for their families from early childhood, while others are employed in animal rearing and other petty works.So the Commission suggested that parents of these children should be boosted to send their wards in schools.It also provided suggestion to revise the stipend rate for the backward castes students, which is as follows:

Table: 5.2

	Students studying in day school	Students residing in hostels
Upto Class 4	Rs. 6.00 per month	Undecided, because students are not expected to reside in hostel
Upto Class 7	Rs. 15.00 per month	Rs. 40.00 per month
Upto Class 11	Rs. 20.00 per month	Rs. 40.00 per month

1) Only those students of backward caste will be given stipend whose parents/guardians donot submit their income tax/agriculture tax/sales tax. For this there should be provision by the State Government to allocate sufficient fund for this purpose so that atleast 75.0 percent can get the benefit.

2) For poor students whose parents do not submit their income tax a lumpsum stipend should be provided within a month of the start of the session, so that they will be able to purchase books and stationery on time. For this one time stipend of Rs. 20 should be provided to the students studying in class VI & VII., this amount will be Rs.25 for class VIII & IX students and for Class X & XI it should be Rs.30.

3) All such students should be exempted from depositing tution fee and university examination fee, who want to continue their study after doing their matriculation.If it

is not possible for the State Government due to financial constraint, then only those students should be provided benefit whose parents annual income(of five members) is less than Rs. 12000.This limit for the most backward communities should be Rs. 15000.

4) The rate of stipend should be revised from time to time keeping in view the cost of living index.

5) It is essential to open hostels in sufficient numbers for backward communities students, so that they can get the benefit of higher education.In the initial stage these hostels can be opened in districts and at commissionaires level, where no such hostel exists for these communities students.Later on this experiment can be done at block level.

6) Free boarding and lodging as well as books and stationery should be provided to the backward communities students residing in the hostels run by the welfare department of the State Government. Because, mostly they donot get their stipend on time.Whereas the question of reservation of seats for backward communities students in these hostels are concerned, the Commission has suggested following formula:

Castes	allotment of seats
a) Other backward castes	75.0 percent
b) Scheduled Castes	10.0 "
c) Scheduled Tribes	5.0 "
d) Others	10.0 "

The report further says that the most backward communities students should be given preference in this respect.

7) **If sufficient numbers of STs students are not available, the seats in the hostel should be allotted to the SCs students and similarly if they are not available in sufficient numbers, it should be allotted to the backward caste students.Students belonging to upper castes can also avail this facility, if their parents income is less than Rs. 3600 per annum.**

For allocation of seats in the hostels not opened for the backward communities students, the following reservation pattern should be adopted:

Reservation of seats in hostels opened for Scheduled Castes:

Castes	allotment of seats
a) Scheduled Castes	75.0 percent
b) Scheduled Tribes	5.0 "
c) Other backward castes	10.0 "
d) Others	10.0 "

Reservation of seats in hostels opened for Scheduled Tribes:

Castes	allotment of seats
a) Scheduled Tribes	75.0 percent
b) Scheduled Castes	5.0 "
c) Other backward castes	10.0 "
d) Others	10.0 "

The Commission suggested the State Government to construct hostels for the BCs students by taking loans from the financial institutions, as similar steps have been taken by the Governments of Tamilnadu and Madhya Pradesh.

8) **Resedential high schools for the BCs students should be opened and in these schools only such students should be enrolled whose parents are landless or having less than 2.0 acres of land in their possession.If such students**

are not available then those students can also be enrolled whose parents do not file income tax or sales tax return.

9) Studends belonging to the most backward castes who are pursuing higher education in science, engineering and medical streams and whose parents income is less than Rs. 12000 per annum should be provided a lumpsum amount in the form of annual stipend (example; Commission found that in Kerala, Harijan students were provided Rs.90 to 375 per annum for purchasing books).

The State Welfare Department has been set up with an aim to cater the needs of the welfare of scheduled castes, scheduled tribes and other backward classes of the state. Under this department various schemes have been implemented for educational development, economic development and social development.After the bifurcation of the State, the major target groups have been the SCs and OBCs as the STs are now only 0.88 percent of the total population of the State.This has been kept in mind while allocating funds for welfare of these castes categories during the 10th five year plan 2002-2007.

The schemes which are being run, are based on different funding patterns. In fact majority are being funded out of State allocations. Some schemes are funded on 50:50 basis by the Central Govt. and some are based on 100% Central sponsorship. In fact the Welfare Department has planned the schemes as per the local requirement and grants are provided by the State Government accordingly.

Welfare Department is running different educational schemes like stipend, residential schools, hostels, reimbursement of examination fee to boost literacy amongst SCs, STs and OBCs of the State. In fact these schemes have always been the focus area of the department. Apart from plan head, in non-plan also the State Government is earmarking major funds for these schemes.

At present this department is running 51 residential schools for SCs, 15 residential schools for STs and 12 residential schools for OBCs.At the same time 146 hostels for SCs, 13 for STs and 5 for OBCs are in operation.During 2001-02 a 100 bed OBCs hostel has been sanctioned for construction in Rohtas district.

As stated above, stipend schemes are the major schemes identified for the educational development of SCs, STs and OBCs of the State.It has been seen that the students are not taking full advantage of the schemes which shows their lack of awareness. For this reason, the department is regularly advertising in the local newspapers.

Secondly, the bottlenecks has been the release of Central share in the 50:50 schemes.If the Central share is released on time, the schemes can be sanctioned.

OBC girl's residential high schools exclusively for OBC girls have been sanctioned and will be completed during the 10th plan period (12 in numbers).

Apart from stipend schemes, reimbursement of examination fees will also be in operation so that the poor students can complete their studies.

During the 9th five year plan Welfare Department implemented a number of schemes for SCs, STs and OBCs.During this period, it has been found that the schemes under the C.S.S.(50:50) Government of India released the funds either late or did not release at all though the State made provisions for those schemes.

Welfare department is also running different income generating schemes through two of its corporations, i.e; Bihar State Scheduled castes Cooperative Development Corporation, Patna and Bihar State Backward Classes Finance & Development Corporation, Patna.

After Scheduled Castes and Scheduled Tribes the Other Backward Classes of Bihar have been denied their share in the society since long.For them different types of stipend schemes have been implemented, which are as follows:

Table : 5.3

1. **Stipend Scheme:**

Sl.No.	Schemes	Rate/Student/ month(Rupees)
1.	Primary Schools(class 1 to 1V)	15
2.	Middle Schools(V to VI)	30
3.	High Schools(VII to X)	55
4.	Stipend to Hostelers (Classes 1 to X)	80
5.	Stipend to technical students	150

The proposed outlay and physical target for the year 2002-03 for the schemes are as follows:

Stipend	Proposed (Rs. In Lakhs)	Physical target Outlay
High School	50.00	7575
Middle & Primary School	128.30	47518

The proposed outlay and physical target for the tenth five year plan 2002-07 for the schemes are as follows:

Stipend	Proposed Outlay (Rs. In Lakhs)	Physical target
High School	1200.00	170000
Middle & Primary School	2300.00	707000

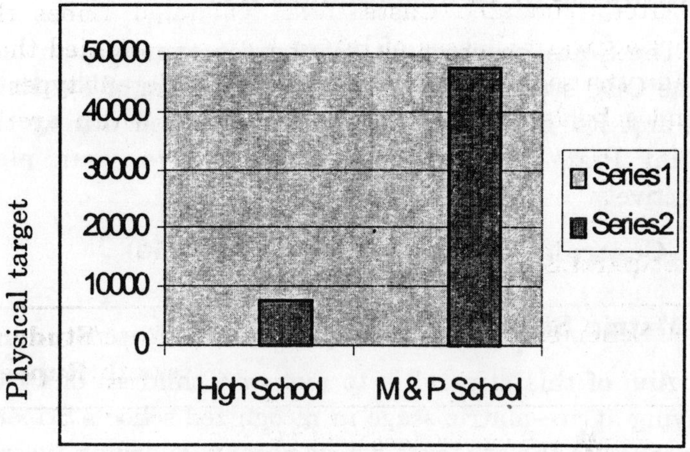

Year 2002-03

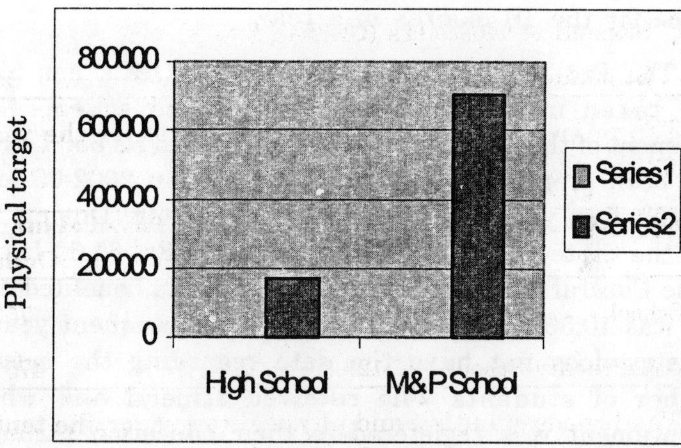

Year 2002-07

2. Establishment of 12 OBC Girls' residential schools

For the financial year 2002-03, a sum of Rs. 68.54 lakhs has been proposed for the establishment of 12 girls residential schools for OBCs.For this a sum of Rs. 1000 lakhs has been proposed during the 10th five year plan 2002-07.

Reimbursement of examination fee:

The State government reimburses examination fees for the OBC students. For this scheme a sum of Rs. 10.00 lakh and Rs. 500 lakhs have been proposed during the Annual Plan 2002-03 and the 10th five year plan respectively.

Centrally Sponsored Scheme (50:50)

Pre-Matric Stipend

Aim of this stipend is to motivate children of OBCs studying at pre-matric stage in recognized schools.Stipend is awarded to the students whose parents/guardian income does not exceed the prescribed limits set up by the State government.This stipend terminate at the end of class X.It will be for the 10 months in a year.

The Pre-Matric Stipend scheme for OBCs has also been taken up as a centrally sponsored scheme.For fulfillment of this scheme Rs.125.00 lakhs and Rs.850 Lakhs have been proposed during the Annual Plan 2002-03 and the 10th five year plan 2002-07 respectively. During IX plan the State Government was provided Rs. 84.60 lakhs as the Central share and the OBCs students benefited out of it was 10,566 in 1998-99.But for the subsequent years, Ministry does not have the data regarding the actual number of students who received stipend and what improvement was registered in their education through this scheme. In 1999-2000 and 2000-01, no fund was released.One reason may be that the State plan does not contain approved outlays to enable the State Government to match the funds available from the Ministry.The remedy for this difficulty is either to ensure that State plan do have outlays for meeting the share of each scheme for which the fund is provided on matching basis and such State plan outlay is cumulatively equal to the outlay in the Central plan of the Ministry or to convert this scheme into 100.0 percent centrally funded scheme.

For **post-matric**, Central share of Rs. 196.50 lakh was released during 1998-99 and the total beneficiaries were 14, 410, whereas for the subsequent years, i.e; 1999-2000 & 2000-01 it was nil.

Construction of OBC Boy's Hostel under C.S.S (50:50).

During the Annual Plan 2002-03 and the 10th five year plan for the construction of OBC boy's hostels, a sum of Rs.230.00 lakhs and Rs. 1250.00 lakhs respectively have been proposed as State share. The Central share will be provided by the government of India.

Construction of Girl's hostel under C.S.S (50:50)

During the financial year 2002-03, for construction of OBC's girl's hostel, a sum of Rs. 230.00 lakhs have been proposed as the State share. The Central share will be provided by the government of India. For this scheme, a sum of Rs. 1250.00 lakhs has been proposed during the 10th five year plan 2002-07.

During IX th Plan, in the year 1998-99, an amount of Rs. 120.53 lakhs was released under the above schemes and the number of students who availed the facility was 300 and 3 hostel was built for this purpose. For the years 1999-2000 and 2000-01 the funds released for this purpose was nil.The remarks made for the pre-matric stipend scheme hold good for this scheme also.

Construction of Residential School for OBC Students

For construction of residential school for OBC, a sum of Rs.3600.00 lakhs has been proposed during the 10th five year plan 2002-07.

Renovation of Schools, hostels of SCs, STs and OBCs

For this scheme an outlay of Rs. 1250.00 lakhs has been proposed during the 10th five year plan 2002-07.

Dr.S.P. Jain in his article "Backward Classes:Problems of Education", says that the school-college level curriculam mainly in subjects like languages, civics, history etc; should be proportionately balanced representing the concerns and aspirations of different sections of students.But in reality they represent the interests of the dominant social groups.Also among the teachers in Bihar the total female representation is less than 20.0 percent and in my opinion it has not changed much in these years.This has its negative impact on the education of girls.The data shown below reveals this fact:

Table: 5.4
Percentage of teachers on the basis of caste and sex

SC	ST	OBC	Female
7.50	7.27	27.72	19.75

Mostly the backward communities in Bihar had their own traditional occupations, and some of the artisans were highly proficient in their works.They were engaged either in cottage industries or handicrafts. But due to industrialization, they could not faced the competition posed by big factories and become unemployed.In search of employment they moved to the cities and became rickshawpuller, servants, joined Government services as peon, and also joined industrial establishments as an unskilled worker or labourer.And those who were left behind joined the rank of landless labourers, thus increasing burden on the rural economy of the State.

Keeping in view the above facts, the Mungerilal Commission opined that a finance corporation with the share capital of Rs. 5.0 crores should be established by the State Government to provide financial help to the backward castes, so that they can revive their traditional occupations as well as start other businesses. The main aim of this corporation will be as follows:

- To construct houses for the backward castes on its own or by providing financial help to other agencies for doing this job.
- To start and develop poultry, and dairy farms.
- For purchasing autorickshaw, motorcar, lori and truck, sewing machine, printing press, leth machine and other instruments, provision of finance on installment to the backward castes be mode.
- Help in starting and developing village and cottage industry, such as Bamboo work, leather work besides industry based on use of soil and jute etc;
- To provide financial help for building houses and for purchase of agricultural land.
- To lend money for purchasing or starting hotel, wine shop, grocery shop etc.
- For starting intensive work on agriculture land and for its development.
- To provide money on interest to those persons from backward castes who are doctors, engineers, chartered accountant or wish to start such other beneficial occupations.

No interest should be payable on the financial help upto Rs. 1000 and be provided without guarantor.Financial help above this amount should not be provided without any guarantor or interest.

Reservation should be applied in allotment of vacant land to the most backward castes, the percent of which can be determined in the following ways:

All districts except Chhotanagpur and Santhal pragana

SCs	50.0 percent
STs	10.0 "
OBCs	30 "
Others	10.0 "

For Chhotanagpur and Santhal pragana

SCs	25.0 percent
STs	40.0 "
OBCs	25.0 "
Others	10.0 "

It should also be kept in mind while allocating land to the landless labourers who owns less than 2.0 acres of land that preference should be given to them.

Besides the above the Commission also proposed to provide financial help to individuals belonging to the backward castes for purchase of agricultural equipments, HYV seeds, Oxen, milch animals and others.

Later on State Government on the recommendation of Mungerilal Commission, established a financial corporation for the welfare of Backward castes known as **Bihar State Backward Classes Finance & Development Corporation, Patna**.

This corporation has been established to provide financial assistance to Other Backward Classes and registered under the company Act of 1956 in 1993.It has an authorized share capital of Rs. 25.00 crores. Till 1999-2000 the State Government towards its share capital has earmarked a sum of Rs. 13.36 crores. The corporation implement the schemes after getting term loan from National Backward Classes Finance & Development Corporation. The margin money is provided out of the share capital. The company function as a State channelising agent (SCA) for granting loan and margin money to members of the backward castes, for setting up income generating viable economic projects/schemes, as approved by NBCFDC. The agreement stipulated that if the State Channelising Agency drew or received any loan as financial assistance from the NBCFDC and did not disburse it further to the ultimate beneficiary or utilize for the purpose for which it was drawn within a period of two months, the SCA will have to pay interest at the normal bank rate, not below 18.0 percent per annum to the NBCFDC on the undisbursed or unutilized amount for the period it was not disbursed or utilized after the expiry of two months..

A study conducted by Haryali, Delhi on behalf of PREM Division of the Ministry of Social Justice & Empowerment on the grant provided to some NGOs, working in Bihar for upliftment of backward castes reveals the following facts:

State-Bihar

Sl.	Name of Organisation & Address	1.Training Grade, 2.Year wise grant received 3.No. of trainees sanctioned per year	Strength & Weakness	Grade
1	Adarsh Sarwangin Mahila Evam Bal Vikas Samiti, Belwamore, Lauria, Dist. W.Champaran	1.TradeCraft-tailoring &cutting 2.Grant received 2000-01-Nil 2001-02-Rs.114030 2002-03 & 03-04–grant not received 3.No. of trainees-50	Strength: The organization. having solid organizational support, despite not receiving grant for three years imparted training to the needy and out of the total, who received training, 64.0 percent got employment. Weakness;Partial amount of stipend was disbursed by the organization and also the attendance was low, i.e;68.0 percent on the inspection day.	B
2.	Bihar Jansahyog Avam Kalyan Prathisthan, Kailgarh, PO:KailgarhBazar, Dist.Siwan	Craft training centre	Untraceable	C

3.	Rajendra Shiksha Evam Samaj Kalyan, PO:DumriKalan, Dist.Sitamarhi.	1. Craft-Tailoring & Cutting 2. Grant received 2000-01-Nil 2001-02-Rs.123232 2002-03 & 03-04 –grant not received 3. No. Of trainees-50	A well established organization imparted training to the trainees satisfactorily.It also followed training syllabus approved by the State government. Weakness: Selected training programme without proper assessment about its demand and another organization was started in the same locality by the secretary's wife, i.e; Vishwa Bandhu Ramavatar Jamuna Madhya Vidayalaya with same trade. The percentage of attendance was also low on the day of inspection(58.0%)	B

Note: Another organization run by the same organization with more or less the same feature as mentioned at Sl.No.3 (Col.3) has been left out.

The above example shows that how the money received by the Ministry of Social Justice & Empowerment towards development of vocational skills, is used by the NGOs and upto what extent it is beneficial to the needy persons of the society.

Keeping in view the problems faced by the backward castes, Working Group on Empowerment of Backward Classes in Tenth five year Plan (2002-07), Ministry of Social Justice & Empowerment has worked out following solutions to amelioerate their grievances:

> The OBCs are mainly farmers or artisans, small cultivators, agricultural labourers, weavers, tailors, potters, carpenters, blacksmith, mud & stone querry workers, construction workers etc;. Many of them are nomadic & semi-nomadic with poor literacy and surrounded by the vicious circle of poverty.For these occupational groups of OBCs, the working group for the development and welfare of the backward classes (2002-07) has identified the following objectives for their empowerment :
>
> 1) Removal of the conditions under which they are collectively distinguishable from the advanced social category as socially backward.
>
> 2) To make the above objevctive achievable, removal of the educational backwardness of the BCs as a whole and of each BC.
>
> 3) To make the above two objectives achievable, removal of the economic underdevelopment, economic dependency, economic inadequacy and economic exploitation from which the BCs suffer- this is to be done in respect of the BCs as a whole and in respect of each BC.

a) As one aspect of this, strengthening BCs communities in their respective traditional occupations (except those occupations which are stigmatized as unclean and from which they should be liberated) and securing for them control and mastery over their respective traditional fields of economy.

b) As another aspect of this, liberating those BCs communities which have been traditionally condemned to highly stigmatized occupations like manual handling of human refuse and providing them training to shift in other occupations without loss of employment or income.

c) Providing opportunities through education and training and appropriate economic measures for BCs to diversify them into a variety of modern occupations unconnected with their caste traditions and that too have social prestige attached to it.

d) Creating a situation in which BC as a whole and each BC is found initially with the help of supportive measures and ultimately on their own strength, in due proportion in all types of occupations including occupations of social prestige.

On the above, the working group recommended that the planning commission and the Government of India as a whole and every Ministry there/of and similarly the State Government and the State Planning Commission/Planning Board/ Department and every State Department should specifically and clearly without reservation adopt the objectives enlisted above and be guided by the vision of development and empowerment in formulating plans for them.

References

- Annual Report 2003-04: Ministry of Social Justice & Empowerment, Government of India, New Delhi.
- Approach papers of different five years plan, Planning Commission, Government of India, New Delhi.
- Chairperson: P.S.Krishnan, Working Group on Empowerment of Backward Classes in Tenth Plan(2002-07), Ministry of Social Justice & Empowerment, New Delhi.
- Mungerilal Commission Report, Part-III, Bihar Government Publication, Patna.
- Sinha, S.K.(2005) Backward Classes in India: Various Dimensions, Raj Publications, New Delhi.
- *www.bihar.nic.in(Information* on various welfare measures on OBCs of the State).

Epilogue

Caste is the basic pillar of Indian society which is undergoing a continuous process of transformation. At present the system of social transformation is not only based on the notion of ritual purity and pollution, but also on secular considerations of economic and occupational status, educational achievement and political power. In spite that, social inequality persists and different castes are involved in their own occupation prescribed for them since time immemorial with few changes in recent years due to globalization and liberalization of market economy. Jajmani system, as conceptualise by Wiser, bears the testimony of this unequal social relationship in rural India.

Bihar is grasped with many problems including lack of investment leading to low productivity and incomes and poverty and this situation has been further aggravated during the last 15 years (1990-2005). Besides crimes and scams, criminals and bahubalis too became part of the nexus, says Shaibal Gupta. "They are useful in mobilizing the right contacts and crowds during the election campaigns".

These intermediate caste/class with growing economic strength became significant political force since it realized the power of its votes and began to assert itself independence and became less deferential to the upper caste/class. This cultivating intermediate caste/class broke with the Congress Party over its neglect of agriculture and formed separate political party and also backed up those party who served their interest.

Now Bihar has moved into post-Mandalism - a paradigm or framework which makes a clear break with the politics of social justice based on the self-assertion of underprivileged social layers. In this second phase of Mandal politics, probably the Most Backward Castes/Classes will play an important role in the State politics with support from other social groups.These scattered castes/classes are now asserting themselves in all sphere of activities. Soon they could articulate their specific demands or insists on political self-representation. Perhaps, this may lead to some more violence in the State if it is not tackled in the best possible manner. Dipankar Gupta is of the view that the so-called intermediate backward castes having hold on rural economy, may perhaps on occasion become more brutal in their prosecution of the SCs and MBCs than the Brahmins.

By virtue of centuries of oppression, SCs and STs were singled out for reservation in the Indian Constitution but there were no consensus on this matter for OBCs. However they also got it by their own virtue and in this process the caste became synonymous with the class for the purpose of reservation. There is enough evidence to suggest that OBCs such as yadavs, Kurmis, Koeries and some other upper backwards in Bihar have benefited greatly from the reservation and at present can not be considered backward anymore. They have become dominant groups in term of political and economic sense but the tool of creamy layer, that exit for the purpose of exclusion of these castes, is toothless in the sense as it has not been used effectively by the State Government. And those who for various reasons have not been able to profit from reservation continue to languish. These groups known as MBCs are now uniting themselves for asserting their power to achieve their rights. As stated above, it is the right time to rethink over these caste groups and policy should be framed accordingly. To channelise their energy in the right direction, and for arousal of their caste identity, political and cultural nationalism is must, as it will also create a sense of confidence and pride among them, which will be helpful in diluting the aggressiveness of this caste groups with OBCs and other groups of the State. This will also contribute in overall development of the State.

References

* Bidwai, Praful "Heading for Mandal Mark-II? Frontline, Vol-22, Issue-25, November 5th,2005.
* "Caste Vs. Class, Times of India, June 14th, 2006. N. Delhi edition
* Gupta, Dipankar "Sweeping Statements" Hindustan Times, 12-6-2006, N. Delhi.
* K.K. Mohanti (1993) Social Mobility and Caste Dynamics, Rawat Publications, Jaipur/Delhi.
* Rudolph & Rudolph (1967) The Modernity of Tradition-Political Development in India, Orient Longman Ltd.; Bombay.
* Singh, Amrendra Kumar (2005) Discrimination Amongst Harijans, Sunrise Publications, Delhi.

Annexure - 1

पत्रांक-11/वि0-पि0व0आ0-6/2005का0.....1800..............

बिहार सरकार

कार्मिक एवं प्रशासनिक सुधार विभाग

प्रेषक

सरयुग प्रसाद,
सरकार के उप सचिव ।

सेवा में,

सभी आयुक्त एवं सचिव
अध्यक्ष लोक उद्यम ब्यूरो
सभी प्रमण्डलीय आयुक्त
सभी विश्वविधालयों के कुलपति
सभी जिला प्रदाधिकारी
सचिव, बिहार लोक सेवा आयोग, पटना
परीक्षा नियंत्रक,
बिहार संयुक्त प्रवेश प्रतियोगिता परीक्षा पर्षद

सचिव कर्मचारी चयन आयोग, पटना
सदस्य सचिव पिछड़े वर्गो के लिए राज्य आयोग, पटना
निबंधक महाधिवक्ता बिहार का कार्यालय
उच्च न्यायालय, पटना।

पटना -15, दिनांक-01 सितम्बर, 2005

विषय:- बिहार पदों एवं सेवाओं को रिक्तियों में आरक्षण (अनुसूचित जातियों/अनुसूचित जनजातियों एवं अन्य पिछड़े वर्गो के लिए (अधिनियम -1991) बिहार अधिनियम-2/1992 की अत्यंत पिछड़े वर्गो की सूची (अनुसूची-1)एवं अन्य पिछड़े वर्गो की सूची (अनुसूची -2) का सम्प्रेषण।

महोदय

निदेशानुसार उपर्युक्त विषय के संबंध में कहना है कि कार्मिक एवं प्रशासनिक सुधार विभाग के पत्रांक-5 दिनांक-18.2.1999 द्वारा राज्य में अधिवासित अत्यन्त पिछड़े वर्गो एवं पिछड़े वर्गो की सूची परिचालित की गई थी। कालक्रम से बिहार अधिनियम-3/1992 में अधिसूचित अत्यन्त पिछड़े वर्गो एवं पिछड़े वर्गो की सूची में संशोधन किया जाता रहा है जिसे जन साधारण की जानकारी के लिए पुन: परिचलित किये जाने की आवश्यकता महसूस की गई है।

2. उक्त परिप्रेक्ष्य में बिहार अधिनियम -3, 1992 के अन्तर्गत अत्यन्त पिछड़े वर्गो की सूची (अनुसूची-1) एवं पिछड़े वर्गो की सूची (अनुसूची-2) की अद्यतन सूची सुलभ प्रसंग हेतु सम-प्रेषित की जा रही है।

अनुरोध है कि इसे अधीनस्थ कार्यालयों/ पदाधिकारियों के, बीच परिचालित कर दिया जाए ताकि संबंधित व्यक्तियों को जाति प्रमाण-पत्र प्राप्त करने में कोई असुविधा न हों। परन्तु किसी जाति विशेष के संबंध में संदेह होने पर मूल अधिनियम तथा संकल्प की प्रविर्ष्टि को संदर्भ किया जाए।

विश्वासभाजन

हस्ताक्षर/-

सरकार के उप सचिव।

सीधी भर्ती के लिए आरक्षण (1) किसी स्थापना में सेवाओं और पदों की सभी नियुक्तियां, जो सीधी भर्ती के द्वारा भरी जाने वाली हों, निम्नलिखित रूप से विनियमित की जायेगी यथा:-

(क) खुली गुणागुण कोटि से - 50 प्रतिशत

(ख) आरक्षित कोटि से - 50 प्रतिशत

(2) आरक्षित कोटि की 50 प्रतिशत रिक्तियों में से आरक्षित उम्मीदवारों की विभिन्न कोटियों की रिक्तियां इस अधिनियम के अन्य उपबंधों के अध्याधीन निम्नलिखित रूप में होंगी:-

		झारखण्ड़ बंटवारा के पूर्व A		झारखण्ड़ बंटवारा के बाद B
(क)	अनुसूचित जातियाँ	14%	-	16% (+2)
(ख)	अनुसूचित जन जातियाँ	10%	-	01% (-9)
(ग)	अत्यन्त पिछड़ा वर्ग	14%	-	18% (+4)
(घ)	पिछड़ा वर्ग	10%	-	12% (+2)
(ड़)	पिछड़े वर्गो की महिलाएँ	02%	-	03% (+1)
		कुल -50%		कुल -50%

This change will be done by amending section 4 of the sub-section (2) in Bihar ordinance 3, of 1992.

अत्यन्त पिछड़े वर्गो की सूची

(अनुसूची-1)

1.	कपारिया	kapadia
2.	कानू	kanu
3.	(विलोपित)	Deleted
4.	कलन्दर	kalander
5.	कोछ	kochh
6.	कुर्मी (महतो)झारखंड स्वशासी क्षेत्र	kurmi (Mahto) (Jharkhand autonomous area)

7.	केवट (कउट)	kewat (kaut)
8.	कादर	kadar
9.	कोरा	kaura
10.	कोरक	korku
11.	केवर्त	kaibart
12.	(विलोपित)	deleted
13.	खटवा	khatwa
14.	(विलोपित)	deleted
15.	खतौरी	khatouri
16.	खंगर	khangar
17.	खटिक	khatik
18.	खेलटा	khelta
19.	खतवे	khatwe
20.	(विलोपित)	Deleted
21.	गोड़ी (छावी)	Gorhi (chhabi)
22.	गंगाई (नगेश)	Gangai (Nagesh)
23.	गंगोता	Gangota
24.	गोड़ या गोंड़ (सारण तथा रोहतास जिले में)	Gour or Gonr (In saran & rohtas districts)
25.	गधर्व	Gandharb
26.	गुलगुलिया	Gulgulia
27.	गोड़	Gour
28.	चाय	Chain
29.	चपोता	Chapota
30.	चन्द्रवंशी (कहार, कमकर)	Chandrabansi (Kahar, Kamkar)
31.	टिकुलहार	Tikulhar
32.	ढेंकारू	Dhekaru
33.	ताती(ततवा)	Tanti (Tatwa)
34.	तमरिया	Tamaria
35.	तुरहा	Turha
36.	तियर	Tiar
37.	(विलोपित)	Deleted

38.	धानुक	Dhanuk
39.	धामिन	Dhamin
40.	धीमर	Dhimar
41.	धनवार	Dhanwar
42.	नोनिया	Nonia
43.	नइया	Naiya
44.	नाई	Nai
45.	नामशुद्र	Namsudar
46.	पाण्डी	Pandi
47.	पाल(भेड़िहार, गड़ेरी)	Pal(Bherihar, Gareri)
48.	प्रधान	Pradhan
49.	पिनगनिया	Pingania
50.	पहिरा	Pahira
51.	वारी	Bari
52.	बेलदार	Beldar
53.	बिन्द	Bind
54.	(विलोपित)	Deleted
55.	सखड़ा	Shekhra
56.	बागदी	Bagdi
57.	भुईयार	Bhuiyar
58.	भार	Bhar
59.	(विलोपित)	Deleted
60.	भास्कर	Bhaskar
61.	माली(मालाकार)	Mali (malakar)
62.	मांगर	Mangar
63.	मदार	Madar
64.	मल्लाह (सुरहिया)	Mallah(Surhia)
65.	मझवार	Majhwar
66.	मारकन्डे	Markandey
67.	मोरियारी	Moriyari
68.	मलार (मालहोर)	Malar(Malher)
69.	मौलिक	Molik

70.	राजधोबी	Rajdhobi
71.	राजभर	Rajbhar
72.	रंगवा	Rangwa
73.	वनपर	Banpar
74.	(विलोपित)	Deleted
75.	सौटा(सोता)	Shota (Shota)
76.	संतराश(केवल नवादा जिले के लिए)	Sang-trash for Nawada only)
77.	(विलोपित)	Deleted
78.	अघोरी	Aghouri
79.	अबदल	Abdal
80.	कसाब (कसाई)(मुस्लिम)	Kasab(kasai)(Muslim)
81.	चीक (मुस्लिम)	Chik(Muslim)
82.	डफाली(मुस्लिम)	Dafali(Muslim)
83.	धुनिया(मुस्लिम)	Dhunia(Muslim)
84.	धोबी (मुस्लिम)	Dhobi(Muslim)
85.	नट (मुस्लिम)	Nut(Muslim)
86.	पमरिया(मुस्लिम)	Pamaria(Muslim)
87.	भठियारा(मुस्लिम)	Bhathiara(Muslim)
88.	भाट(मुस्लिम)	Bhat(Muslim)
89.	महतर, लालबेगीया, हलालखोर, भंगी (मुस्लिम)	Mehater,Lalbegia, Halalkhor, Bhangi(Muslim)
90.	मिरियासीन (मुस्लिम)	Miriasin(Muslim)
91.	मदारी(मुस्लिम)	Madari(Muslim)
92.	मीरशिकार(मुस्लिम)	Meershikar(Muslim)
93.	साई/फकीर/दिवान/मदार/(मुस्लिम)	Saeen/Fakir/Diwan/Madar(Muslim)
94.	मोमिन (मुस्लिम)(जुलाह/अंसारी)	Momin (Muslim)(Julaha/Ansari)
95.	अमात	Amat
96.	चुड़ीहार(मुस्लिम)	Churihar(Muslim)
97.	प्रजापति(कुम्हार)	Prajapati(Kumhar)
98.	राईन या कुंजरा(मुस्लिम)	Raeen or Kunjara(Muslim)
99.	सोयर	Soyar
100.	ठकुराई (मुस्लिम)	Thakurai(Muslim)

101. नागर	Nagar
102. शेरशाहबादी	Shershahbadi
103. बक्खो (मुस्लिम)	Bakkho(Muslim)
104. अदरखी	Adrakhi
105. छीपी	Chhipi
106. तिली	Tili
107. इदरीसी या दर्जी (मुस्लिम)	Idrisi or Darji(Muslim)
108. सैकलगर(सिकलगर)(मुस्लिम)	Saikalgar(Sikalgar)(Muslim)
109. रंगरेज(मुस्लिम)	Rangrej(Muslim)
110. सिदुरिया बनिया	Sinduria Bania
111. मुकरी(मुस्लिम)	Mukeri(Muslim)
112. ईटफरोश/ईटाफरोश/ गदेहड़ी / ईटपज इब्राहिमी(मुस्लिम)	Itfarosh/Itafarosh/Gadheri/ Itpaj Ibrahimi(Muslim)

नोट:-उन जातियों तथा वर्गो को जिन्हें मुस्लिम नहीं लिखा गया है, हिन्दु तथा मुस्लिम दोनों जातियों का समझना चाहिए, जैसे तेली में दोनों:- हिन्दु तथा मुसलमान तेली।

(1) बिहार पदों एवं सेवाओं की रिक्तियों में आरक्षण (अनुसूचित जातियों/अनुसूचित जनजातियों एवं अन्य पिछड़े वर्गो के लिए) अधिनियम-1991(बिहार अधिनियम-3/1992) के अत्यन्त पिछड़े वर्गो की सूची(अनुसूची-1) में जिन जातियों/वर्गो का समावेशन किया गया है, उसका विवरण निम्नांकित है।

सूची क्रमांक	जाति का नाम	अधिनियम/संकल्प संख्या
6.	कुर्मी (महतो) केवल छोटानागपुर	संकल्प सं0-110, दि0-24.7.1997 डिविजन के लिए विलोपित कर कुर्मी (महतो) झझरखंड स्वशासी क्षेत्र अंकित किया गया।
30.	कर्मकर	संकल्प सं0-8, दि0-8.1.2004
93.	फकीर, दिवान, मदार(मुस्लिम)	संकल्प सं0-97, दि0-3.3.2003
94.	जुलाहा/अंसारी	संकल्प सं0-432, दि0-16.9.2002

95.	अमात	बिहार अधिनियम-6/1996 96.
96.	चुड़ीहार(मुस्लिम)	बिहार अधिनियम-6/1996
97.	प्रजापति (कुम्हार)	बिहार अधिनियम-6/1996
98.	राईन या कुंजरा(मुस्लिम)	बिहार अधिनियम-6/1996
99.	सोयर	बिहार अधिनियम-6/1996
100.	ठकुराई (मुस्लिम)	संकल्प सं0-178, दि0-18.12.1995
101.	नागर	संकल्प सं0-135, दि0-4.9.1996
102.	शेरशाहबादी	संकल्प सं0-135, दि0-4.9.1996
103.	बक्खो (मुस्लिम)	संकल्प सं0-183, दि0-27.11.1996
104.	अदरखी	संकल्प सं0-183, दि0-27.11.1996
105.	छीपी	संकल्प सं0-183, दि0-27.11.1996
106.	तिली	संकल्प सं0-109, दि0-24.07.1997
107.	इदरीशी या दर्जी(मुस्लिम)	संकल्प सं0-34, दि0-17.03.1998
108.	सैकलगर(सिकलगर)(मुस्लिम)	संकल्प सं0-165, दि0-20.12.1997
109.	रंगरेज (मुस्लिम)	संकल्प सं0-211, दि0-10.04.2001
110.	सिन्दुरिया बनिया	संकल्प सं0-129, दि0-2.04.2002
111.	मुकेरी(मुस्लिम)	संकल्प सं0-673, दि0-23.11.2001
112.	ईटफरोश/ईटाफरोश/ गदेहड़ी / ईटपज इब्राहिमी(मुस्लिम)	संकल्प सं0-499, दि0-16.10.2003

नोटः- बिहार पदों एवं सेवाओ की रिक्तियों में आरक्षण (अनुसूचित जातियों/अनुसूचित जनजातियों एवं अन्य पिछड़े वर्गो के लिए) अधिनियम-1991(बिहार अधिनियम-3/1992) के अत्यन्त पिछड़े वर्गो की सूची(अनुसूची-1) के क्रमांक-3, 12, 14, 20, 37, 54, 59, 74, 77, पर अंकित जातियों को भारत सरकार द्वारा अनुसूचित जाति/अनुसूचित जनजाति की सूची में सम्मिलित किये जाने के फलस्वरूप स्वतः विलोपित समझे जायेंगे।

पिछड़े वर्गों की सूची
(अनुसूची-2)

1.	(विलोपित)	Deleted
2.	कागजी	Kagji
3.	कमार(लोहार और कर्मकार)	Kamar(Lohar-Karmkar)
4.	कुशवाहा (कोईरी)	Kushwaha (Koiri)
5.	कोस्ता	Kosta
6.	गद्दी	Gaddi
7.	घटवार	Ghatwar
8.	विलोपित	Deleted
9.	चनउ	Chanau
10.	जदुपतिया	Jadupatia
11.	जोगी(जुगी)	Jogi(Jugi)
12.	तमोली	Tamoli
13.	तेली	Teli
14.	देवहार	Dewhar
15.	नालबंद(मुस्लिम)	Nalband(Muslim)
16.	विलोपित	Deleted
17.	परथा	Partha
18.	बढ़ई	Barhi
19.	बरई	Barai
20.	बनिया- (सूढ़ी, हलवाई, मोदक/मायरा, रोनियार, पनसारी, मोदी, कसेरा, केशरवानी, ठठेरा, कलवार, (कलाल/एराकी), वियाहुत कलवार), पटवा, कमलापूरी वैश्य, माहुरीवैश्य, अवधबनिया, बंगीवैश्य (बंगालीबनिया), वर्नवाल, अग्रहरीवैश्य, पोद्दार, कसौधन, गंधबनिक, बाथम वैश्य, गोलदार(पूर्वी/पश्चिमी चम्पारण हेतु) कैथल वैश्य/ बनिया, सामरीवैश्य)	Bania (Sundi, Halwai, Modak/ Maira, Roniar, Pansari, Modi, Kasera, Kesarwani, Thathera, Kalwar (Kalal/ Eraki (Biahutkalwar), Patwa, Kamalapuri Vaishya, Mahuri Vaishya, AwadhBania, Bangi Vaishya (Bengali Bania), Barnwal, Agrahari Vaishya, Poddar, Kath Kasaudhan, Gandh banik, Batham Baishya, Goldar

		(East/West Champaran) Kaithal Vaishya/Bania, Samari Vaishya)
21.	विलोपित	Deleted
22.	यादव-(गोला, अहीर, गोरा, घासी, मेहर, सदगोप, लक्ष्मी नारायण गोला)	Yadav- (Gwala, Ahir, Gora, Ghosi, Mehar, Sodgop, lakshmi Narain gola)
23.	राजवंशी(रिसिया या पोलिया)	Raj banshi (Ristia or polia)
24.	विलोपित	Deleted
25.	रौतिया	Rautia
26.	विलोपित	Deleted
27.	लहेड़ी	Laheri
28.	शिवहरी	Shivahari
29.	सोनार	Sonar
30.	सूत्रधार	Sutradhar
31.	सुकियार	Sukiar
32.	विलोपित	Deleted
33.	ईसाई धर्मावलंबी(हरिजन)	Isai Dharmawalambi(harijan)
34.	ईसाई धर्मावलंबी(अन्य पिछड़ी जाति)	Isai Dharmawalambi (Anya pichari Jati)
35.	कुर्मी (महतो)	Kurmi(Muslim)
36.	भाट(हिन्दू)	Bhat (Hindu)
37.	दांगी	Dangi
38.	कुल्हैया	Kulhaiya
39.	जट (हिन्दू) (सहरसा, सुपौल, मधेपुरा और अररिया जिलों के लिए)	Jat (Hindu) (for saharsa, supaul, madhepura and araria districts)
40.	जट (मुस्लिम) (मधुबनी, दरभंगा, सीतामढ़ी, खगड़िया एवं अररिया जिलों के लिए	Jat(Muslim) (for Modhubani, Darbhanga, sitamarhi, Khagaria and Araria district)
41.	मडरिया (मुस्लिम) (मात्र भागलपुर जिला के सन्हौला प्रखंड एवं बांका जिला के धोरैया प्रखंड के लिए)	(only for Sanhaula Block of Bhagalpur Madaria (Muslim) district and Dhoraia Block of Banka district)
42.	दोनवार (केवल मधुबनी और	Donwar (only for Madhubani

	सुपौल जिलों के लिए)	and Supaul districts)
43.	सुरजापुरी मुस्लिम (शेख, सैयद, मल्लिक, मोगल, पठान को छोड़ कर) केवल पूर्णिया, कटिहार, किशनगंज एवं अररिया जिलों के लिए)	Surjapuri Muslim (excluding Shedh, Syed, Mllik, Mogal, Pathan) only for Purnea, Katihar, Kishanganj and Araria districts)

नोटः- उन जातियों तथा वर्गो को जिन्हें मुस्लिम नहीं लिखा गया है, हिन्दू तथा मुस्लिम दोनों जातियों का समझना चाहिए। जैसे तेली में दोनों :- हिन्दू तथा मुसलमान तेल।

2. बिहार पदों एवं सेवाओ की रिक्तियों में आरक्षण (अनुसूचित जातियों/अनुसूचित जनजातियों एवं अन्य पिछड़े वर्गो के लिए) अधिनियम-1991(बिहार अधिनियम-3/1992) के पिछड़े वर्गो की सूची (अनुसूची-2) में जिन जातियों का समावेशन किया गया है, उनका विवरण निम्नांकित है:-

सूची क्रमांक	जाति का नाम	अधिनियम/ संकल्प संख्या
36.	भाट (हिन्दु)	बिहार अधिनियम-7/1994
20.	कसौधन	बिहार अधिनियम-6/1996
37.	दांगी	बिहार अधिनियम-6/1996
38.	कुल्हैया	संकल्प सं0-135, दिनांक-4.9.1996
20.	कलाल/एराकी	संकल्प सं0-164, दिनांक-17.10.1996
20.	गंधबनिक	संकल्प सं0-110, दिनांक-24.7.1997
20.	वियाहुत कलवार	संकल्प सं0-79, दिनांक-28.5.1998
20.	मोदक/ मायरा	संकल्प सं0-615, दिनांक-15.10.2001
20.	बाथम वैश्य	संकल्प सं0-102, दिनांक-21.3.2001
20.	गोलदार (पूर्वी/पश्चिमी चम्पारण हेतु)	संकल्प सं0-01, दिनांक-02.01.2002
20.	कैथल वैश्य/ कथ बनिया	संकल्प सं0-248, दिनांक-24.6.2002

20.	सामरी वैश्य	संकल्प सं0-03, दिनांक-09.01.2001
22.	सदगोप	संकल्प सं0-283, दिनांक-5.6.2003
22.	लक्ष्मी नारायण गोला	संकल्प सं0-328, दिनांक-22.12.2000
22.	जट (हिन्दु) (सहरसा, सुपौल, मधेपुरा और अररिया जिलों के लिए)	संकल्प सं0-277, दिनांक-6.11.2000
40.	जट (मुस्लिम) (मधुबनी, दरभंगा, सीतामढ़ी, खगड़िया एवं अररिया जिलों के लिए	संकल्प सं0-277, दिनांक-6.11.2000
41.	मडरिया (मुस्लिम) (मात्र भागलपुर जिला के सन्हौला प्रखंड एवं बांका जिला के धोरैया प्रखंड के लिए)	संकल्प सं0-177, दिनांक-13.5.2002
42.	दोनवार (केवल मधुबनी और सुपौल जिलों के लिए)	संकल्प सं0-530, दिनांक-26.11.2002
43.	सुरजापुरी मुस्लिम (शेख, सैयद, मल्लिक, मोगल, पठान को छोड़ कर) (केवल पूर्णिया, कटिहार, किशनगंज एवं अररिया जिलों के लिए)	संकल्प सं0-500, दिनांक-16.10.2003

नोट:- पिछड़े वर्गो के अनुसूची -2 क्रमांक-1, 8, 16, 20 (सिन्दुरिया बनिया) 21, 24, 26 एवं 32 में अंकित जातियों को विलोपित कर अत्यन्त पिछड़ा वर्ग की सूची (अनुसूची-1) के क्रमांक-क्रमशः 95, 96, 97, 110, 111, 109, 98 एवं 107 पर समावेशित किया गया।

Annexure - 2

बिहार राज्य की पिछड़ी जातियों की सूची (1951 में तैयार की गयी)

एनेक्सर (-1)

जाति तथा वर्ग का नाम।]

		मान्यता का क्षेत्र]
1.	बारी	सारे राज्य में।]
2.	वनपर	„
2.क.	वेदिया	„
3.	बेलदार	„
4.	भठियारा (मुस्लिम)	„
5	भेड़िहार (गड़ेरी)	„
6.	बिन्द	„
7.	चीक (मुस्लिम)	„
8.	डफाली (मुस्लिम)	„
9.	धानुक	„

10. धोबी (मुस्लिम) .. .. „
11. धुनिया (मुस्लिम) .. .. „
12. गोंढ़ी (छावी) .. .. „
13. नाई .. .. .. „
14. कहार. . . .. .. „
15. कसाब. . .. .. „
16. केवट (कउट) .. .. .. „
17. खटिक .. .. .. „
18. माली (मालाकार) .. .. „
19. मल्लाह (सुरहिया) .. .. „
20. मदारी (मुस्लिम) .. .. „
21. मेहतर, लालवेगी, हलालखोर और भंगी „
(मुस्लिम) .. .. „
22. मिरियासिन (मुस्लिम) .. .. „
23. नट (मुस्लिम) .. .. „
24. नोनियां . .. . „
25. पमरिया (मुस्लिम) .. .. „
26. बेखड़ा . . .. .. „
27. तांती (ततवा) .. .. „
28. तुरहा . . .. .. „
29. अबदल .. .. .. पूर्णियाँ।
30. अगरिया . . .. .. लातेहार और गुमला।
31. अघोरी. . . . . पटना तथा तिरहुत डिवीजन।
32. बागदी .. . . धनबाद।
33. बनजारा . . . . संताल परगना।
34. भार . . . . छोटानागपुर।
35. भास्कर. . . .. .. पलामू।
36. भुईहार . . . . छोटानागपुर।

37. भूइयो . . .	. . . .	तिरहुत, भागलपुर और छोटानागपुर डिवीजन में पलामू जिले को छोड़कर।
38. चांय . . .	. . . .	उत्तर तथा दक्षिण बिहार।
39. चपोता . .	. . . .	मुख्यतः संताल परगना में।
40. प्यामीन . .	. . . .	उत्तरी बिहार।
41. धनवार . .	. . . .	छोटानागपुर।
42. ढेकारू. .	. . . .	दुमका।
43. धीमर . .	. . . .	दरभंगा।
44. गंधर्व . .	. . . .	उत्तरी बिहार और भागलपुर।
45. गंगाई(गनेरा) . .	. . . .	पूर्णियां एवं सहरसा।
46. गंगौता(गंगौता)	. . . .	भागलपुर डिवीजन।
47. गुलगुलिया . .	. . . .	छोटानागपुर
48. जदुपतिया. .	. . . .	संताल परगना।
49. कादर	. . . .	भागलपुर और संताल परगना।
50. कैबर्त	. . . .	धनबाद, भागलपुर, पूर्णिया और सहरसा।
51. कलन्दर. .	. . . .	नवादा और सिवान।
52. कौरा	. . . .	सिंहभूम ।
53. कवार	. . . .	छोटानागपुर।
54. खटवा . .	. . . .	उत्तरी बिहार।
55. खेतौरी . .	. . . .	छोटानागपुर और संताल परगना।
56. खेलटा . .	. . . .	संताल परगना।
57. कोछ	. . . .	पूर्णियां।
58. कोरकू. .	. . . .	भभुआ।
59. कुमार भाग पहाड़िया	. . . .	संताल परगना जिले में ।
60. कुर्मी (महतो)	. . . .	छोटानागपुर डिवीजन।
61. मझवार. .	. . . .	

62. मलार(मालहोर).	.. ..	
63. मांगर (मागर)	.. ..	चम्पारण।
64. मारकण्डे. .	.. ..	संताल परगना, भागलपूर, पूर्णिया और सहरसा।
65. मौलिक . .	.. ..	संताल परगना और गया।
66. मदार	.. ..	दरभंगा।
67. मोरियारी. .	.. ..	संताल परगना और गया।
68. नामशुद्र . .	.. ..	किशनगंज।
69. नइया	.. ..	भागलपुर डिविजन।
70. प्रधान. .	.. ..	छोटानागपुर।
71. पहिरा. .	.. ..	धनबाद और रांची।
72. पाण्डो. .	.. ..	रांची।
73. पिनगनिया. .	.. ..	रांची।
74. सौटा (सोता). .	.. ..	रांची और सिंहभूम।
75. तमरिया. .	.. ..	छोटानागपुर।
76. थारू	.. ..	चम्पारण।
77. तियर	.. ..	भागलपुर डिवीजन।
78. राजधोबी. .	.. ..	सहरसा जिला के सुपौल, मधेपुरा अनुमंडल, जिला के सदर और अररिया अनुमंडल ।
79. खंगर	.. ..	पूर्णियां।

नोट –उन जातियों तथा वर्गो को, जिन्हें मुस्लिम नहीं लिखा गया है, उन्हें हिन्दु तथा मुसलमान दोनों जाति का समझना चाहिए।

एनेक्सर – 2

1. अहीर (ग्वाला, यादव, गौरा, धासी और मेहर),
2. अमान,
3. बढ़ही,
4. बरई,

5. बनिया, (सूड़ी हलवाई, रौनियार, पंसारी, मोदी, कसेरा, केसरवानी, ठठेरा, कलवार, पटका वर्णवाल)
6. भाट,
7. चुड़िहारा (मुस्लिम),
8. देवहार,
9. पटवार,
10. इदरिसी या दर्जी (मुस्लिम)
11. जोगी (जुगी), (11-क) कागजी,
12. कानू,
13. कमार (लोहार और कर्मकार),
14. कोईरी,
15. कुम्हार, (15-क) कुर्मी (छोटानागपुर के बाहर),
16. लहेरी,
17. मीरशीकार (मुस्लिम)
18. मोमीन (मुस्लिम)
19. नालबंद (मुस्लिम)
20. परवा,
21. राजवंशी (रेसिया और पोलिया)
22. रंगरेज (मुस्लिम)
23. रौतिया,
24. राइन या कुंजरा(मुस्लिम), (24-क) साई (मुस्लिम),
25. सोनार,
26. सुकिआर,
27. तमोली,
28. तेली
29. ईसाई धर्मांवलम्बी हरिजन,
30. कोस्टा,

नोट -उन जाति तथा वर्गो को जिन्हें मुस्लिम नही लिखा गया है उन्हें हिन्दु तथा मुसलमान दोनों ही जाति का समझना चाहिए जैसे तेली से दोनों हिन्दु तथा मुस्लिम तेली।

Annexure - 3

सं. 3। एस-2-119।70-नि0-22297

नियुक्ति विभाग।

संकल्प 1

23 दिसम्बर 1971

विषय - पिछड़ा वर्ग आयोग का गठन ।

1 राज्य सरकार ने अपने संकल्प संख्या 9355, दिनांक 1 जून 1971 के द्वारा एक पिछड़ा वर्ग आयोग का गठन किया था, जिसमें 20 सदस्य मनोनीत किये गये थे।

2. जिन उद्देश्य की प्राप्ती हेतु आयोग का गठन किया गया था उसे स्वीकार करते हुए राज्य सरकार ने पुनर्विचार कर यह निर्णय लिया कि 20 सदस्यों की बड़ी समिति के माध्यम से यह प्रयोजन सिद्ध नहीं होगा। अतः नियुक्ति विभाग के संकल्प संख्या 11441, दिनांक 25 जून 1971 के द्वारा मनोनयन सम्बन्धी अधिसूचना रद्द कर दी गयी एवं एक छोटी समिति गठित करने का निर्णय लिया गया।

3. अनुसूचित जाति, अनुसूचित जन-जाति एवं अन्य पिछड़ी जाति के लोगों के हित तथा कल्याण की रक्षा सम्बंधी सरकारी आदेशों के अनुपालन में हुई त्रुटियों के कौन-कौन कारण है तथा इन जातियों के सर्वागीण अभ्युदय के लिये और कौन-कौन सी सुविधाएँ दी जाये, इन पर विचार करने के लिये राज्य सरकार ने पुन: एक पिछड़ा वर्ग आयोग का गठन किया है, जिसमें निम्नलिखित सज्ञन सदस्य होंगे:-

(1) श्री मुंगरी लाल- अध्यक्ष ।

सदस्यगण।

(2) श्री अब्दुल क्यूम अंसारी।

(3) श्री धनिक लाल मंडल ।

(4) श्री देवशरण सिंह ।

(5) श्री करमचन्द्र भगत।

(6) श्री वैद्यनाथ दास।

(7) श्री यमुना प्रसाद सिंह।

4.। आयोग का मुख्यालय पटना होगा। आयोग जिन बिन्दुओं पर जांच-पड़ताल की अनुशंसा देगा उनका उल्लेख अनुलग्नक में है।

5.। आयोग की कालावधि 31 दिसम्बर 1972 तक होगी ।

आदेश- इस संकल्प को "बिहार गजट" में प्रकाशित किया जाये एवं इसकी एक प्रतिलिपि सभी सरकारी विभाग/सभी प्रमंडलीय आयुक्त / सभी जिला पदाधिकारी / बिहार विधान परिषद् तथा महालेखापाल, बिहार को सूचनार्थ भेजी जाये ।

बिहार-राज्य पाल के आदेश से,

शिवनाथ सैगल

सरकार के सचिव

पिछड़ा वर्ग ग्रायोग के ग्रध्यक्ष एवं सदस्यों के नाम तथा कालावधि ।

क्र संख्या।	नाम।	पदनाम।	ग्रवधि।
1-	श्री मुंगेरी लाल	. .ग्रध्यक्ष. . .	दिनांक 30 दिसम्बर 1971 से ग्रन्तिम तिथि तक।
2-	श्री ग्रब्दुल क्यूम ग्रन्सारी	. .सदस्य . .	दिनांक 30 दिसम्बर 1971 से दिनांक 18 जनवरी 1973 तक।
3-	श्री देवशरण सिंह	. .सदस्य . .	दिनांक 30 दिसम्बर 1971 से दिनांक 9 जुलाई 1975।
4-	श्री यमुना प्रसाद सिंह	. .सदस्य . .	दिनांक 30 दिसम्बर 1971 से दिनांक 29 जून 1976 तक।
5-	श्री धनिक लाल मंडल	. .सदस्य . .	दिनांक 30 दिसम्बर 1971 से ग्रन्तिम तिथि तक।
6-	श्री करम चन्द भगत	. .सदस्य . .	दिनांक 30 दिसम्बर 1971 से दिनांक 24 फरवरी 1975।
7-	श्री पृथ्वी चन्द किस्कु	. .सदस्य . .	दिनांक 25 फरवरी 1975 से दिनांक 10 जून 19761
8-	श्री वैद्यनाथ दास	. .सदस्य . .	दिनांक 30 दिसम्बर 1971 से ग्रन्तिम तिथि तक।
9-	*श्री शमसूल होदा ग्रस्थानवी	. .सदस्य . .	दिनांक 28 मई 1973 से ग्रन्तिम तिथि तक।
10-	श्री ठाकुर प्रसाद	. .सदस्य-सचिव	दिनांक 20 जनवरी 1972 से ग्रन्तिम तिथि तक।

* (दिनांक 20 जनवरी 1972 से दिनांक 31 दिसम्बर 1972 तक उप-सचिव कार्मिक विभाग के रूप में अपने कर्त्तव्य के अतिरिक्त सदस्य-सचिव के रूप में भी कार्य करते थे। सेवा-निवृत्ति होने के बाद दिनांक 1 जनवरी 1973 से अवैतनिक सदस्य-सचिव के रूप में अन्तिम तिथि तक कार्य करते रहे।)

Annexure - 4

बिहार गजट

असाधारण अंक (बिहार सरकार-द्वारा प्रकाशित)

पटना शनिवार 21 अगस्त, 1993

विधि विभाग

(अधिसूचनाएं)

संख्या एल. जी. 1-03/93 पेज-376- बिहार विधान मंडल द्वारा यथा-पारित निम्नलिखित अधिनियम जिस पर राज्यपाल 19 अगस्त 1993 को अनुमति दे चुके हैं, इसके द्वारा सर्व-साधारण की सूचना के लिये प्रकाशित किया जाता है।

[Bihar Act 12, 1993]

THE STATE COMMISSION FOR BACWARD CLASSES BILL, 1993

A

BILL

TO CONSTITUTE A STATE COMMISSION FOR

BACKWARD CLASSES OTHER THAN THE SCHEDULED CASTES AND THE SCHEDULED TRIBES AND TO PROVIDE FOR MATTER'S CONNECTED THERE-WITH OR INCIDENTAL THERETO ....

Be it enacted by the legislature of the State of Bihar in the forty fourth year of the Republic of India as follows.

CHAPTER I

Preliminary

1. Short title, extent and commencement.- (1) This Act may be called the State Commission for Backward Classes Act, 1993

   (2) It extends to the whole of the State of Bihar

   (3) It shall come into force at once

2. Definitions.- In this Act, unless the context otherwise requires-

   (a) "Backward Classes " means such backward Classes other than the Scheduled Castes and the Schduled Tribes specified or to be specified in the Schedule appended to Bihar Act 3, 1992.

   (b) "Commision" means the State Commission for Backward Classes constituted under section-3

   (c) "Lists" means Lists prepared by the State Government from time to time for purposes of making provision for the reservation of appointments or posts in favour of backward Classes of citizens which, in the opinion of the Government, are not adequately represented in the services under the State Government and any local or other authority within the State or under the control of the State Government;

   (d) "Member" means a Member of the Commission

and includes the Chairperson;

(e) "Prescribed" means prescribed by rules made under this Act.

CHAPTER II

The State Commission for Backward Classes

3. Constitution of the State Commission for Backward Classes.-(1) The State Government Shall constitute a body to be known as the State Commission for Backward Classes to exercise the powers conferred on and to perform the functions assigned to it under this Act.

(2) The Commission shall consist of the following members nominated by the State Government:-

(a) A Chairperson ;

(b) A social scientist;

(c) Two persons, who have special knowledge in matters relating to backward classes and

(d) a Member-Secretary, Who is or has been an officer of the State Government in the rank of a Secretary, Special Secretary, Additional Secretary or joint Sscretary to the Government of Bihar.

4. Term of Office and conditions of service of Chairperson and Members.- (1) Every Member shall hold office for a term of three year from the date he assumes office.

(2) A member may, by writing under his hand addressed to the State Government, resign from the office of Chairperson or, as the case may be, of Member at any time.

(3) The State Government shall remove a person from the office of Member, if that person-

(a) Becomes an undischarged insolvent;

(b) is convicted and sentenced to imprisonment for an offence Which, in the opinion of the State Government involves moral turpitude.

(c) Becomes of unsound mind and stands so declared by a competent court.

(d) Refuses to act or becomes incapable of action..

(e) is, without obtaining leave of absence from the Commission, absent from three consecutive meetings of the Commission; or

(f) has, in the opinion of the State Government so abused the position of chairperson or Member as to render that person's continuance in office detrimental to the interests of backward classes or the public interest:

Provided that no person shall be removed under this clause until that person has been given an opportunity of being heard in the matter.

(4) A vacancy caused under sub-section (2) or otherwise shall be filled by fresh nomination.

(5) The salaries and allowances payable to and the other terms and conditions of service of the Chairperson and Members shall be such as may be prescribed.

(1) Officers and other employees of the Commission.- (1) The State Government shall provide the Commission with such officers and employees as may be necessary for the efficient performance of the function of the Commission.

(2) The salaries and allowances payable to and the other terms and conditions of service of the officers and other employees appointed for the purpose of the Commission shall be such as may be prescribed.

6. **Salaries and allowances to be paid out of grants.-** The salaries and allowances payable to the Chairperson and Member and the administrative expenses including salaries, allowances and pensions payable to the officers and other employees referred to in Section 5, shall be paid out of the grants referred to in sub-section (1) of Section 12.

7. **Vacancies, etc. not to invalidate proceedings of the Commission.-** No act or proceeding of the Commission shall be invalid merely on the ground of the existence of any vacancy or defect in the constitution of the Commission.

8. **Procedure to be regulated by the Commisssion.-** (1) The Commission shall meet as and when necessary at such time and place as the Chairperson may think fit.

   (2) The Commission shall regulate its own procedure.

   (3) All orders and decisions of the Commission shall be authenticated by the Member-Secretary or any other officer of the Commisssion duly authorised by the Member-Secretary in this behalf.

CHAPTER III

Functions and Powers of the Commission

9. **Functions of the Commission.-** (1) The Commission shall examine request for inclusion of any class of citizen as backward class in the lists and hear complaints of over inclusion or under-inclsion of any backward class in such lists and tender such advice to the State Government as it deems appropriate.

   (2) The advice of the Commission shall ordinarily be binding upon the State Government.

10. **Powers of the Commission.-** The Commission shall, while performing its functions under sub-section (1) of Section 9, have all the powers of a Civil Court trying a suit and in particular, in respect of the following matters, namely:-

(a) Summoning and enforcing the attendance of any person and examining him on oath,

(b) Requiring the discovery and production of any document,

(c) Receiving evidence on affidavits;

(d) Requisitioning any public record or copy thereof from any court or office;

(e) Issuing commissions for the eexamination of witnesses and documents; and

(f) Any other matter which may be prescribed.

2. Periodic revision of lists by the State Government.- (1) The State Government may at any time, and shall at the expiration of ten years from the coming into force of this Act and every succeeding period of ten years thereafter, undertake revision of the lists with a view to excluding from such lists those classes who have ceased to be backward classes.

(2) The State Government shall, while undertaking any revision referred to in sub-section (1) consult the Commission

CHAPTER IV

Finance, Accounts, and Audit

12 Grants by the State Government.- (1) The State Government shall pay to the Commission by way of grants such sums of money as the State Government may think it for being utilised for the purposes of this Act.

(2) The Commission may spend such sums as it thinks fit for performing the functions under this Act and such sums shall be treated as expenditure payable out of the grants referred to in sub-section (1)

13. Accounts and Audit.- (1) The Commission shall maintain proper accounts and other relevant records and prepare an annual statement of accounts in such form as may be prescribed by the State Government in consultation with the Accountant-General, Bihar.

    (2) The accounts of the Commission shall be audited by the Accountant-General, Bihar at such intervals as may be specified by him and any expenditure in connection with such audit shall be payable by the Commission to the Accountant-General, Bihar.

    (3) The Accountant-General and any person appointed by him in conection with the audit of the accounts of the Commission under this Act shall have the same rights and privileges and the authority in connection with such audit as the Accountant-General, Bihar generally has in connection with the audit of Government accounts and, in particular, shall have the right to demand the production of books, accounts, connected vouchers and other document and papers and to inspect any of the offices of the Commission.

14. Annual report.-The Commission shall prepare, in such form and at such time, for each financial year, as may be prescribed, its annual-report, giving a full account of its activities during the previous financial year and forward a copy thereof to the State Government.

15. Annual report and audit report to be laid before State Legislature.-The State Government shall cause the annual report, together with a memorandum of action taken on the advice tendered by the Commission under-section 9 and the reasons for the non acceptance, if any, of any such advice, and the audit report to be laid as soon as may be after they are received before each House of State Legislature.

CHAPTER V

Miscellaneous

16. **Chairperson, Members and employees of the Commission to be public servants.-** The Chairperson, Members and employees of the Commission shall be deemed to be public servants within the meaning of section 21 of the Indian penal Code (45 of 1860).

17. **Power to make rules.-**

(1) The State Government may by notification in the official Gazette, make rules for carrying out the provisions of this Act.

(2) In particular, and without prejudice to the generality of the foregoing powers, such rules may provide for all or any of the following matters; namely:-

(a) salaries and allowances payable to, and others terms and conditions of service of the Chairperson and Members under sub-section (5) of section 4 and of officers and other employees under sub-section (2) of section 5;

(b) The form in which the annual statement of accounts shall be maintained under sub-section (1) of section 13;

(c) The form in, and the time at which the annual report shall be prepared under section 14;

(d) Any other matter which is required to be or may be prescribed.

(3) Every rule made under this Act shall be laid, as soon as may be, after it is made before each House of State Legislature while it is in session for a total period of fourteen days which may be comprised in one session or in two or more succesive sessions and if before the expiry

of the session immediately following the session or the successive sessions aforesaid both Houses agreed in making any modification in the rule or both House agree that the rule should not be made, the rule shall thereafter have effect only in such modified form or be of no effect, as the case may be so, however, that any such modification or annulment shall be without prejudice to the validity of anything previously done under rule.

18. Power to remove difficulties.-

(1) If any difficulty arises in giving effect to the provisions of this Act, the State Government may,by order published in the official Gazette, make provisions not inconsistant with the provisions of this Act as appear to it to be necessary or expedient for removing the difficulty.

(2) Every order made under this section shall, soon as may be after it is made, be laid before each House of State Legislature.

19. Repeal and Savings.-

(1) The State Commission for Backward classes second Ordinance, 1993(Bihar Ordinance No. 17,1993) is hereby repealed.

(2) Notwithstanding such repeal, anything done or any action taken in the exercise of any power conferred by or under the said Act shall be deemed to have been done or taken in the exercise of the powers conferred by or under this Act, as if this ordinance were in force on the day on which such thing or action was done or taken.

बिहार राज्यपाल के आदेश से

वि0 प्र0 यादव,

सरकार के प्र0 संयुक्त सचिव।

Annexure - 5

No.36033/3/2004-Estt.(Res.)

Government of India

Ministry of personnel, Pubic Grievances and Pensions

Department of personnel and Training

North Block, New Delhi,

Dated: 9th March, 2004.

OFFICE MEMORANDUM

Subject: Revision of Income criteria to exclude socially advanced persons/ sections (Creamy Layer) from the purview of reservation for Other Backward Classes (OBCs).

The undersigned is directed to invite attention to this Department's O.M.No.36010/22/93-Estt.(SCT) dated 8th September, 1993 which inter alia provides that sons and daughters of persons having gross annual income of Rs. 1.0 lakh or above for a period of three consecutive years fall within the creamy layer and are not entitled to get the benefit of reservation available to the Other Backward

Classes. It has been decided to raise the income limit from Rs. 1 lakh to Rs. 2.5 lakh for determining the creamy layer amongst the OBCs. Accordingly the following entry is hereby substituted for the existing entry against Category VI in the Schedule to the above referred O.M.:

Category	Description of category	To whom the rule of exclusion will apply
VI.	Income/Wealth Test	Son (s) and daughter(s) of (a) Persons having gross annual income of Rs.2.5 lakh or above or possessing wealth above the exemption limit as prescribed in the Wealth Tax Act for a period of three consecutive years. (b) Persons in categories I, II, III and V A who are not disentitled to the benefit of reservation but have income from other sources or wealth which will bring them within the income/wealth criteria mentioned in (a) above. Explaination: Income from salaries or agricultural land shall not be clubbed.

2 The provisions of this Office Memorandum take effect from the 4th February, 2004.

3 All the Ministries / Departments are requested to bring the contents of this Office Memorandum to the notice of all concerned.

(K.G. Verma)

Deputy Secretary to the Government of India

Tele: 23092797

To

1. All the Ministries / Departments of the Government of India.
2. Department of Economic Affairs (Banking Division), New Delhi.
3. Department of Economic Affairs (Insurance Division), New Delhi.
4. Department of Public Enterprises, New Delhi.
5. Railway Board.
6. Union Public Service Commission / Supreme Court of India / Election Commission / Lok Sabha Secretariat / Rajya Sabha Secretariat/ Cabinet Secretariat/ Central Vigilance Commission / President's Secretariat/ Prime Minister's Office / Planning Commission.
7. Staff Selection Commission, CGO Complex, Lodi Road, New Delhi.
8. Ministry of Social Justice and Empowerment, Shastri Bhavan, New Delhi.
9. National Commission for SCs and STs, Lok Nayak Bhavan, New Delhi.
10. National Commission for Backward Classes, Trikoot-1, Bhikaji Cama Place, R.K. Puram, New Delhi.

11. Office of the Comptroller and Auditor General of India, 10, Bahadurshah Zafar Marg, New Delhi -110002.

12. Information and Facilitation Centre, DOPT, North Block, New Delhi . (100 copies)

13. Spare copies -400

Annexure - 6

भारत का राजपत्र

The Gazette of India

असाधारण

EXTRAORDINARY

भाग १–खण्ड् १

PART 1-Section 1

प्राधिकार से प्रकाशित

PUBLISHED BY AUTHORITY

सं. 186] नई दिल्ली, सोमवार, सितम्बर 13, 1993/ भाद्रा 22, 1915

No. 186] NEW DELHI, MONDAY, SEPTEMBER 13, 1993/BHADRA 22, 1915

कल्याण मंत्रालय

संकल्प

नई दिल्ली, 10 सितम्बर, 1993

संख्या 12011/68/93-बी.सी.सी. (सी):---भारत सरकार के ग्रधीन सिविल पदों और सेवाओं में अन्य पिछड़े वर्गो को 27% आरक्षण प्रदान किये जाने के संबंध में इंदिरा साहनी और अन्य बनाम भारत सरकार तथा अन्य (संख्या 1990 का 930 के मामले में उच्चतम न्यायालय द्वारा दिनांक 16-11-92 को दिये गए निर्णय पर भारत सरकार विचार कर रही थी।

2. भारत सरकार के कार्मिक लोक शिकायत तथा पेंशन मंत्रालय (कार्मिक और प्रशिक्षण विभाग) द्वारा 8 सितम्बर, 1993 के कार्यालय ज्ञापन संख्या 36012/12/93-स्थापना (एस.सी.टी.) के माध्यम से जारी किये गये आदेशों के अनुसार पूर्वोक्त आरक्षण के उद्देश्य से प्रथम चरण में अन्य पिछड़े वर्गो के अंतर्गत उन जातियों और समुदायों को रखा जाएगा जो मंडल आयोग की रिपोर्ट और राज्य सरकारों की सूची दोनो में शामिल हों।

3. न्याय मूर्ति (सेवानिवृत्त) आर.एन. प्रसाद की अध्यक्षता में "सम्पन्न वर्ग" (क्रीमी लेयर) संबंधी विशेषज्ञ समिति की (स्थापना निम्नलिखित राज्यों के संबंध में समान सूचियां अनुबन्ध संलग्न) तैयार करने हेतु की गई जिन्होंने उच्चतम न्यायालय के निर्णय की तारीख तक राज्य सेवाओं में आरक्षण के उद्देश्य से अन्य पिछड़े वर्गो की सूची अधिसूचित कर दी थी :-

1-आन्ध्र प्रदेश

2-असम

3-बिहार

4-गोवा

5-गुजरात

6-हरियाणा

7-हिमाचल प्रदेश

8-कर्नाटक

9-केरल

10-मध्य प्रदेश

11-महाराष्ट्र

12–पंजाब

13–तमिलनाडू

14–उत्तर प्रदेश

4. समिति द्वारा तैयार की गई समान सूची सरकार द्वारा स्वीकार कर ली गई है। सरकार ने पूर्वोक्त कार्यालय ज्ञापन के कार्यान्वयन के संदर्भ में अन्य पिछड़े वर्गो की संलग्न सूची को अधिसूचित करने का निर्णय लिया है। ये सूचियां 8 सितम्बर, 1993 से लागू मानी जाएंगी।

5. पूर्वोक्त मामले में उच्चतम न्यायालय द्वारा दिये गये निर्देश के अनुपालन में राष्ट्रीय पिछड़ा वर्ग आयोग अधिनियम, 1993 के प्रावधानों के अंतर्गत स्थापित राष्ट्रीय पिछड़ा वर्ग आयोग नागरिकों के अन्य पिछड़े वर्गो की सूचियों में शामिल किये जाने संबंधी अनुरोध तथा अधिक संख्या और कम संख्या में शामिल किये जाने संबधी शिकायतों की जाँच और सिफारिश करेगा।

आदेश

यह आदेश दिया जाता है कि संकल्प की एक प्रति सभी राज्य सरकारों सघं राज्य क्षेत्र प्रशासनों/मंत्रालय/विभागों की भेजी जाये।

यह भी आदेश दिया जाता है कि सार्वजनिक सूचना हेतू इस संकल्प का भारत के राजपत्र में प्रकाशन किया जाये।

एम० एम० पंडित,

संयुक्त सचिव

Annexure - 7

भारत का राजपत्र

The Gazette of India

असाधारण

EXTRAORDINARY

भाग1–खण्ड1

PART I-Section 1

प्राधिकार से प्रकाशित

PUBLISHED BY AUTHORITY

सं. 83] नई दिल्ली, मंगलवार, मई 16,1995/वैशाख 26,1917

No.83] NEW DELHI, TUESDAY, MAY 16,1995/ VAISAKHA 26, 1917

MINISTRY OF WELFARE

CORRIGENDUM

New Delhi, the 15th May, 1995

No. 12011/21/95-BCC:- In the resolution of the Government of India, Ministry of Welfare, bearing

No. 12011/68/93-BCC(C) dated 10th September, 1993, published in Extraordinary issue of the Gazette of India, Part I, Section I.No. 186, Monday, September, 13,1993/ Bhadra 22, 1915,the following corrections are made:-

Line 1 For "Ministry of Social Welfare" Read "Ministry of Welfare".

Line 7-8 For "relatin" Read "relating".

Line 10 For "OBCs" Read "(OBC)"

Line 22 delete "(Appendix Allahabad)"

For “Appendix” Read “Appendix”

List of States of OBCs".

List of OBCs of states"

STATE	Bihar	Common List
SI.No.	For	Read
8.	Kalbartta	Kaibartta
27.	Khetauri Khataur	Khetauri, Khatauri
34.	Gourh	Gonrh
48.	Tanti (Tatwa) Tati, Tatin	Tanti (Tatwa) Tati, Tatin
60.	Dhaukar	Dhankar
93.	Mirisin (Muslim)	Miriasin (Muslim)
95.	Malai (Malhai)	Malar (Malhar)
107.	Risija	Risiya
109.	Rangrez (Muslim)	Rangrez (Muslim)
119.	Idaisi	Idrisi
	Footnote below the Bihar: Common List	
Line 1	which	while
Line 2	OBG	OBC

Line 2 (except Dhanwar) (except Dhanwar)

BHAGWATI PRASAD

Jt. Secretary

Order that this corrigendum be published in the Gazettee of India for gereral information.

Also ordered that a copy of the corrigendum be communicated to all State Governments/ UTs, Ministries/ Departments of the Government of India, UPSC, SSC etc. for information and record.

BHAGWATI PRASAD

Jt. Secretary

भारत का राजपत्र

The Gazette of India

असाधारण

EXTRAORDINARY

भाग 1-खण्ड 1

PART I Section 1

प्राधिकार से प्रकाशित

PUBLISHED BY AUTHORITY

सं. 129] नई दिल्ली, मंगलवार, जुलाई 8, 1997/ आषाढ़ 17, 1919

No. 129] NEW DELHI, TUESDAY, JULY 8, 1997/ ASADHA 17, 1919

कल्याण मंत्रालय

शुद्धि-पत्र

नई दिल्ली, 8 जुलाई, 1997

सं. 12011/68/93-बी.सी.सी.:- भारत सरकार, कल्याण मंत्रालय के संकल्प संख्या 12011/68/93-बी. सी. सी. दिनांक 10 सितम्बर, 1993/भाद्र 19, 1915 जो भारत के राजपत्र असाधारण भाग-1 खण्ड 1, सं. 186 नई दिल्ली सोमवार, 13 सितम्बर, 1993/भाद्र 22, 1915 द्वारा प्रकाशित हुआ है, में निम्नलिखित शुद्धियां की जाती हैं:-

राज्य: बिहार

क्रम संख्या	के स्थान	पर पढ़ें
76	BEKHRA	SHEKHRA
76	बैखड़ा	शेखड़ा

डा0 एम0 एस0 अहमद, संयुक्त सचिव

Annexure - 8

भारत का राजपत्र

The Gazette of India

असाधारण

EXTRAORDINARY

भाग 1-खण्ड 1

PART I-Section I

प्राधिकार से प्रकाशित

PUBLISHED BY AUTHORITY

सं. 270] नई दिल्ली, सोमवार, दिसम्बर 6,1999/अग्रहायण 15, 1921

No. 270] NEW DELHI, MONDAY, DECEMBER 6,1999/AGRAHAYANA 15, 1921

सामाजिक न्याय और अधिकारिता मंत्रालय

संकल्प

नई दिल्ली, 6 दिसम्बर, 1999

सं. 12011/88/98-बी. सी. सी. -भारत सरकार ने कार्मिक, लोक शिकायत तथा पेंशन (कार्मिक एवं प्रशिक्षण) मंत्रालय के अ. शा. स. 36012/22/93-स्था. (एस.सी.टी.) दिनांक 8 सितम्बर, 1993 के तहत अन्य पिछड़े वर्गो के पक्ष में सीधी भर्ती के माध्यम से भरी जाने वाली केन्द्रीय सरकार के अधीन सिविल पदों और सेवाओं में 27% रिक्तियां आरक्षित की है। इस संबंध में 26 राज्यों/संघ राज्य क्षेत्रों से संबंधित सूचियों को कल्याण मंत्रालय के संकल्प सं. 12011/68/93-बी. सी. सी. (सी.) दिनांक 10 सितम्बर, 1993, सं. 12011/9/94-बी.सी.सी.दिनांक 19 अक्टूबर, 1994, सं. 12011/7/95-बी.सी. सी.दिनांक 9 मार्च , 1996, सं. 12011/44/96-बी.सी.सी.दिनांक 6 दिसम्बर 1996, तथा सं. 12011/11/99/94-बी.सी.सी.दिनांक 11 दिसम्बर, 1997, एवं 12011/68/98-बी.सी.सी.दिनांक 27 अक्टूबर, 1999, के तहत जारी की गई है।

2. राष्ट्रीय पिछड़ा वर्ग आयोग की स्थापना राष्ट्रीय पिछड़ा वर्ग आयोग अधिनियम, 1993 के उपबंध के अंतर्गत अन्य पिछड़े वर्गो की केन्द्रीय सूची में शामिल करने तथा कम शामिल करने के लिए अनुरोधों को प्राप्त करने, जांचने और उन पर सिफारिश करने के लिए की गई थी ।

3. राष्ट्रीय पिछड़ा वर्ग आयोग ने आन्ध्र प्रदेश, बिहार, चण्डीगढ़, गोवा, गुजरात, कर्नाटक, केरल, मध्य प्रदेश, उड़ीसा, पांडिचेरी, पंजाब, राजस्थान, सिक्किम, तमिलनाडु, त्रिपुरा, उत्तर प्रदेश और पश्चिम बंगाल से संबंधित अन्य पिछड़े वर्गो की केन्द्रीय सूची में शामिल करने /संशोधन करने के लिए जातियों /समुदायों (उप जातियों/पर्यायों सहित) के नामों की सिफारिशों को स्वीकार कर लिया है और उपर्युक्त राज्यों/संघ राज्य क्षेत्रों से संबंधित अन्य पिछड़े वर्गो की केन्द्रीय सूची में अनुबंध में दिए गए अन्तर्वेशनों /संशोधनों को अधिसूचित करने का निर्णय किया है। ये अंतर्वेशन/संशोधन इस संकल्प के जारी होने की तारीख से प्रभावी होंगे।

धर्मेन्द्र देव, संयुक्त सचिव

उपबन्ध

निम्नलिखित राज्यों /संघ राज्य क्षेत्रों से संबंधित अन्य पिछड़े वर्गो की केन्द्रीय सूची में शामिल करना /संशोधन करना।

1 आन्ध्र प्रदेश

2	बिहार
3	चण्डीगढ़
4	गोवा
5	गुजरात
6	कर्नाटक
7	केरल
8	मध्य प्रदेश
9	उड़ीसा
10	पांडिचेरी
11	पंजाब
12	राजस्थान
13	सिक्किम
14	तमिलनाडु
15	त्रिपुरा
16	उत्तर प्रदेश
17	पश्चिम बंगाल

अन्य पिछड़े वर्गों की केन्द्रीय सूची में जातियों / समुदायों (उप-जातियों/पर्यायों सहित) के नाम

क्र. सं	पुरानी प्रविष्टि	नई प्रविष्टि
	राज्य : बिहार : अन्य पिछड़े वर्गों की केन्द्रीय सूची	
1.	32 गंगई (नागेश)	32 गंगई (गणेश)
2.	83 कलवार (सुदी का प्रर्याय)	124. (क) कलवार, (ख) कलाल, इराकी
3.	90 मल्लाह (सुर्हिया)	90 मल्लाह (सुर्हिया, केवट, मुरावरी)
4.	-शुन्य-	125. कुलहिया
5.	-शुन्य-	126. शेरशाहबादी
6.	-शुन्य-	127. सुकियार

MINISTRY OF SOCIAL JUSTICE & EMPOWERMENT

RESOLUTION

New Delhi, the 6th December, 1999

No. 12011/88/98-BCC.-The Government of India, vide the Ministry of personnel, Public Grievances and Pension (Department of Personnel and Training) OM NO. 36012/22/93-Estt.(SCT), dated the 8th September, 1993, have reserved 27% of vacancies in Civil Posts and Services under the Central Government, to be filled through direct recruitment, in favour of the Other Backward Classes(OBCs). In this regard the lists in respect of 26 States/UTs have been notified vide Ministry of Welfare Resolutions No. 12011/68/93-BCC (C) dated the 10th September, 1993, No. 12011/9/94-BCC dated the 19th October, 1994, No. 12011/7/95-BCC dated the 24th May, 1995, No.12011/96/94-BCC dated the 9th March, 1996, No. 12011/44/96-BCC dated the 6th December, 1996, No. 12011/99/94-BCC dated the 11th December, 1997 and No. 12011/68/98-BCC dated the 27th October, 1999.

2. The National Commision for Backward Classes was set up under the provisions of the National Commission for Backward Classes Act, 1993 to entertain, examine and recommend upon the requests for inclusion and complaints of over inclusion and under inclusion in the Central List of Other Backward Classes.

3. The National Commission for Backward classes have recommended names of castes/communities (including sub-castes/synonyms)for inclusion/amendment in the Central Lists of OBCs in respect of Andhra pradesh, Bihar, Chandigarh. Goa, Gujarat, Karnataka, Kerala, Madhya pradesh, Orissa, Pondicherry, Punjab, Rajasthan, Sikkim, Tamil Nadu, Tripura, Uttar Pradesh and West Bengal. The

Government have accepted the recommendations of the commission and have decided to notify annexed inclusions/ amendments in the Central Lists of OBCs in respect of aforesaid States/UTs. These inclusions/amendments shall take effect from the date of issue of this Resolution.

DHARMENDRA DEO, Jt. Secy.

Inclusion/Amendment in Central List of Other Backward Classes (OBCs) in respect of under mentioned States/UTs:

1. Andhra pradesh
2. Bihar
3. Chandigarh
4. Goa
5. Gujarat
6. Karnataka
7. Kerala
8. Madhya pradesh
9. Orissa
10. Pondicherry
11. Punjab
12. Rajasthan
13. Sikkim
14. Tamil Nadu
15. Tripura
16. Uttar pradesh
17. West Bengal

Name of Castes/ Communities (including sub-castes/ synonyms) in the Central list of OBCs.

1.	32. Gangai (Nagesh)	32.	Gangai (Ganesh)

2.	83. Kalwar (synonym of Sudi)	124. (a) Kalwar (b) Kalal, Eraqui
3.	90. Mallah (Surhia)	90. Mallah (Surhiya, Kewat, Murawari)
4.	Nil	125. Kulahia
5.	Nil	126. Shershahbadi
6.	Nil	127. Sukiyar

भारत का राजपत्र

The Gazette of India

असाधारण

EXTRAORDINARY

भाग 1-खण्ड 1

PART I-Section I

प्राधिकार से प्रकाशित

PUBLISHED BY AUTHORITY

सं. 71] नई दिल्ली, मंगलवार, अप्रैल 4, 2000/चैत्र 15, 1922

No. 71] NEW DELHI, TUESDAY, APRIL 4, 2000/ CHAITRA 15, 1922

सामाजिक न्याय और अधिकारिता मंत्रालय

संकल्प

नई दिल्ली, 4 अप्रैल, 2000

संख्या 12011/36/99-बी.सी.सी.-भारत सरकार ने कार्मिक, लोक शिकायत तथा पेंशन (कार्मिक एवं प्रशिक्षण) मंत्रालय के अ.शा.सं. 36012/22/93-स्था. (एस.सी.टी.) दिनांक 8 सितम्बर, 1993 के तहत अन्य पिछड़े वर्गो के पक्ष में सीधी भर्ती के माध्यम से भरी जाने वाली केन्द्र सरकार के अधीन सिविल पदों और सेवाओं में 27% रिक्तियाँ आरक्षित की हैं।

2. राष्ट्रीय पिछड़ा वर्ग आयोग की स्थापना राष्ट्रीय पिछड़ा वर्ग आयोग अधिनियम, 1993 के उपबंध के अंतर्गत अन्य पिछडे वर्गो की केन्द्रीय सूची

में शामिल करने तथा कम शामिल करने के लिए अनुरोधों को प्राप्त करने,जांचने और उन पर सिफारिश करने के लिए की गई थी।

3. इस संबंध में 26 राज्यों/संघ राज्य क्षेत्रों से संबंधित सूचियों को कल्याण मंत्रालय के संकल्प सं.12011/68/93-बी.सी.सी. (सी.) दिनांक 10 सितम्बर, 1993, सं. 12011/9/94-बी.सी.सी.दिनांक 19 अक्टूबर, 1994, सं. 12011/7/95-बी.सी.सी.दिनांक 24 मई, 1995, सं. 12011/96/94/-बी.सी.सी. दिनांक 11 मार्च, 1996 के तहत जारी किया गया। उपर्युक्त सूचियों को राष्ट्रीय पिछड़ा वर्ग आयोग की सिफारिशों के आधार पर संशोधित किया गया था और समय-समय पर संकल्प संख्या 12011/96/94-बी.सी.सी. दिनांक 9 मार्च, 1996, सं. 12011/44/96-बी.सी.सी. दिनांक 6 दिसम्बर, 1996, सं. 12011/13/97-बी.सी.सी. दिनांक 3 दिसम्बर, 1997 तथा 12011/68/98-बी.सी.सी. दिनांक 27 अक्टूबर, 1999, सं. 12011/88/99-बी.सी.सी. दिनांक 6 दिसम्बर, 1999 के तहत जारी की गई है।

4. राष्ट्रीय पिछड़ा वर्ग आयोग ने आन्ध्र प्रदेश, बिहार, दिल्ली, गुजरात, हरियाणा, हिमाचल प्रदेश, कर्नाटक, केरल, मध्य प्रदेश, महाराष्ट्र, उड़ीसा, पांडिचेरी, राजस्थान, सिक्किम, त्रिपुरा, उत्तर प्रदेश और पश्चिम बंगाल से संबंधित अन्य पिछड़े वर्गो की केन्द्रीय सूची में शामिल करने/संशोधन करने के लिए जातियों /समुदायों (उपजातियों /पर्यायों सहित) के नामों की सिफारिश की है।

5. सरकार ने आयोग की सिफारिशों को स्वीकार कर लिया है और उपर्युक्त राज्यों/संघ राज्य क्षेत्रों से संबंधित अन्य पिछड़े वर्गो की केन्द्रीय सूची में अनुबन्ध में दिए गए अंतर्वेशनों /संशोधनों को अधिसूचित करने का निर्णय किया हैं। ये अंतर्वेशन/ संशोधन इस संकल्प के जारी होने की तारीख से प्रभावी होंगे।

एस. के. पंडा, संयुक्त सचिव

State : Bihar

S.No.	Old Entry	New Entry
5.	128. Nil	128. Nagar (This does not include Maithili Brahmins and immigrant Nagars from other States who are Brahmins and Baniyas)

भारत का राजपत्र

The Gazette of India

असाधारण

EXTRAORDINARY

भाग 1-खण्ड 1

PART I-Section 1

प्राधिकार से प्रकाशित

PUBLISHED BY AUTHORITY

सं. 9] नई दिल्ली, मंगलवार, जनवरी 13, 2004/पौष 23, 1925

No. 9] NEW DELHI, TUESDAY, JANUARY 13, 2004/ PAUSA 23, 1925

सामाजिक न्याय और अधिकारिता मंत्रालय

संकल्प

नई दिल्ली, 13, जनवरी, 2004

सं. 12011/4/2002-बी.सी.सी.- भारत सरकार ने कार्मिक, लोक शिकायत तथा पेंशन (कार्मिक एवं प्रशिक्षण) मंत्रालय के का.ज्ञा. सं. 36012/22/93-स्था. (एस.सी.टी.) दिनांक 8 सितम्बर, 1993 के तहत अन्य पिछड़े वर्गों के पक्ष में सीधी भर्ती के माध्यम से भरे जाने वाले केन्द्र सरकार के अधीन सिविल पदों और सेवाओं में 27% रिक्तियाँ आरक्षित की हैं।

2. राष्ट्रीय पिछड़ा वर्ग आयोग की स्थापना राष्ट्रीय पिछड़ा वर्ग आयोग अधिनियम, 1993 के उपबंधों के अनुसार अन्य पिछड़े वर्गों की केन्द्रीय सूचियों में शामिल करने के अनुरोधों तथा अधिक शामिल करने और कम शामिल करने की शिकायतों को प्राप्त करने, जांचने और उनकी सिफारिश करने के लिए की गई थी।

3. इस संबंध में 26 राज्यों/संघ राज्य क्षेत्रों से संबंधित अन्य पिछड़े वर्गों की सामान्य केन्द्रीय सूची को कल्याण मंत्रालय के संकल्प सं. 12011/68/93-बी. सी.सी.(सी.) दिनांक 10 सितम्बर, 1993, सं. 12011/9/94-बी.सी.सी. दिनांक 19 अक्टूबर, 1994, सं. 12011/7/95-बी.सी.सी. दिनांक 24 मई 1995, सं.

12011/99/94-बी.सी.सी. दिनांक 11 दिसम्बर, 1997, के तहत अधिसूचित किया गया। उपर्युक्त सूचियों को राष्ट्रीय पिछड़ा वर्ग आयोग की सिफारिशों के आधार पर संशोधित किया गया था और समय-समय पर संकल्प सं. 12011/96/94-बी.सी.सी. दिनांक 9 मार्च, 1996, सं. 12011/44/96-बी.सी.सी. दिनांक 6 दिसम्बर, 1996, सं. 12011/13/97-बी.सी.सी. दिनांक 3 दिसम्बर, 1997, सं. 12011/68/98-बी.सी.सी. दिनांक 27 अक्टूबर, 1999, सं. 12011/88/99-बी.सी.सी. दिनांक 6 दिसम्बर, 1996, 1999, सं. 12011/36/99-बी.सी.सी. दिनांक 4 अप्रैल, 2000, सं. 12011/44/99-बी.सी.सी. दिनांक 21 दिसम्बर, 2000, सं. 12015/9/2000-बी.सी.सी. दिनांक 06-09-2001 तथा 12011/1/2001-बी.सी.सी. दिनांक 19-06-2003 के तहत जारी की गई।

4. राष्ट्रीय पिछड़ा वर्ग आयोग ने तदन्तर आंध्र प्रदेश, बिहार, पंजाब, सिक्किम, तमिलनाडु और उत्तर प्रदेश से संबंधित अन्य पिछड़ें वर्गो की केन्द्रीय सूची में शामिल करने/संशोधन करने के लिए जातियों/समुदायों (उपजातियों /पर्यायों सहित) की सिफारिश की है।

5. सरकार ने आयोग की सिफारिशों पर विचार किया है और उन्हें स्वीकार कर लिया है। तदनुसार उपर्युक्त राज्यों से संबंधित अन्य पिछड़े वर्गो की केन्द्रीय सूची में अनुबंध में दिए गए अंतर्वेशनों /संशोधनों को एतद्द्वारा अधिसूचित किया है। ये अंतर्वेशन/संशोधन इस संकल्प के जारी होने की तारीख से प्रभावी होंगे।

सपना राय, संयुक्त सचिव

निम्नलिखित राज्यों के संबंध में अन्य पिछडें वर्गों की केन्द्रीय सूची में समावेशन/संशोधनः-

1. आंध्र प्रदेश
2. बिहार
3. पंजाब
4. सिक्किम
5. तमिलनाडु
6. उत्तर प्रदेश

MINISTRY OF SOCIAL JUSTICE AND EMPOWERMENT

RESOLUTION

New Delhi, the 13th January, 2004

No. 12011/4/2002-BCC.- The Government of India, vide the Ministry of Personnel, Public Grievances and pension (Department of Personnel and Training) OM No. 36012/22/93-Estt. (SCT) dated the 8th september, 1993 have reserved 27% of vacancies in Civil Posts and Services under the Central Government, to be filled through direct recruitment in favaur of the Other Backward Classes (OBCs).

2. The National Commission for Backward Classes(NCBC) was set up as per the provisions of the NCBC Act, 1993 to entertain, examine and recommend upon the requests for inclusion and complaints of over-inclusion and under-inclusion in the Central Lists of OBCs.

3. The common Central List of OBCs in respect of 26 State/UTs were notified vide Ministry of welfare Resolution No.12011/68/93BCC. (c) dated the 10th September, 1993, No.12011/9/1994-BCC.dated the 19th October, 1994, No. 12011/7/1995-BCC.dated the 24th May, 1995, No. 12011/99/94-BCC.dated the 11th December, 1997.The said lists were modified on the basis of the recommendations of the NCBC and notified from time to time vide Resolutions No. 12011/96/94-BCC.dated the 9th March, 1996, No. 12011/44/96-BCC dated the 6th December, 1996, No. 12011/13/97-BCC dated the 3rd December, 1997, No. 12011/68/98-BCC dated the 27th October, 1999m No. 12011/88/99-BCC dated the 6th December, 1999, No. 12011/36/99-BCC dated the 4th April,2000, No. 12011/44/99-BCC dated the 21st September, 2000, No. 12015/9/2000-BCC dated the 6th September, 2001 and No. 12011/1//2001-BCC dated the 19th June, 2003.

4. The NCBC have subsequently recommended castes/ communities (including sub-castes/synonyms)for inclusion/ amendment in the Central Lists of OBCs in respect of Andhra Pradesh, Bihar, Punjab, Sikkim, Tamil Nadu and Uttar Pradesh.

5. The Government have considered and accepted the recommendation of the Commission. Accordingly, the inclusions/ amendments in the Central Lists of OBCs in respect of aforesaid States as given in the Annexure is hereby notified. These inclusions/amendments shall take effect from the date of issue of this Resolution.

Sapna Ray, Jt. Secy.

Inclusion/Amendment in Central List of Other Backward Classes (OBCs) in respect of under mentioned States

1. Andhra Pradesh
2. Bihar
3. Punjab
4. Sikkim
5. Tamil Nadu
6. Uttar Pradesh

S.No.	Name of the State	Old Entry	New Entry
1.	Bihar	104.Yadav (Gwala, Ahir, Gope,	104. Yadav (Gwala, Ahir Sadgope, Gope)
		129. Nil	129. Saikalgar (Sikligar) (Muslim)

भारत का राजपत्र

The Gazette of India

असाधारण

EXTRAORDINARY

भाग 1-खण्ड 1

PART I- Section 1

प्राधिकार से प्रकाशित

PUBLISHED BY AUTHORITY

सं. 10] नई दिल्ली, मंगलवार, जनवरी 17, 2006/पौष 27, 1927

No. 10] NEW DELHI, TUESDAY, JANUARY 17, 2006/ PAUSA 27, 1927

सामाजिक न्याय और अधिकारिता मंत्रालय

संकल्प

नई दिल्ली, 16 जनवरी, 2006

सं. 12011/9/2004-बी.सी.सी.- भारत सरकार ने कार्मिक, लोक शिकायत तथा पेंशन (कार्मिक एवं प्रशिक्षण) मंत्रालय के का.ज्ञा.सं. 16012/22/93-स्था (एस.सी.टी.) दिनांक 8 सितम्बर, 1993 के तहत अन्य पिछड़े वर्गों के पक्ष में सीधी भर्ती के माध्यम से भरे जाने वाले केन्द्र के अधीन सिविल पदों ओर सेवाओं में 27% रिक्तियाँ आरक्षित हैं।

2. राष्ट्रीय पिछड़ा वर्ग आयोग की स्थापना राष्ट्रीय पिछड़ा वर्ग आयोग अधिनियम, 1993 के उपबंधों के अनुसार अन्य पिछड़े वर्गो की केन्द्रीय सूचियों में शामिल करने के अनुरोधों तथा अधिक शामिल करने और कम शामिल करने की शिकायतों को प्राप्त करने,जाँचने और उनकी सिफारिश करने के लिए की गई थी।

3. इस संबंध में 26 राज्यों/संघ राज्य क्षेत्रों से संबंधित अन्य पिछड़े वर्गों की सामान्य केन्द्रीय सूची को कल्याण मंत्रालय के संकल्प सं. 12011/68/93-बी.सी.सी (सी.) दिनांक 10 सितम्बर, 1993 सं. 12011/9/94-बी.सी.सी. दिनांक 19 अक्टूबर, 1994, सं. 12011/7/95-बी.सी.सी. दिनांक 24 मई 1995, सं. 12011/99/94-बी.सी.सी. दिनांक 11 सितम्बर, 1997 के तहत अधिसूचित किया गया। उपर्युक्त सूचियों को राष्ट्रीय पिछड़ा वर्ग आयोग की सिफारिशों के आधार पर संशोधित किया गया था और समय-समय पर संकल्प सं. 12011/96/94-बी.सी.सी. दिनांक 9 मार्च, 1996, सं. 12011/44/96-बी.सी.सी. दिनांक 6 दिसम्बर, 1996, सं. 12011/13/97-बी.सी.सी. दिनांक 3 दिसम्बर, 1997, सं. 12011/68/98-बी.सी.सी. दिनांक 27 अक्टूबर, 1999, सं. 12011/88/99-बी.सी.सी. दिनांक 6 दिसम्बर, 1999, सं. 12011/36/99-बी.सी.सी. दिनांक 4 अप्रैल, 2000, सं. 12011/44/99-बी.सी.सी. दिनांक 21 सितम्बर, 2000, सं. 12015/9/2000-बी.सी.सी. दिनांक 6 सितम्बर, 2001, सं. 12011/1/2001-बी.सी.सी. दिनांक 19 जून, 2003 तथा सं. 12011/4/2002-बी.सी.सी. दिनांक 13 जनवरी, 2004 के तहत जारी की गई।

4. राष्ट्रीय पिछड़ा वर्ग आयोग ने तदन्तर आंध्र प्रदेश, बिहार, राष्ट्रीय राजधानी क्षेत्र दिल्ली, गोवा, गुजरात, कर्नाटक, मध्य प्रदेश, महाराष्ट्र, उड़ीसा, पांडिचेरी तथा उत्तर प्रदेश से संबंधित अन्य पिछड़े वर्गों की केन्द्रीय सूची में शामिल करने/संशोधन करने के लिए जातियों/समुदायों (उपजातियों/पर्यायों सहित) की सिफारिश की है।

5. सरकार ने आयोग की सिफारिशें पर विचार किया है और उन्हें स्वीकार कर लिया है। तदनुसार उपर्युक्त राज्यों/संघ शासित क्षेत्रों से संबंधित अन्य पिछड़े वर्गों की केन्द्रीय सूची में अनुबंध में दिए गए अंतर्वेशनों/संशोधनों को एतद्द्वारा अधिसूचित किया है। ये अंतर्वेशन /संशोधन इस संकल्प के जारी होने की तारीख से प्रभावी होंगे।

जी.एन. पेगू, संयुक्त सचिव

निम्नलिखित राज्यों के संबंध में अन्य पिछड़ें वर्गों की केन्द्रीय सूची में समावेश/ संशोधन :-

1. आन्ध्र प्रदेश

2. बिहार
3. राष्ट्रीय राजधानी क्षेत्र दिल्ली
4. गोवा
5. गुजरात
6. कर्नाटक
7. मध्य प्रदेश
8. महाराष्ट्र
9. उड़ीसा
10. पांडिचेरी तथा
11. उत्तर प्रदेश

क्रम सं0.	राज्य का नाम	पुरानी प्रविष्टि	नई प्रविष्टि
2–	बिहार	125. कुलहिया	125. कुल्हैया
		130. शून्य	130. बाखो (मुस्लिम)
		131. शून्य	131. ठकुराई (मुस्लिम)
		15. कुर्मी (महतो), कुर्मी (महतो) (केवल छोटा नागपुर प्रभाग में)	15. कुर्मी, कुर्मी (महतो) (केवल छोटा नागपुर प्रभाग में)

Annexure - 9

REPORT

OF

THE EXPERT COMMITTEE

FOR SPECIFYING

THE CRITERIA FOR IDENTIFICATION OF

SOCIALLY ADVANCED PERSONS

AMONG

THE SOCIALLY AND EDUCATIONALLY

BACKWARD CLASSES

The 10th March, 1993

MINISTRY OF WELFARE

Justice Ram Nandan Prasad
Former Judge,
Patna High Court,
CHAIRMAN

Expert Committee on
Socially & Educationally
Backward Classes
New Delhi-110001

Dated 10th March, 1993

Dear Hon'ble Minister,

I have the privilege of presenting the Report of the Expert Committee Constituted under Resolution No. 12011/16/93-BCC(C), dated 22nd February, 1993 of the Ministry of Welfare, Government of India. I and the other Members of the Committee, namely, Dr M.L. Shahare, Shri P.S. Krishnan and Shri R.J. Majithia, assumed charge on 23rd February, 1993 and from day one, we got down to serious work. as all of us were fully conscious that the Report has to be completed and presented by the 10th March, 1993.

2. Needless to say, all of us had to work very hard to complete the Report and in this difficult and daunting task, we received full cooperation from you as well as all the officers and staff of the Ministry of Welfare. We justifiably feel happy that we have completed the work within the targeted time.

3. We hope that our labour will serve the purpose and our Report will enable the Government to commence implementation of the policy of reservation for Socially & Educationally Backward Classes at the earliest, fulfilling the directions of the Supreme Court.

With regards,

Yours sincerely,

Sd/-

(Ram Nandan Prasad)

Shri Sitaram Kesari,
Minister of Welfare,
Government of India,
New Delhi-110001

No. 12011/19/93-BCC(C)

GOVERNMENT OF INDIA

MINISTRY OF WELFARE

New Delhi, the 22nd February, 1993

RESOLUTION

The Supreme Court, in its Majority Judgement in writ petition (Civil) No. 930 of 1990, Indra Sawhney and Others etc. Vs. Union of India and Others etc., delivered on 16th November 1992 has, inter alia, directed that "Within four months from today the government of india shall specify the bases, applying the relevant and requisite socio-economic criteria to exclude Socially advanced persons/ sections ('creamy layer') from 'Other Backward Classes' and further that the implementation of the impugned O.M. dated 13th August, 1990 shall be subject to exclusion of such socially advanced persons (creamy layer')".

2. Having regard to the fact that a lot of specialised inputs would be needed to determine the bases viz., socio-economic criteria for identification of the 'creamy layer', it has been decided to set up an Expert Committee consisting of:

1. Justice Ram Nandan Prasad (Retd.)
   High Court Patna. — Chairman

2. Shri M.L Sahare (Social Scientist)
   Former Chairman, U.P.S.C. — Member

3. Shri P.S. Krishnan, Former Secretary
(Welfare) Govt.of India. Member

4. Shri R.J. Majithia, former
Chairman Revenue Board,
Government of Rajasthan Member-Secretary

to make recommendations to the Govt. of India, in regard to the said socio-economic criteria. The Committee will also give recommendations on such other matters relating to the implementation of the judgement of the Supreme Court, as the Government of India may consider necessary.

3. The Headquarters of the Committee will be located at Delhi.

4. The Committee will devise its own procedures in the discharge of its functions. All the Ministries and Departments of the Government of India will furnish such information and documents and provide such assistance as may be required by the committee. It is hoped that the State Governments and Union Territory Administrations and other concerned will extend their fullest cooperation and assistance to the Committee.

5. The Committee shall submit its report on the socio-economic criteria for exclusion of the 'creamy layer' from Other Backward Classes latest by 10th March, 1993.

Sd/-

(M.S. PANDIT)

Jt. Secy. (M&BC)

ORDER

ORDER that a copy of the resolution be communicated to all Ministries/ Departments of the Government of India/ State Governments and U.T.Administrations.

ORDERED also that the resolution be published in the Gazette of India for general information.

Sd/-

(M.S.PANDIT)

Jt. Secy. (M&BC)

Report of the Expert Committee for specifying the criteria for identification of socially advanced persons among the socially and educationally backward classes.

The 9-Member Constitution Bench of the Supreme Court of India delivered its historic judgement in the Reservation case relating to Socially and Educationally Backward Classes(Indra Sawhney and Others vs. the Union of India and Others) on the 16th of November ,1992. The case arose out of several Writ Petitions filed to challenge the office Memorandum dated 13th August, 1990 and the office memorendum dated 25th September, 1991 issued by the GOI for implementing, according to the respective modes prescribed in the two office Memoranda, the recommendations for reservation for Socially and Educationally Backward Classes (SEBCs) in public employment, made by the Second Backward Classes Commission appointed under Article 340 of the Constitution, popularly known as the Mandal Commission.

2. The Supreme Court while upholding by majority the basic principle of reservation for the SEBCs have at the same time, directed that the socially advanced persons of the (SEBCs) category ought not to be given the benefit of reservation. In order to carry out this directive and specifiying and determining as to who from amogst the SEBCs would be liable to be excluded from the benefit of reservation, the Government has appointed the Expert Committee as per Resolution No. 12011/16/93-BCC(C),

dated the 22nd February, 1993 of the Ministry of Welfare, Government of India. The Court has also directed that the reservation shall not become operative till the criteria to exclude the socially advanced persons are ascertained and specified.

3. Four Hon'ble Judges who were members of the Special Bench, namely, the then Hon'ble Chief Justice Shri M.H. Kania, Hon'ble Justice M.N. Venkatachaliah(now Chief Justice), Hon'ble Justice A.M. Ahmadi and Hon'ble Justice B.P. Jeevan Reddy, delivered a common Judgement written out by Hon'ble Justice B.P. Jeevan Reddy and this is known as the majority judgement and we shall refer to it as such in our report. Hon'ble Justice S.R. Pandian and Hon'ble Justice P.B. Sawant have, no doubt, written out separate judgements of their own, but they have in substance supported most of the conclusions of the majority judgement and we will refer to the judgements of these two Hon'ble Justice T.K. Thommen, Hon'ble Justice Kuldip Singh and Hon'ble Justice R.M. Sahai have a common operative order and this is known as the dissenting judgement and we shall refer, if need be, to the same in the above terminology. When we refer to the ratio deciding of the entire judgement we will be referring to it as the judgement of the Court.

4. It is neccessary to bear in mind that the Court has accepted the principle of reservation on the reasoning that the SEBCs on account of their social and educational backwardness are truly in need of reservation. In other words, the dominant consideration for upholding the reservation is the social and educational backwardness and not the income test, although in actual life it mostly happens that economic backwardness is a natural consequence of the social and educational backwardness. It logically follows, therefore, that for determining who from amongst the SEBCs shall be denied the benefit of

reservation, the basics again would be the social and educational factors and only when the advancement in this regard is such as to put that person at par with the forward classes that he may be placed in the excluded category. In the majority judgement, it has been observed that only when a person's social and educational advancement is such that it totally snaps the connnecting link of backwardness between him and other members of his community, he can then be said to be a misfit in his own class and so ought to be taken out from there and placed in "Creamy Layer" category. The following passage in the judgement of Hon'ble Justice Sawant (paragraph 522 Judgement Today Vol. VI No.9 30th Novermber, 1992) elaborates the point more succintly:-

"The correcet criterion for judging the forwardness of the forwards among the Backward classes is to measure their capacity not in terms of the capacity of others in their class, but in terms of the capacity of the members of the Forward classes, as stated earlier. If they cross the Rubicon of backwardness, they should be taken out from the Backward Classes and should be made disentitled to the provisions meant for the said classes".

Hence while determining the criteria of exclusion we have kept in mind the guiding principle laid down by the Hon'ble Court as mentioned above. However, if economic betterment flows from social and educational advancement, then this also has to be taken note of.

5. Before specification of the actual determinants is taken up, it will be useful, say necessary, to indicate and explain what exactly the term 'Creamy Layer' or the Rule of Exclusion in actual application would imply. When a person has been able to shed off the attributes of social and educational backwardness and has secured employment or has engaged himself in some trade / profession of high status, as categorised by us below, he, at that stage is

normally no longer in need of reservation for himself. For example, if a person gets appointed as a Class I officer either on open competition basis or reservation basis, the question of excluding him on the ground that he forms part of the 'Creamy Layer' does not at all arise. But since he himself has come into the socially advanced category he will be in a position to provide the means, the equipment and the opportunities which are necessary for the uplift of his offspring from the level of social and educational backwardness. As such, the question of applying the Rule of Exclusion will arise only in the case of his of spring. In the present social set-up, when the joint family system, particularly among the upper strata of society has been breaking up, we are regarding the family to constitute husband, wife and children and on that basis applying the exclusion principle. In other words, even if a person, say Mr. "X", will or will not get the benefit of reservation shall depend upon the status of their parents.

6. Now we proceed to indicate and define the criteria of the Rule of Exclusion. The rise in social and educational status may result from different kinds of positions and placements in life and we shall deal with them one by one as noted below. To the categories listed below, the Rule of Exclusion will apply unless exceptions are specifically indicated.

I. Constitutional Posts

7. President , Vice-President, Judges of the Supreme Court and High Courts, Chairman/Members of the Union public Service Commission and State Public Service Commissions, Chief Election Commissioner, Comptroller and Auditor General of India and persons holding Constitutional Positions of like nature.

The Constitutional posts of Governor, Minister, and

Membership of Legislatures, are, in the very nature of things, temporary and often transitory. Further, in most cases such persons would be covered in one or the other categories which have been enumerated in this report. Hence such persons have not been separately categorised.

II. Service Category

A. Group A/Class 1 Officers of the All-India, Central and State Services (Direct Recruits)

8. If either of the spouses is a Class I officer rule of exclusion will apply. Where Both spouses are Class I officers and one of them dies the situation remains unchanged and the rule of exclusion will apply. However, if both of them die then obviously, the offspring are not only left to suffer mental agony and hardship in different ways but they are also denied the benefits and status resulting from the posts of their parents, and due to this disadvantage thrust upon them, the children shall not be denied the benefits of reservation, i.e., the rule of exclusion will not apply to them. It may be noted that if permanent incapacitation occurs which results in putting an officer out of sevice, then it shall be treated as equivalent to death so far as the application of rule of exclusion to the offspring is concerned. Hereafter, wherever death has been mentioned it shall include permanent incapacitation as stated above.

To the unfortunate situation of death or permanent incapacitation of the only spouse who is in this category of service, or of both spouses who are in this category of service, an exception has to be recorded. If before the unfortunate event of death of either of or both such spouses occurs, either of the spouses has had the benefit of employment in any international organisation like the UN, IMF, World Bank etc., for a period of not less than five years then exclusion from the benefit of reservation will continued to apply to the offspring.

9. It sometimes may happen that a lady who has got married to a Class I officer may herself like to apply for a job. If she belongs to SEBC category, she will not be disentitled by the rule of exclusion. The reason for saying so is that originally having been a member of SEBC, she carries with here the attributes of backwardness even after she is married to a Class I officer and though she may economically be in a better position, the initial attributes of social backwardness continue to linger on and will not get shaken off during the short period (in view of the age limit) which will be available to her for getting into any service employment. Therefore, we consider that such a person more so because she is a lady (which in our society may be generally regarded as a weaker class) should not be denied the benefit of reservation. Therefore, to such a lady rule of exclusion will not apply.

B. Group B/ ClassII- Central Services and State Services (Direct Recruitment)

10. If both spouses are Class II officers then rule of exclusion will apply to their offspring. If only one of the spouses is a Class II officers it will not apply, but if a male officer from Class II category gets into Class I category at the age of forty or earlier, then the rule of exclusion will apply to his offspring. Where both spouses are Class II officers and one of them dies, it is better to let the children have the benefit of reservation which means rule of exclusion will not apply; however, If either of the spouses has had the benefit of employment in any international organisation, as indicated above, for a period of not less than five year, then even in the event of death the application of the rule of exclusion will not apply to the off spring even if one of the spouses has had the benefit of employment in an international organisation.

11. Where the husband is a Class I officer (Direct Recruit or pre-forty promoted) and the wife is a Class II officers and the husband dies, the rule of exclusion will not apply. And when the wife is a class 1 officer (i.c., Direct Recruit or pre-forty promoted) and the husband is a Class II officer and the wife dies the rule of exclsion will not apply but if the husband dies the rule of exclusion will apply on the principle that one of the parents, namely the mother continues to be a Class I officer.

C. Employment in Public Sector Undertakings etc.

12. The service category is not confined to employment under the Government only, whether at the Union or at the State level. The criteria enumerated above will apply mutatis mutandis to officers holding equivalent or comparable posts in public sector undertakings, banks, insurance organisations, universites, etc. and also to equivalent or comparable posts and positions under private employment.

13. The evaluation of the posts on equivalent or comparable basis is bound to take some time. In order that this may not become a ground for postponing the implementation of reservation in respect of persons under this category, it is made clear that so long as the evaluation process is not completed and made operative, the income/ wealth test under Item VI will govern the persons under this category. In other words, even during the interim period, the employees under this category will get the benefit of reservation, and if any exclusion is to be made it shall be on the basis of the criterion under item VI.

3. Armed Forces Including Para Military Forces (this will not include persons holding civil posts)

14. The exclusion rule will apply at the level of Colonel and above in the Army and to equivalent posts in the

Navy and the Air Force and the para Military Forces. If the wife of an Armed Forces officer is herself in the Armed Forces (i.e., the category under consideration the rule of exclusion will apply only when she herself has reached the rank of Colonel; the service ranks below Colonel of husband and wife shall not be clubbed together. Even if the wife of an officer in the Armed Forces is in civil employment, this will not be taken into account for applying the rule of exclusion, unless she falls in the service category under item No.II in which case the criteria and conditions enumerated therein will apply to her independently. In making these recommendations, we have borne in mind the peculiar nature of the service and hardships faced by the members of the Armed Forces and the Para Military Forces. It has also to be remembered that there is no reservation in recruitment to the Armed Forces, which means that a person at the stage of recruitment in these services is denied the benefit of reservation even though he may otherwise be entitled to it.

4. Professional Class and Those Engaged in Trade, Business and Industry

15. This will include persons not in service employment either Government or private, but those who are engaged in professions as a doctor, lawyer, chartered accountant, income-tax consultant, financial or management consultant, dental surgeon, engineer, architect , computer specialist, film artiste and other film professional, author, playwright, sports person, sports professional, media professional or any other vocations of like status. All these persons for the purpose of determining whether they will fall in the disentitlement category or not will be governed by the income/wealth criterion as noted in item No. VI. Likewise, persons engaged in trade, business and industry will be governed by the income/ wealth criterion.

16. In a situation where the husband is in some profession and the wife is in a Class II or lower grade employment, the income/wealth test will apply only on the basis of the husband's income; in other words, the wife's employment will not be taken into account. If the wife is in any profession and the husband is in employment in a Class II or a lower rank post, then the income/wealth criterion will apply only on the basis of the wife's income and the husband's income will not be clubbed with it. The rationale is to avoid discouragement of women entering service or professions in a gender discriminating society such as ours.

5. Property Owners
A. Agricultural Land Holdings

17. It may not only be difficult but hazardous to prescribe any criteria on the basis of income from agricultural land holdings and this is borne out by the following observations in paragraph 809 of the majority judgement (Judgements Today):-

> "Further, income from agriculture may be difficult to assess and, therefore, in the case of agriculturists, the line may have to be drawn with reference to the extent of holding. While the income of a person can be taken as a measure of his social advancement, the limit to be prescribed should not be such as to result in taking away with one hand what is given with the other."

So we proceed to indicate the criteria on the basis of the extent of land holding.

18. If a person belongs to a family (father, mother and minor children) which owns only irrigated land, and the extent of irrigated land is equal to or more than 65% of the statutory ceiling area. than the disentitlement will occur. It generally happens that a person holds different

types of irrigated land. In such a situation, the different types of lands should, on the basis of the conversion formula existing, be brought into a single type of irrigated land as a common denominator and on the basis of such denominator, the above cut-off point of 65% will have to be determined.

19. The rule of exclusion will not disentitle persons belonging to families owning only unirrigated land irrespective of the area of such land. This is on account of the constraints imposed on and implicit in unirrigated cultivation.

20. In the case of members of a family owning both irrigated and unirrigated land, the exclsion rule will apply where the pre-condition exists that the irrigated area(having been brought to a single type under a common denominator) is 40% or more of the statutory ceiling limit for irrigated land (this being calculated by excluding the unirrigated portion). If this pre-condition of not less than 40% exists, then only the area of unirrigated land will be taken into account. This will be done by converting the unirrigated land on the basis of the conversion formula existing, into the irrigated type. The irrigated area so computed from unirrigated land shall be added to the actual area of irrgated land, and if after such clubbing together the total area in terms of irrigated land is 65% or more of the statutory ceiling limit for irrigated land, then the rule of exclusion will apply and disentitlement will occur.

21. On the basis of data supplied to us, we find that there is no Ceiling Law in the States of Nagaland, Mizoram, Meghalaya, Arunachal Pradesh and Goa and in the Union Territories of Andaman & Nicobar Islands, Lakshadweep, Daman & Diu. Apparently this is on account of the peculiar situation prevailing in these areas including topography, climatic conditions, etc. Under the circumstances the

exclusion rule on the basis of land holding will not be applicable here. However, if at a future date Ceiling Law is enacted for any of such States or Union Territories, it would then have to be considered and determined if the rule of exclusion on the basis o land holding criterion will be made applicable or not and if so, in what manner.

B. Plantations

22. The plantations like coffee, tea, rubber, etc. which are not regarded as agricultural holdings will come under this category. Since they are not regarded as agricultural holdings, they are not covered by ceiling laws. Therefore, the criterion of income/ wealth under item No.VI will apply.

23. From the data supplied to us, it appears that mango, citrus, apple plantations, etc., are regarded as agricultural holdings and they will be covered by the criterion at 'A' above.

C. Vacant land and/or buildings in urban areas or urban agglomeration

24. To identify those who come under this category the criterion of income/wealth under item No. VI will apply. When we refer to a bulding it is made clear that the building may be used for residential, industrial or commercial purposes and the like, or two or more such purposes.

6. Income/Wealth Test

25. This criterion is on the basis of income or wealth. we are conscious of the fact that in the majority judgement of Pandian and Sawant, JJ it has been clearly emphasised that when placing a person in the excluded category, it should be unmistakable evident that social backwardness has come to an end. Their Lordships have emphasized that unless there is social advancement to such a degree as to bring a member of the SEBC more or less at par with the

members of the forward classes, he should not be denied the benefit of reservation.

26. Since the people of this country are engaged in innumerable types of vocations and calling, it is simply not possible to assess the degree of social backwardness or advancement by specifiying each one of such vocations for callings and under these circumstances, we have to take recourse to the only discernible criterion available, namely the criterion of income or wealth. As such, this category may be said to be the residuary category. However, while prescribing the limit for this category, it has been kept in view that improvement in economic condition is so marked as to necessarily imply social advancement. Thus, here the rise in social status is presumption based indicating that it has followed necessarily from the economic betterment. The aspect of treating social advancement on the basis of presumption has been kept in mind in prescribing the limit of gross income. In this connection, the following passage occurring in paragraph 809 of the majority judgement may be usefully quoted:

> "The basis of exclusion should not merely be economic, unless of course the economic advancement is so high that it necessarily means social advancement."

(Vide Judgement Today Vol. VI, No. 9, Nov. 30,1992)

Hence, persons having gross annual income of Rs. 1 lakh or above or possessing wealth above the exemption limit as prescribed in the Wealth Tax Act will be exclueded from the benefit of reservation. Only when such level of income or wealth has a consistency for a reasonable period will it be justifiable to regard a person as socially advanced on the basis of income. we consider a period of three consecutive years to be a reasonable period for the purpose of the application of the criteria under consideration.

27. In addition to the above, we have to say that the income / wealth test governs categories IV, VB and VC as stated carlier. For the remaining categories, namely, I,II,III and VA. specific criteria have been laid down: however, if in these categories, any person, who is not disentitled to the benefit of reservation, has income from other sources or wealth which will bring him within the criterion under item No. VI, then he shall be disentitled to reservation, in case his income- without clubbing his income from salaries or agricultural land -or his wealth is in excess of cut- off point prescribed under the income/ wealth criteria.

28. Since the rupee value is bound to undergo change the income criterion in terms of the rupee as stated above will accordingly stand modified with change in the value. The modifiction exercise may, normally speaking, be undertaken every three years but if the situation so demands the interregnum may be less.

29. Persons working as artisans or engaged in the hereditary occupations, calling, etc.. like potters, washermen, barbers, etc.. are exempted from application of the rule of exclusion.

30. The Supreme Court Judgement indicates that classifying the socially and educationally back ward classes into two or more categories (backward, more backward, most backward and if necessary, further sub-categorisation) is not only desirable but pehaps actually necessary. As and when such categorisaton is done we feel that for those fall in the two lowest strata having the maximum backwardness, the application of the rule of exlusion may be kept in abeyance on the reasoning that the process of "creamy layer" formation will take more time in their case. While doing so the Government may examine its legal permissibility in terms of the Supreme Court Judgement.

31. We are aware of the strain imposed on candidates who seek certificates of caste, etc. The strain for them and the existing administrative machinaery will be all the more where certification is required not only of caste but that the candidate is or is not affected by any of the criteria of exclusion. In order that SEBC candidates are not put to any harassment in this regard, we recommend that Government may make smooth and satisfactory arrangements for the issue of such certificates without delay and without any difficulty. Government have created a single window system for entrepreneurs applying for certificates and facilities for setting up new industries. Similarly, an appropriate single window system needs to be created at State/ District level and necessary guidelines to be issued to see that correct certificates are issued promptly, and without harassment to the applicants.

32. We are also aware of the fact that in some cases false certificates of caste are issued to candidates who do not belong to the reserved categories. In order to prevent this and to ensure that certificates of caste as well as exclusion criteria are factually corect, innovative arrangements such as transparency through steps like publication in the village/ mohalla/ panchayat raj offices,etc., may be considered.

Conclusion

33. In specifying the determinants and prescribing the different formulations therein, we have adopted a pragmatic approach and we have considered it prudent as well as desirable to err on the right side. In other words, where it appeared while defining the criteria that more strict formulation would have the possible effect of excluding more than it ought to, we have choosen not to adopt such a course. And for this approach of ours we find support from observations in different judgments of the Special Bench as well as from other sources.

34. Reservation has been adopted as a remedy for curing the historical discrimination and its continuing ill-effects in public employment. That being the object in view, the denial of reservation to any member of a socially and educationally backward class is and has to be, treated as an exception. In identifying such an exception, i.e., applying the rule of exclusion, it has to be ensured that the ill-effects have been fully and finally eliminated and no grey zone is discernible. The nature of such an exercise itself makes the rule of caution inherent.

35. Hon'ble Mr. Justice Pandian does not subscribe to the "creamy layer" theory. dealing with the oft-repeated criticism that the reserved posts are lapped up by the socially advanced ("creamy layer") among the socially and eductionally backward classes, Pandian J. has quoted with approval the observation of Chinnappa Reddy J. in the case of Vasant Kumar. The relevant passage is given below:-

> ".........That a few of the seats and posts reserved for backward classes are snatched away by the more fortunate among them is not to say that reservation is not necessary. This is bound to happen in a competitive society such as ours. Are not the unreserved seats and posts snatched away, in the same way, by the top creamy layers amongst them on the same principle of merit on which the non-reserved seats and taken away by the top layers of society. How can it be bad if reserved seats and posts are snatched away by the creamy layer of backward classes, if such snatching away unreserved posts by the top creamy layer of society itself is not bad?"

Pandian J. says " The above observation, in my view, is an apt reply to such a criticism with which I am in full agreement."

(Paragraph 229 and 230 Judgements Today)

36. Another passage from the judgement of Hon'ble Mr. Justice Pandian Justifies the rule of caution and of

erring on the right side adopted by us. The passage is as below:

> "It is after 42 years since the advent of our Constitution, the Government is taking the first step to implement this scheme of reservation for OBCs under Article 16(4). In fact, some of the States have not even introduced policy of reservation in the matters of public empoyment in favour of OBCs."
>
> (Paragraph 225 Judgement Today)

37. In the above context would it not be proper, say desirable to let there be acceleration and let some distance be covered before we apply the brakes?

38. What the Supreme Court has directed is identification of the "creamy layer". This obviously means that we have not to take note off sprinklings of cream or the mere appearance of cream at the surface. Only when the "creamy layer" is substantial and stable, formed after crossing the Rubicon of social backwardness, then and then alone can it be made the basis for disentitlement. In such a situation,can it be said that adopting a rule of caution and caring on the right side is not justified ? Apprehension has been expressed, and rightly, that applying the rule if exclusion in the ground of social advancement may be counter-productive, in as much as by excluding those who have become capable of facing the fierce competition for appointment in the services what will remain are those of the socially backward who are simply not equipped and ready to face the competition and this will have the effect of many of the reserved seats being left vacant. The well-known writer and columnist, Mr. S. Sahay is one among many who have expressed such an apprehension. In an article entitled "A Moment of Truth" published in the Hindustan Times, Patna Edition dated 26-11-1992, this is what he has to say:

"....... Approval in principle of the concept of backward and more backward is rational and so is the exclusion of the creamy layer. However, the consequences in the immediate future of the exclusion of the creamy layer, even though desirable and necessary, are not going to be happy....... The poor remain both poor and uneducated. Count the cost of education today and realise for yourself whether the boy or girl from the chaupal has ever the chance of getting a higher appointment under the Central Government. Even now the reserved jobs for the Scheduled Castes and Tribes are not fully filled. Would the lot of the OBCs be any better, especialy after excluding the creamy layer?"

39. We can cite many more such quotations and also give more reasons in support of the approach which we have adopted, but in our opinion what we have said above is sufficient to highlight the point under consideration.

40. We are happy to say that all the Members of this Expert Committee have worked day and night in a spirit of cooperation and understanding with each other. There has been free and frank exchange of views on almost every point dealt with in this Report and thereafter the Committee has arrived at a consensus on the basis of which the criteria have been laid down.

41. For its delibrations, the Committee had to gather and examine a large volume of literature and documents including the judgement under consideration (Indra Sawhney & Others), various other related judgements on the subjects, report of the Mandal Commission, report of the Chinnappa Reddy Commission, reports of the various State Commissions on OBCs/SEBCs. we have had also to look into a large amount of data furnished by the Ministry of welfare itself or by other Ministries/ Departments through the Ministry of Welfare which had relevance to or threw light on the points under consideration.

42. It is not out of place to mention that formulation of the criteria for ascertainment of the socially advanced among the SEBC (termed Creamy Layer by the Supreme Court) in the manner it required to be done for practical application, is unique in the sense that to our knowledge, such an exercise has been taken up in this country for the first time. Though we find that in the Report of the Third Backward Classes Commission for Karnataka,1990, there is mention at page 174 Vol. I, of categories among socially and educationally backward Classes who should not be entitled to reservation, but we have undertaken an elaborate exercise to make the formulations as far-reaching and comprehensive as possible. Of course, it may be desirable, perhaps even necessary at a future date, to give a second look to the criteria evolved by us and make suitable changes on the basis of experience of implementation and other relevant factors.

43. We are happy to place on record our gratitude for the unstinted cooperation extended to the Committee in the discharge of its work by the Hon'ble Minister of Welfare, Government of India, Shri Sitaram Kesari and by the Secretary and all other officers and staff of the ministry of Welfare, and it is because of this, we have been able to complete this difficult task within the allotted short time.

Sd/-

(RAMNANDAN PRASAD)

Chairman 10-3-1993

Sd/-

(M.L.SHAHARE) Member 10-3-1993

Sd/-

(P.S. KRISHNAN) Member 10-3-1993

Sd/-

(R.J.MAJITHIA) Member Secretary 10-3-1993

Bibliography

- Aloysius, G.(1997) Nationalism Without A Nation in India, Oxford University Press, Delhi.
- Annual Report 2003-04: Ministry of Social Justice & Empowerment, Government of India, New Delhi.
- Approach papers of different five years plan, Planning Commission, Government of India, New Delhi.
- Aggarwal, SP & JC, Aggrawal (1991) Educational & Social Upliftment of Backward Classes:At What Cost and How, Mandal Commission & After, Concept Publishing Company, New Delhi.
- Akinchan, S (1995) Caste, Class & Politics:Emerging Horizons of Political Sociology, Gyan Publishing House, New Delhi.
- Bakshi, S.R. & Kiran Bala (ed.)2000, Social Status & Development of Backward Classes, Deep & Deep Publications Pvt;Ltd., New Delhi.
- Blair, H."(1980) Rising Kulaks and Backward Classes in Bihar: Social Change in the Late 1970s" Economic and Political Weekly, Vol-XV, No, -2.

- Bhatt, SC. (2000), The Encyclopedic District Gazetteers of India (Eastern Zone, Bihar), Vol. VIII, Gyan Publishing House, New Delhi.
- Backward Classes Commission Report, Part 1& II, Government of India, New Delhi.
- Bourdieu, P (1986) Distinction: A Social Critique of the Judgment of Taste, London
- Beteille, Andre."Caste in Contemporary India' in C.J.Fuller (ed.) Caste Today (1997), Oxford University Press, Delhi.
- Beteille, Andre (1996) Caste, Class & Power: Changing Pattern of Stratification in a Tanjore Village, Oxford University Press, New Delhi.
- Basham, A.L.(1990)The Wonder That was India, Oxford University Press, Delhi.
- Bharti, Indu (Feb.10, 1990) Politics of Anti-Reservation Stir in Bihar, Economic & Political Weekly.
- Burman, BK. Roy(1992) Beyond Mandal & After:Backward Classes in Perspective, Mittal Publications, Delhi.
- Bhattacharya, Jogendra Nath (1995) Hindu Castes and Sects, Munshiram Manoharlal Publishers Pvt; Ltd.
- Barber, Bernard (1968) Social Mobility in the Caste System in India, Mouton Publishers, Hague.
- Chaudhary, R.K.(1958)History of Bihar, Swatantra Nava Bharat Press, Patna.
- Conference on State Politics in India in the1990s; Political Mobilization and Political Competition.
- Chandapuri, Second Freedom Struggle, Mission Prakashan, Saraswati Bhavan, Mandiri, Patna.
- Choudhary, Prasanna, K. Land Reform in Bihar:Need for a Fresh Appraisal, & Iyer, K.Gopal. Concealed Tenancy: Dilemmas of Share-Croppers in Bihar in Yugandhar BN & Iyer, K.Gopal (ed.) 1993, Land Reform in India, Bihar: Institutional Constraints, Vol-1, Sage Publications, New Delhi.
- Chaudhary, Prasanna Kumar & Srikanth, (1998) Bahi Dhar Sangh Triveni Ki, Bihar Mein Samajik Nayaya Ka Pehala Sangharsh, Lok Tantra, Patna.

- Census Report of OBCs, 1951, Registrar General of India, N. Delhi.
- Das A.N. 1992 The Republic of Bihar,, Penguin Books India (p) Ltd; New Delhi.
- Das A.N.& Sita, Deulkar (2002) Caste System: A Holistic View, Dominant Publishers & Distributors, New Delhi.
- Das, A.N. (1983) Agrarian Unrest and Socio-Economic Change in Bihar: 1900-1980, Manohar, New Delhi.
- Das, Bhagwan, Moments in a History of Reservations, Economic & Political Weekly, October 28, 2000.
- Diwakar, R.R (ed.), 1959, Bihar Through the Ages, Orient Longman, Bombay.
- Dirks, Nick (2001) Castes of Mind:Colonialism and the making of Modern India, Princeton University Press, Princeton, NJ.
- Dube, S.C (1990) Indian Society, National Book Trust, Delhi.
- Dreze, Jean & Amartya Sen(1998) India Economic Development & Social Opportunity, Oxford University Press, Delhi.
- Development Conference Report: Bihar, 21st -22nd August, 2005, Development Alternatives-Pricewater House Coopers (P) Ltd, & DFID.
- Dumont, L (1966) Homo Hierarchicus, Gallimard, Paris.
- Encyclopaedia of India and her States, (1998) Shyam Nandan Singh, Politics of Job Reservation for Backward Castes in Bihar: 1977-79, Vol:7, Deep Publications, New Delhi.
- Express News Service, "Zero Growth During Lalu-Rabri Regime: Nitish White Paper, Indian Express, April 4, 2006.
- Frankel, Francine & Rao, M.S. A (eds.) 1989-90, Dominance and State Power in Modern India, Vol.2, Oxford University Press, Delhi
- Galanter, Marc (1991) Competing Inequalities: The Law and the Backward Classes in India, Oxford University Press, Delhi.

- Ghurye, G.S. (1957) Caste and Class in India, Popular Book Depot, Bombay.
- ————(1932) Caste and Race in India, Popular Prakashan, Bombay.
- Gogoi, Troilukya (2005) Reservation Policy & OBC Movement in Assam, Ashish Publishing House, Delhi.
- Gupta Shaibal (January 2002) Subaltern Resurgence: A Reconnaissance of Panchayat Election in Bihar; ADRI, Patna, (working paper no:8), Economic & Political Weekly.
- Gupta Shaibal "Emergence of New Social Elites in Bihar: Crisis or Change", Economic & Political Weekly.
- Gupta, Shaibal (5/12/05) Between the facts and a hard place, The Bihar Times, Patna.
- Gupta Shaibal(December 2004) Nature of Elite Formation in the Hindi Heartland: A Comparative Assessment of Bihar and M.P, ADRI, Patna
- Guha, Ramachandra & Jonathan, P. Parry (1999) Institutions & Inequalities, Oxford University Press, New Delhi.
- Hasan, Zoya(1998), Quest for Power:Oppositional Movements and Post-Congress Politics in UP, Oxford University Press, Delhi.
- Harris, John(2002), Institutions, Politics and Culture:A Case For Old Institutionalism in the Study of Historical Change (Working Paper series), Development Studies Institute, LSE, London.
- Hauser, W.(1967)Dynamics of Social Ranking and Political Power Among Emerging Caste Group in Bihar'.Unpublished paper prepared for the 19th AAS meeting, Chicago.
- Hutton, J.H., (1989), Census of India-1931, Part-1 & II, Gian Publishing House, Delhi.
- Hutton, J.H. (1963) Caste in India, Oxford University Press, Bombay.
- Hussain, Majid (1994) Encyclopaedia of India (Bihar), Vol-XXVI, Rima Publishing House, New Delhi.

- Hooda, Sagar Preet (2001) Contesting Reservations, Rawat Publications, Jaipur.
- Jaiswal, Suvira (2005) Caste:Origin, Function and Dimensions of Change, Manohar, New Delhi.
- J. Prabhash (2001) Affirmative Action and Social Change: Social Mobility of Dalits, Anmol Publications Pvt. Ltd. New Delhi.
- Jaffrelot, Christophe "Positive Discrimination and the transformation of Caste in India.
- ———(2003) India's Silent Revolution : The Rise of the Low Castes in North Indian Politics, Permanent Black, Delhi-92.
- Jain, S.P. Backward Classes: Problems of Education, Times of India(Patna), July 13, 1988.
- Jha, PK (1994) Changing Conditions of Agriculture Labourers in Post-Independence India: A Case Study from Bihar, Ph.D. dissertion, JNU, Centre for Economic Studies and Planning, School of Social Sciences, New Delhi.
- Jha, Makhan (ed.) 1997, Scheduled Castes Today, MD Publications Pvt. Ltd. New Delhi.
- Jha Dayadhar, 1977, State Legislature in India, Abhinav Publication.
- Jha, Hetukar. Lower Caste Peasants and Upper Caste Zamindars in Bihar(1921-1925): An analysis of sanskritization and contradiction between the two groups. Indian Economic and Social History Review, Vol.XIV, No. 4, Delhi.
- Kohli, Atul (1990) Democracy and Discontent: India's Growing Crisis of Governability, Cambridge University Press, Cambridge.
- Kothari, Rajni (ed.)1995, Caste in Indian Politics, Orient Longman Limited, Hyderabad.
- Kumar Suresh "Dalit Discontent and the pattern of Mobilisation: The experience of Bihar" Lal, A.K "Other Backward Classes in Bihar" in Bhosale, BV (2004) (ed)

"Mobilisation of Backward Communities in India", Deep & Deep publications Pvt; Ltd; New Delhi.

- Kumar, Anand.(29-30th Sept;' 2005), Seminar paper "Some aspects of post- conflict face of poverty: A Study of 4 villages of Musahari Block, Muzaffapur (Draft) IIPA, New Delhi.
- Kumar, Dr.Ravi, Failure to Translate Social Justice into Development-Exploring Backward Castes Politics in Bihar, N.R (29th-30th Sept) "Chronic Poverty and Social Conflict in Bihar"(Draft) IIPA, New Delhi.
- Mohanty, K.K.(1993) Social Mobility and Caste Dynamics, Rawat Publications, Delhi/Jaipur.
- Merton, R.K.(1968) Social Theory and Social Structure (ed.) Amerind Publishing Co., New Delhi.
- Mungeri lal Commission Report, Part-III & IV, Government of Bihar, Patna.
- Mammen Mathew "Scramble for Caste icons in Bihar, The Hindustan Times, 28 April, 1998 New Delhi.
- Mandal Judgement, Writ Petition (Civil, 930 of 1990), Vol-1to111, Ministry of Snocial Welfare, Government of India, N.Delhi.
- Milner, Murray Jr. and Sukirti Sahay (1997) "Victory without the spoils? The irony of backward caste politics in a liberalizing economy". Paper presented at a Conference of the American Sociological Association, Toronto, Canada, 9-13 August 1997
- Mukherjee, Ramkrishna (2000). Caste in Itself, Caste and Class, or Caste in Class, in Journal of World Systems Research, Vol-VI, (2).
- National Commission for Backward Classes, Annual Report: 2004-05, Minto Government Press, Minto Road, N.Delhi.
- Panadiker, V.A.Pai(1997)(ed.) The Politics of Backwardness: Reservation Policy in India, Reservation and After; The case of Bihar by Sachchidananda, Konark Publishers Pvt; Ltd;, New Delhi.
- Prasad, H.P (1989) Poor-Peasant Movement in Central Bihar, Unpublished.
- Prasad.H.P, Caste and Class in Bihar, Economic and Political Weekly, 1979.

- Purnima, S.Tripathi "A Vote for Change" Frontline, Vol:22A issue 25, November 5-18, 2005
- Prasad, Ishwari, April 23, 1978, "Job Reservation for Backward in Bihar", Janata, New Delhi.
- Prasad, Anirudh (1997) Reservational Justice to Other Backward Classes (OBCs), Deep & Deep Publications, New Delhi.
- Ramashray Roy, Caste and Political Recruitment in Bihar in Rajni Kothari(ed.) 1970 "Caste in Indian Politics., Orient Longman, New Delhi
- Report of the Backward Classes Commission (BP Mandal) 1980, Part-1 & 11, Manager of Publication, N.Delhi.
- Report of the First Backward Classes Commission, 1955, Vol.2, Ministry of Home Affairs, New Delhi.
- Radhakrishna, R. & Sharma, Alakh.N.(ed.)1998, Empowering Rural Labour in India, Institute of Human Development, New Delhi.
- Rao, MSA(1987)Social Movements and Social Transformation, Manohar, New Delhi.
- Rao, M.S.A.(1958) Political Elite and Caste Associations, Economic & Political Weekly, Vol.3.
- Runciman, W.C.(1966) Relative Deprivation and Social Justice, Routledge & Kegan Paul, London.
- Risley, H.H.(1981) The Tribes & Castes of Bengal, Vol.1, Firma Mukhopadhayay, Calcutta.
- Ramaiah, A(1991) Mandal Commission Recommendations:A Critical view in A.A.Engineer (ed.) Mandal Commission Controversy, Ajanta Publications, Delhi
- Sharma Premlata(2002), The Problems of Dalits and OBCs, Book Enclave, Jaipur.
- Sathyamurthy T V(1996)(ed.) Class Formation and Political Transformation in Post-Colonial India" (Agricultural labour and the Poor Peasant Movement in Bihar), Oxford University Press, New Delhi.
- Shukla, Kiran(1987) Castes Politics in India, Mittal Publications, New Delhi.

- Sharma, K.K., P.P. Singh, & Ranjan Kumar (ed.) (1994) Peasant Struggle in Bihar 1831-1992, Janaki Prakashan, Patna.
- Saif Shahin, Does Bihar Matter? What Ails Bihar? Hindustan Times.
- Sundar, Nandini; The Indian Census, Identity & Inequality in Institutions & Inequalities(1999), Oxford University Press, Delhi
- Sinha S.K., (2004) The Bhumihars: Caste of Eastern India, Raj Publications, New Delhi.
- Sinha, S.K. (2005) Backward Classes in India: Various Dimensions, Raj Publications, New Delhi.
- Sinha, A. (1995) Social Mobilization in Bihar: Bureaucratic Feudalism in Distributive Justice, Economic & Political Weekly, No.31.
- Singh, R.R (1998) Social Intervention for Social Justice, paper presented at National Seminar on Protective Discrimination:Ideology and Praxis, G.B.Pant Social Science Institute, Allahabad, March 24-25.
- Surana, Pushpendra (1983)Social Movement and Social Structure, Manohar, New Delhi.
- Shah, Ghanshyam (ed.) 1997, Social Transformation in India, Vol. 2, Rawat Publications, Jaipur.
- Shah.AM, BS, Baviskar & EA, Ramaswamy (eds.)1997, Social Structure & Change, Vol. 4, Sage Publications, Delhi.
- Sharma, S.R (2002) Protective Discrimination:Other Backward Classes, Raj Publications, New Delhi.
- Souza, Victor, S.D.(1981) Inequality & its Perpetuation, Manohar, Delhi.
- Srinivas, M.N. (1972) Social Change in Modern India, Orient Longman, Hyderabad.
- Study conducted by Haryali, Delhi on behalf of PREM Division(Min; of Social Justice & Empowerment, New Delhi)entitled "State-wise Summary Report of the Voluntary Organizations, State-Bihar.
- Ethnographic & Folk Culture Society, The Eastern Anthropologist, April-September, 2002, Vol-55, No.-2-3 Lucknow.

- Bihar Reboots. Drastically Changed Landscape, The Times of India, New Delhi November 24, 2005.
- Lalu's Voterloo, & MBCs Proved Lalu's Achilles'Heel, The Times of India,, New Delhi, November 23, 2005.
- Verma H.S, (2005) The OBCs and the Dynamics of social exclusion in India, Serials Publications, New Delhi.
- Verma, HS (ed.) The OBCs and the Ruling Classes in India, Rawat Publication, Jaipur/New Delhi.
- Verma K.K. (1979) Changing Role of Caste Association, National Publishing House, New Delhi.
- Verma Binoy N (1993) Agrarian Relation in Transition, Vol-1, Ashish Publishing House, New Delhi.
- Venkitesh Ramakrishan, "A New Era in Bihar", Frontline, Vol: 22A issue 25, November 5-18, 2005.
- V.K.Krishna Ananth, "Shifting Alliances in Bihar", Economic & Political Weekly, January 1, 2005
- Venkitesh Ramakrishnan, Bihar: Power of the Poorest, Frontline, Vol.22, Issues 22, Oct; 22-November 04, 2005.
- W. G. Lacey, 1987 (Rpt.) Census of India; 1931, Part-1.Report, Vol: VII (Bihar & Orissa) Usha Publications, Darya Ganj, New Delhi.
- Walter Hauser (February, 1997) Bihar Changing Images of Caste and Politics, in the State of Bihar, Seminar#450
- Weiner, M(2001) The Struggle for Equality:Caste in Indian Politics in Atul Kohli (ed.): The Success of India's Democracy, Cambridge University Press, Cambridge.
- Working Group on Empowerment of Backward Classes in Tenth Plan (2002-2007),(2001) Chairperson P.S. Krishnan, Ministry of Social Justice & Empowerment, New Delhi.
- www.bihar.nic.in (Information on various welfare measures on OBCs of the State).
- Yadav, K.C. (1994) India's Unequal Citizens: A Study of the Backward Caste, Manohar, New Delhi.
- Yadav Muneshwar, Politics from Below & Cyril Robin, Bihar Elections: Laloo against Who? Economic & Political Weekly, Vol-39, No.51 December18-24, 2004.